REQUIEM
for MARX

To my dear
friends Neal
and Shray with
best regards and
wishes of happiness,
health and
prosperity!

With love to
you and Freedom!

Yuri

REQUIEM
for MARX

Edited with an introduction by
Yuri N. Maltsev

Ludwig von Mises Institute
Auburn University, Alabama 36849-5301

Published by Praxeology Press of the Ludwig von Mises Institute, Auburn University, Auburn, Alabama 36849.

Printed in the United States of America.

Library of Congress Catalog Card Number: 93-083763
ISBN 0-945466-13-7

Contents

The Ludwig von Mises Institute gratefully acknowledges the generosity of its Members, who made the publication of this book possible. In particular, it wishes to thank the following Patrons:

Mark M. Adamo

O. P. Alford, III

Anonymous (2)

Everett Berg
EBCO Enterprises

Burton S. Blumert

John Hamilton Bolstad

Franklin M. Buchta

Christopher P. Condon

Charles G. Dannelly

Mr. and Mrs. William C. Daywitt

Tad Dekko
Kendall, USA

Robert T. Dofflemyer

Mrs. Card G. Elliott, Jr.

Dr. James W. Esler, Jr.

Willard Fischer

James W. Frevert

Thomas E. Gee

Franklin Lee Johnson

Andrew P. Jones

Dr. Richard J. Kossmann

Helen H. Lea

Hugh E. Ledbetter

Charles H. Mason

William W. Massey, Jr.

James R. Merrell

Dr. Matthew T. Monroe

Lawrence A. Myers

Dr. Richard W. Pooley

Dr. Francis Powers

Mr. and Mrs. Harold Ranstad

James M. Rodney

Catherine Dixon Roland

Leslie Rose

Gary G. Schlarbaum

Edward Schoppe, Jr.

Raleigh L. Shaklee

Raymond Shamie

E. D. Shaw
Shaw Oxygen Company

Richard J. Stephenson

Donald R. Stewart, Jr.
Twin Oil Company

David F. Swain, Jr.

Loronzo H. Thomson
L. H. Thomson Company

top dog

Edgar J. Uihlein

Joe Vierra

Paul Vlahos

Robert S. Young
Young Electric Company

Introduction

L enin's slogan, "Marxism is Almighty Because It Is True," was displayed practically everywhere in the former Soviet Union. My first encounter with Karl Marx came in the first grade of elementary school in the city of Kazan on the bank of the great Volga River. His picture was printed on the first page of the first textbook I opened. "Dedushka Marx" (Grandfather Marx), said the teacher pointing to the picture. I was thrilled, for both of my grandfathers died during Stalin's purges in the 1930s. I ran home to my grandma to tell her she was wrong. "I have a grandpa," I said, and with his huge beard and smiling eyes, "he looks like Father Frost" (the Soviet/atheist version of Santa Claus or Saint Nicholas, the patron saint of Russia).

Growing up in the Soviet Union, such early confusions are soon cleared up, for studies in Marxism were an unavoidable experience for everyone irrespective of age, class, social position, or nationality. Even the convicts in prison, including those on death row, studied the "Shining Heights" of the "great liberating teacher." The works of Marx, Engels, and Lenin were published in the USSR in 173 languages with a total output of 480 million copies. Many of them were exported. I once met an Indian translator hired by the Political Publishing House to translate 50 volumes of the *Collected Works of Marx and Engels* into Malaylam. He complained the project was stalled because the Soviet propaganda officers could not find another Malaylam translator to cross check his work.

In the Soviet Union, Marxism was not thought to be just an economic theory. It pretended to be the universal explanation of nature, life, and society.[1] It was also a deadly weapon to be wielded against personal enemies. As in the case of Sergei Vavilov who was starved to death for violating Marxism because he adhered to the science of genetics, "a false science invented by the Catholic monk Mendel." In the name of Marxism, the death toll reached 100 million, the rivers of blood flowed from Russia to Kampuchea, from China to Czechoslovakia.

Hatred was the chief motivator of the socialist revolutionaries and their followers. Lenin regarded politics as a branch of pest control; the aim of his operations was the extermination of cockroaches and bloodsucking spiders, the myriad persons who stood in the way of his political ambitions. Yet Western hagiographers have varnished over this atrocious callousness of Marxists, as historian Richard Pipes has documented.

One of the common denominators between Leninists and government interventionists in the West is the belief that the problems of monopoly are the problems of ownership: only private monopolies acting out of greed are harmful. These institutions are suppressing scientific and technical progress, polluting the environment, and engaging in other conspiracies against public well being. Government monopolies, however, were believed to be ethical and upright; they substituted the "greed" of the profit motive with a "societal interest." Yet group bureaucrats who manage and operate the public sector are no less self interested than those who manage and operate private business. One important difference exists, though: unlike private entrepreneurs, they are not financially responsible for their actions and they operate without institutional constraints of cost control that private property and competition induces. The enlightened minds of planners and technocrats cannot

---

[1]For more on the comprehensive system see Alexander Solzhenitsyn, Mikhail Agursky, et al., *From Under the Rubble* (Boston: Little, Brown, and Company, 1974); Erik von Kuehnelt-Leddihn, *Leftism: From de Sade and Marx to Hitler and Marcuse* (New Rochelle, N.Y.: Arlington House: 1974; 2nd edition, Regnery, 1990); Paul Hollander, *The Many Faces of Socialism* (New Brunswick, N.J.: Transaction, 1983); David Conway, *A Farewell to Marx: An Outline and Appraisal of His Theories* (New York: Viking Penguin, 1987).

overcome the problem of economic calculation without market signals.

The failure of socialism in Russia, and the enormous suffering and hardship of people in all socialist countries, is a powerful warning against socialism, statism, and interventionism in the West. "We should all be thankful to the Soviets," says Paul Craig Roberts, "because they have proved conclusively that socialism doesn't work. No one can say they didn't have enough power or enough bureaucracy or enough planners or they didn't go far enough."[2]

In contrast to the West, where Marxist tenets were doctrines of a counter religion, few in the Soviet Union truly believed in the official ideology: not the state managers, not the professors, not the journalists.[3] It was not necessary that they do so, for Marxism was a means of political rent seeking and of coercive control, not a body of ideas held to by honest men.

The Soviet Union is now gone, as are the huge statues of Marx and Lenin that littered the East, and the good reputation of their systems of thought. This collection of articles is the Requiem for Marx and the social and economic systems created in his name. As with any funeral service, we look back on the life of Marxian ideas. But unlike the ordinary funeral, we are not looking back fondly, for Marxism is as good an example of the maxim that "ideas have consequences" as can be found. It does not speak well of the intellectual class that no body of ideas attracted a greater following in this century.[4]

It is beyond the capacity of economic analysis to calculate the opportunity costs of the socialist experiment in Russia. But the human toll from Stalin's collectivization, purges, and Gulags is estimated by Russian historian Roy Medvedev at forty-one

---

[2]Paul Craig Roberts, in the *Wall Street Journal*, June 28, 1989.

[3]See Martin Malia, "From Under the Rubble, What?", in *Problems of Communism*, January–April 1992; Peter Rutland, *The Myth of the Plan* (La Salle, Ill.: Open Court, 1985).

[4]A striking example of Western infatuation with Soviet socialism is Sidney and Beatrice Webb, *Soviet Communism: A New Civilization?* (New York: Charles Scribner's Sons, 1936).

million people. A popular Russian aphorism says: "The only lesson of history is that it does not teach us anything." "Despite the recent collapse of socialism and communism in Soviet Russia and Eastern Europe, socialism is alive and growing,"[5] Gary Becker has said. It presents a mortal danger to economic freedom and the quality of life and will for generations to come.

The scholars contributing to this volume write in the economic and historical tradition of the Austrian school, founded by Carl Menger with his book *Principles of Economics* (1875). The tradition emphasizes a deductive method, role of choice and uncertainty in economic affairs, the power of market prices to coordinate economic activity, and the essential nature of private property for forming the basis of rational calculation. The Austrian school is also the historical *bete' noire* of the Marxian school. Long before any other school came around to understanding the deep flaws in the Marxian approach, the Austrians had devoted an enormous amount of intellectual power to exposing its fallacies and dangers. Carl Menger refuted the labor theory of value, his student Eugen von Böhm-Bawerk demolished Marx's views of capital, F. A. Hayek showed the incompatibility between socialism and political freedom, and Ludwig von Mises attacked the core of socialist economic theory.[6]

---

[5] Gary Becker, "The President's Address," The Mont Pelerin Society Newsletter, vol. 46, no. 1, February 1993.

[6] Austrian contributions to this debate include: Eugen von Böhm-Bawerk, *Karl Marx and the Close of His System* (New York: Augustus M. Kelley, 1949; Philadelphia, Penn.: Orion Editions, 1984); Peter J. Boettke, "The Austrian Critique and the Demise of Socialism: The Soviet Case," in Richard M. Ebeling, ed. *Austrian Economics: Perspectives on the Past and Prospects for the Future* (Hillsdale, Mich.: Hillsdale College Press, 1991); F. A. Hayek, *New Studies in Philosophy, Politics, Economics, and the History of Ideas* (University of Chicago Press, 1978); Trygve J. B. Hoff, *Economic Calculation in a Socialist Society* (Indianapolis, Ind.: LibertyPress, 1981); Hans-Hermann Hoppe, "De-Socialization in a United Germany," *Review of Austrian Economics* 5, no. 2 (1991): 77–106 and *A Theory of Socialism and Capitalism* (Boston, Mass.: Kluwer Academic Publishers, 1989); Israel M. Kirzner, "The Economic Calculation Debate: Lessons for Austrians," *Review of Austrian Economics* 2 (1988): 1–18; Don Lavoie, *Rivalry and Central Planning: The Socialist Calculation Debate Reconsidered* (New York: Cambridge University Press, 1985); Murray N. Rothbard, "The End of Socialism and the Calculation Debate Revisited," *Review of Austrian Economics* 5, no.2 (1991): 51–70), "Lange, Mises and Praxeology: The Retreat from Marxism," *Toward Liberty*, vol. 2 (Menlo Park, Calif.: Institute for Humane Studies, 1971), pp. 307–21,

It was Mises's criticism which has proven to be the most prescient. In his 1920 essay "Economic Calculation in the Socialist Commonwealth," he argued that the socialist economy cannot properly be called an "economy" at all, since the system provides no means for rationally allocating resources. It abolishes private property in capital goods, thereby eliminating the markets which produce prices with which to calculate profit and loss. The absence of rational economic calculation, and the institutional structures that undergird it, prevents any realistic assessment of the proper uses and opportunity costs and resource allocation options. "As soon as one gives up the conception of a freely established monetary price for goods of a higher order," Mises wrote "rational production becomes completely impossible." The central planners of an industrial economy will find themselves in a perpetual state of confusion and ignorance, "groping in the dark."

"One may anticipate the nature of the future socialist society," he said seventy years before the rest of the world was to become convinced. "There will be hundreds and thousands of factories in operation. Very few of these will be producing wares ready for use; in the majority of cases what will be manufactured will be unfinished goods and production-goods.... Every good will go through a whole series of stages before it is ready for use. In the ceaseless toil and moil of this process, however, the administration will be without any means of testing their bearings."

From my life and study in Moscow, I can attest to the truth of this prediction. In an economy, nearly every consumption good requires several stages of production. The more natural

---

and "Ludwig von Mises and Economic Calculation Under Socialism," *The Economics of Ludwig von Mises* (Kansas City: Sheed and Ward, 1976), pp. 67–78; Ludwig von Mises, "Middle-of-the-Road Policy Leads to Socialism," *Two Essays by Ludwig von Mises* (Auburn, Ala.: The Ludwig von Mises Institute, 1991), *Socialism* (Indianapolis, Ind.: Liberty Press/Liberty Classics, 1981), "Economic Calculation in the Socialist Commonwealth," F. A. Hayek, ed., *Collective Economic Planning* (Clifton, N.J.: Kelley Publishing Company, 1975), pp. 87–130, and (Auburn, Ala.: The Ludwig von Mises Institute), and "One Hundred Years of Marxian Socialism," *Money, Method, and the Market Process*, Richard M. Ebeling, ed. (Boston, Mass.: Kluwer Academic Publishers, 1990), pp. 215–32.

resources used and the more complex the technology involved, the more stages of production are required. Yet lacking an ability to see a production process through to ends that consumers desire, Soviet socialism gave only military hardware, useless goods, goods to make other goods, while consumers were deprived of bare essentials.[7]

In the late 1980s, when *glasnost* at last permitted Soviet economists to speak out, they confirmed the death sentence that Mises pronounced. As Martin Malia put it, "through the voices of Nikolay Shmelev, Gavriil Popov, Vasiliy Selyunin, Grigory Khanin, Larisa Piyasheva, Mikhail Berger, and subsequently Grigoriy Yavlinksy and Yegor Gaydar, they offered us a portrait of the Soviet that was in full accord with the evaluations of . . . Ludwig von Mises, whose book contains hardly a single figure and not a word about GNP."[8] This powerful confirmation, Malia points out, led to "methodological *smuta*" (in Russian) in Western economics.

A common mistake Western observers made was to think the Soviet Union's fundamental problem was a lack of democracy. They completely overlooked that the institutional structure of the political system cannot overcome the problem inherent in an economic system with no means of rational calculation. The Soviet Union had a number of leaders that promised political reform, but none was able to put bread on the table. In fact, the primary problem in the Soviet Union was socialism, and it is still far from being dismantled in the nations that once made up that evil empire.

The present "capitalist revolution" in Russia was best described by Russian publicist Viktor Kopin: it is a "quasi-democratic society with a quasi-market of quasi-legality and quasi-morality. The

---

[7]On the failure of the Soviet model, see: Zbigniew Brzezinski, *The Grand Failure: The Birth and Death of Communism in the Twentieth Century* (New York: Macmillan, 1989); Sven Rydenfelt, *A Pattern for Failure: Socialist Economies in Crisis* (San Diego: Harcourt, Brace, Jonvanovich, 1984); Nick Eberstadt, *The Poverty of Communism* (New Brunswick, N.J.: Transaction, 1988).

[8]Martin Malia, "From Under the Rubble, What?", in *Problems of Communism*, January–April 1992, p. 96.

predominant conclusion out of this is that freedom leads to the destruction of spirituality, crime, pauperization of the masses, and the emergence of a class of fat cats."

The decades-long effort to eliminate markets has resulted in the destruction of the work ethic, the mass misallocation of resources through centralized investment, the demolition of the base for private capital accumulation, distorted means of economic calculation, and technology so obsolete that the capital value of industrial enterprises is zero or negative. Most heavy industries were built during Stalin's Industrialization Program in the 1930s and have not been remodeled since. A huge part of Russian industrial stock is as productive as an industrial history museum.

The crisis in socialist agriculture goes back to the 1920s and 30s, when millions of the most productive peasant households were maimed as "kulaks," and exiled to Siberia. Most of them could not survive the hardships and purges and perished there. Agriculture still has not recovered from this collectivization and blanket nationalization of property that turned owners into prison laborers. At the beginning of the century, Russia exported wheat, rye, barley, and oats to the world market. Today Russia is the world's largest importer of grain.

Russia's consumer prices index registered the inflation rate to be 1,240 percent in 1992, instead of the promised 100 percent. Even as the chairman of the Russian Central Bank blamed the government for not pumping enough liquidity into the system, Russia's printing presses have not been able to keep up with demand. Credit markets remain centrally controlled, and serious monetary reform is nowhere in sight.

Larisa Piyasheva—the only visible economist close to the Austrian school in present day Russia—believes that total privatization alone will not solve all the problems, but without it, there is no hope. She was fired by Yeltsin's government due to "budget cuts."[9]

[9]*Stolitsa* No. 37, 1992, p. 4.

If the present looks bleak, the recent history of the Soviet Union remains widely misunderstood. No one figure represents the confusion better than Mikhail Gorbachev. In the West, he was and is considered the great reformer—witness the title of Princeton Professor Stephen Cohen's *New York Times* op-ed, "Gorbachev the Great." If Gorbachev was a reformer, he was hardly the first Soviet politician to use so-called reforms to maintain power. Lenin was a reformer too, and he resorted to extraordinary means to save communism. As a result of Lenin's efforts to impose real utopian socialism—not the bureaucratized model that existed until recently—the entire population was dying out. Had he continued on that course, he would not have had any subjects to rule. That's when he initiated the New Economic Policy, which allowed markets and private property.[10]

According to historian Alec Nove, Lenin "kept stubbornly on the course of all-round nationalization, centralization, the elimination of money, and above all, the maintenance of [grain requisitioning]. There was no pressure on him from his colleagues to change this policy. Events, rather than the central committee, provided a potent means of persuasion."

Gorbachev too tried to save communism through other means. That was the original point behind *glasnost* and *perestroika* (and probably why these petty measures were so heralded in the West). Even the KGB understood the need for reform. As the chief ideologue of the KGB, Philip Bobkov, has said "The KGB understood very well, back in 1985, that the USSR would not be able to make further progress without perestroika."

By the people in the Soviet Union Gorbachev was rightly considered to be just another Communist Party hack. His "reforms" were never fundamental, but only strategic measures to preserve the centrality of the Soviet Communist Party and to salvage what was left of the socialist system. Gorbachev was

[10]Peter J. Boettke, *The Political Economy of Soviet Socialism: The Formative Years 1918–1928* (Boston: Kluwer, 1990).

only willing to "reform" when the world was falling apart around him.

He was in a good position to know better. He was from a peasant family in South Russia, where he witnessed first hand the malnutrition, hunger, and even starvation that socialism caused. His grandfather was killed in Stalin's purges, so he knew the brutality of Communist politics. Yet he chose to make politics his life's work. For Gorbachev, the exercise of power has always been more important than good sense or morality.

It was a Western fantasy that the man named to be general secretary of the Communist Party would not be a devoted Communist. As in joining a street gang, you must demonstrate that you are absolutely loyal to the club (all its associated crimes) and that your conscience can be overridden. During Gorbachev's long political climb, he passed more than one hundred such political and security clearances.

The main difference between Gorbachev and his predecessors was that he was smarter and smoother. He was also the first one with university education: a masters in law and masters in agriculture. Given Soviet education, that is probably why the first thing he did was ruin the agricultural distribution system.

While he was in agricultural school in Stavropol, Russia, he was chief of the local Communist Party. His colleagues report that he ordered his professors to come from the university to Gorbachev's office to tutor and test him.

Gorbachev became secretary of agriculture under the Yuri Andropov regime, and endeared himself to the Party Secretary by promoting a cult of Andropov. He promoted films about him and mandated that streets be named after him. Andropov returned the favor by promoting Gorbachev in the Party bureaucracy. Of course Andropov is one of the most hardened of all Soviet leaders. As ambassador to Hungary, he ordered the invasion of that great country in 1956, and while head of the KGB in 1968, he persecuted dissidents by the tens of thousands (including Solzhenitsyn), presiding over the darkest period in KGB history).

Later, Gorbachev became secretary of ideology during the Chernenko regime, and as early as 1984, he was making overtures to Margaret Thatcher. What Thatcher did not know, or refused to believe, was that Gorbachev's goal was to save Soviet communism (meaning the power of the Party) and given the dire circumstances he faced, that meant "reform." Yet a reformist communist is only marginally better than an orthodox one. His goals and methods should have been condemned, just as one condemn's a successor to Hitler who claimed to be a "reformist Nazi."

Gorbachev never learned economics in school. In all my dealings with him I had never seen even a slight flash of economic insight, or even the desire to learn more about economics. He preferred to think like a communist: everything can be done by issuing orders and demanding obedience, no matter how perverse, contrary to human nature, and brutal they may be.

Beginning with the day he assumed power, he positioned himself as an opponent of freedom and the market. He single-handedly destroyed what little market activity existed in the Soviet Union, wrecked the already miserable lives of the public, presided over appalling violence against innocent people in the Baltic states, and openly supported old-guard communists. Yet the Western media decided not to be skeptical about his aims.

Gorbachev's original theory was that the socialist system was in good working order, but the people, the cogs in the communist machine, had taken to laziness, drunkenness and were accumulating "dishonest income" in violation of socialist ethics. His first reform was to call "a restructuring of people's thinking."

The anti-alcohol campaign began right away. Party bosses sternly announced that they didn't want any "drunks" in their country. Their enforcers began a concerted effort to discover everyone with the smell of alcohol on their breath and haul them into the police station. When the police stations became over-crowded, it became a routine practice to drive thousands of people about fifteen miles out of town and drop them in the dark cold. Nearly every night, you could see armies of so-called drunks walking miles back to town in the middle of winter.

Over 90 percent of liquor stores were closed. The Party bosses did not anticipate what happened next: sugar, flour aftershave, and window cleaner immediately disappeared from the shelves. Using these products, the production of moonshine increased by about 300 percent in one year.

The predictable result was a heavy loss of life. From 13,000 to 25,000 people died from drinking poisoned surrogate alcohol. Many more died standing in lines for five hours to get the little bit of official liquor that was left. Meanwhile, Gorbachev and loyal Party bureaucrats—who said the dead deserved their fate—would get expensive liquor from the West delivered to their homes and offices. Many families would spend up to 75 percent of their official income on alcohol. But with Gorbachev's campaign, every second household began moonshining.

Revenues from alcohol sales (taxed up to 6,000 percent) was a major source of funding for the central government, generating enough to fund the entire medical budget. The campaign ended when the government realized it was costing too much. The government's budget began to lose 25-30 billion rubles per year. Moreover, Gorbachev learned what previous regimes had understood: it is easier to govern people who are drunk because they withstand humiliation and abuse better. When people are sober they begin to care about politics and are not nearly as passive. So Gorbachev did an about-face and ordered a massive increase in alcohol production. And he had the government make it available to be sold everywhere, even toy shops and bakeries.

The anti-alcohol campaign did irreparable damage to the economy. With state revenues having been severely curtailed, an economic chain reaction set in that hurt every sector. The central bank began to print money, leaving too much money chasing too few goods. Consumers used to get enough to survive from state stores, but new disposable income saved from not buying alcohol was spent on goods. The end result was massive shortages. And to correct for the deficit, services were drastically cut, even while Gorbachev restricted private alternatives.

Then Gorbachev began a campaign against "dishonest income." Like Stalin and Khrushchev before him, he declared all sources of income other than official salary to be an evil to be stamped out. For example, if a person rented a room out in his house, he received "dishonest income" and all parties would be severely punished. The problem was not a single person in the Soviet Union was untainted by unofficial economic activity. The official economy did not produce enough of anything desirable, so if a person was untainted, he was probably already dead.

Party bureaucrats bulldozed thousands of gardens in the backyards of peasant's homes, often filled with fresh fruits and vegetables. "Illicit" farmers' markets were closed. The bureaucrats cracked down on such activity as currency exchanges and unofficial transportation. Chaos reigned in the housing market, where the penalty for renting out an apartment for profit would be to have your whole home confiscated.

To make sure that all goods sold were licitly produced, bureaucrats enforced a system of applying certificates to all goods. To get one, a person had to prove that whatever he was selling at the market was approved ahead of time. But the system was evaded like everything else: the certificates were sold by petty bureaucrats for high bribes. Even after the Chernobyl nuclear accident, a vendor could pay a bureaucrat a fee to have food declared radiation free.

Price controls in cooperative markets were strictly enforced, so that all prices had to be the same as in state stores. For example, beef was supposed to be 4 rubles per kilo. As a working economist in Moscow, my first thought was, "all beef will disappear from the market." But when I went to the market to see what was going on, to my surprise beef was available. It turns out that farmers were shrewdly selling 4-rubles worth of beef, but attached would be a huge dinosaur-sized bone that brought the total weight to one kilo. With a complex system of selling meat plus huge bones, supply and demand met and there were no meat shortages.

Things were different in the market for rabbit meat, which was supposed to sell for 3 rubles per kilo. It was impossible to find a bone heavy enough to add to the total weight that could also have plausibly come from a rabbit. Rabbit meat disappeared very quickly. The campaign against dishonest income made the unofficial economy even more unofficial and therefore less efficient. For customers it meant very high prices, because anybody left in the underground added a large risk premium to their products.

The most visible results of the campaign against dishonest income was an increase in bribes and a reshuffling of power in favor of the bureaucrat-led mafia. Soviet bureaucrats were always pleased when new laws were passed because it gave them a chance to extract even more bribes. It was especially helpful when the punishments for violating the law were severe; it provided an opportunity to scare people. People in higher positions could use information to control underlings, or even to leap frog to higher positions. So many of Gorbachev's people used their information to extract bribes and advance their careers.

Within the first year, 150,000 people went to prison for making dishonest income, 24,000 of whom were top bureaucrats. Nobody went to jail in the name of enforcing the law or the Constitution. They were sent because they were unable to evade someone else's personal vendetta, or they were destroyed by bribes demanded by their black-market competition.

Government officials were reluctant to take cash bribes because it would mean going to prison. So they worked through intermediaries like the police. A policemen would come to visit someone in their home or office, and threaten him with severe punishment for some alleged indiscretion. The accused must come up with enough bribe money to clear his name.

I once knew a man who was head of a huge, multi-hundred thousand ruble furniture manufacturing enterprise. He did his best to stay away from underground activities, and on his salary he could afford to. But he had an enemy in the Party, and one day he got a visit from a policeman accusing him of dishonesty in record keeping. (Police work is a highly valued occupation because of the opportunity for receiving bribes.) Instead of paying the appropriate bribe, the man maintained his innocence. Then a team of six accountants came into his offices and combed through his records over a period of weeks. Finally, they found a 34 ruble mistake, which they said was deliberate dishonesty.

After a hearing, the state attorney threatened the man with eight years in prison. His own attorney, who he had to bribe, told him the best solution was to pay 15,000 rubles—divided among the prosecutors, the bureaucrats, and the judge—so the affair could end. The man finally gave in and paid the bribe. Still, the judge punished him for his prior intransigence by giving him a one-year suspended sentence.

The law against dishonest income even affected academia, where many professors took bribes for good grades. After the law took effect, a tremendous reshuffling took place at universities, based on a complex matrix of exchanges of information and bribes.

It is easy to see how the campaign completely discouraged people from any kind of economic activity. Since the state sector was heavily subsidized, and price controls were enforced at cooperatives, a sizable portion of what market did exist was destroyed. And this was under Gorbachev's hand. The campaign, began in 1986, lasted only one year.

After wreaking havoc on the economy through his other campaigns, Gorbachev initiated a third: in favor of "labor discipline," that is, forcing people to show up on time and work harder. In this, Gorbachev was following a similar campaign by his mentor Andropov (who had people rounded up in the streets and destroyed their lives for not acting like slaves). Gorbachev initiated harsh measures against "lazy" people, making it easier to find and prosecute anybody the government did not like. If a person was absent for three hours, they would lose their job. Instead of giving two weeks notice to change jobs, employees had to give two months. Enterprises would hold three-hour meetings, on paid time, to denounce one person for being ten minutes late to work and blame him for all problems. People walking around in midday were questioned and harassed.

This campaign came to a quick halt because it antagonized many people and did not seem to be helping the economy. In fact, the problem was not labor discipline. The problem was Gorbachev's absurd campaigns in favor of a failed economic system.

Gorbachev's final effort, before he began speaking about "the market," was a short-lived campaign for new "quality" standards. The central plan had always emphasized the quantity of output, but never the quality. So 150,000 new bureaucrats were hired to oversee the "quality of output." Every state enterprise had a special division on quality that would police the factory, providing ever more opportunities for bribes—resulting in more bribes and more failure.

That was the last attempt to resuscitate the communist world through conventional means. Yet Gorbachev still had not gotten the message. At a closing speech to the Central Committee in June 1987, Gorbachev said that he would "rebuff anyone who offers us anti-socialist alternatives."

When all else was exhausted, Gorbachev began to speak about markets—a "planned, regulated, socialist market." He had his paid academics find quotes from Marx and Lenin to support his new idea, which is easy to do since together their work makes up 105 volumes. No one takes Marx and Lenin as gospel, but the head communist always has to justify his deeds with the Holy Writ of communism.

The first effort in the creation of this new market was to enact huge "budget cuts." Even government propaganda reinforced the change. Films showed Party chiefs as beggars on the street, sitting with their derbies in hand, while rich, fat free marketeers generously flipped them kopeks. Everyone was paralyzed with fear that they would be fired, and so by the second half of 1987, most people simply stopped working.

The budget cuts appeared to be a reality when Gorbachev sacked 600,000 bureaucrats from central operations of the ministries—which amounts to 30 percent to 50 percent of each department. Alongside that, however, he also created a set of new mega- enterprises to substitute for the ministries. A study I did of these new enterprises at the time showed they hired 720,000 people, most of them just-fired bureaucrats, but with a generous 35 percent salary increase. Gorbachev's "cuts" actually represented a twenty percent increase in the managerial sector of the Soviet State, which was exactly the point of the move. The old structures of the command economy began to evaporate with all these changes, reversals, and talk of creating a market. But since no market was actually set up, everything came to a standstill.

The Law on Cooperatives—a new regulation allowing pseudo-private ownership—seemed to be a step in the right direction. But in fact, the newly created cooperatives became an organized mafia themselves, extracting and paying out bribes at an unprecedented rate. As soon as a person would start a business, the fire department would arrive to close everything down and then wait for bribes. A person could sue the fire department, but he would have to pay a bride to the judge. In the Soviet Union, people learned that it is better to pay bribes directly. Thus Gorbachev's new "market" was not an authentic one. It piled new regulations and ministries on top of the old, and never allowed private property and real buying and selling.

A young man from a peasant family I knew had heard that market activity was legal, and decided to raise a pig to sell in the market. For six months, this hopeful entrepreneur devoted his time and money to caring for it and feeding it, hoping he would earn twice his money back by selling it. Never was a man so happy as when he took the pig to market one morning. That night I found him drunk and depressed. He was not a drinker, so I asked him what happened. When he arrived at the market, a health inspector immediately chopped off a third of the pig. The inspector said he was looking for worms. Then the police came and picked the best part of it, and left without even saying thank you. He had to pay bribes to the officials in charge of the market to get a space to sell what was left. And he had to sell the meat at state prices. By the end of the day, he earned barely enough to buy one bottle of vodka, which he had just finished drinking. This was Gorbachev's new market in a nutshell.

Long before the coup that ousted Gorbachev, thwarted by Yeltsin and leading to the end of the Soviet Union, talk of creating a market ceased, and all real reformers had resigned their positions in the government. Gorbachev used the term "markets," a term which Western reporters liked, as an excuse for more repression. To this end, he undertook a totalitarian effort to withdraw all 50- and 100-ruble notes from circulation, giving people only three days to turn them in, give a full accounting of where they got their money, and get very little money back. This was necessary said Gorbachev, to eliminate "speculation, corruption, smuggling, forgery, unearned income, and normalizing the monetary situation and the consumer market." All money unaccounted for was confiscated. Because there were no goods in the market to buy with rubles, people had stockpiled them. Gorbachev's measures wiped out thousands of people's life savings.

It was nothing more than an explicit attempt to wipe out the "underground economy," which in fact was the only real market in the Soviet Union and the only source of real production. The last Soviet dictators to do this were Khrushchev in 1961, and before him, Stalin in 1947–48. Both permitted a ten-for-one exchange of old notes for new, and the result was an explosion of political oppression of the government's enemies.

Gorbachev's last gasp on behalf of the "market" was a one-time price reform to bring them in line with prices in the West. But it was no more an improvement than when the U.S. Post Office raises the price of stamps. It was not a step in the right direction; it only indicated a continued desire to control the economy from above.

It was the first time since 1961 that the prices of basic

goods changed. Yet the prices for basic goods in the Soviet Union were already extremely high. A person had to work 12 times longer there to buy beef than here, 18 to 20 times longer for poultry, seven times longer for butter, three times longer for milk, 16 times longer for a color television, and 180 times longer for a car. With the new price hikes, the required work hours multiplied by two or three times. It is easy to understand why one fifth of the population lived at the poverty line, below which meant serious malnutrition. The government said 85 percent of the new revenues would go back into raising the wages of workers and peasants, but, in fact, most of it went back into government coffers to pay the military and run failed state enterprises.

The Soviets also cut subsidies to key staple goods, and that is partly why people saw this as a pro-market reform. But under state ownership, in effect, all goods produced are subsidized, that is, not tested by the competitive market. Instead of directly financing production out of the state budget, they did it by arbitrarily increasing the prices for monopoly goods.

The Gorbachev government implemented the "reform" to raise revenue to pay for its fiscal shortfall. The Soviets expected revenue of 23.4 billion rubles in the first two months of 1991, but they only received 7 billion, or less than one third the expected amount. The central government did not receive any of the 48 billion rubles it expected from the republics for a fund to implement the new union treaty. And the official budget deficit showed it was already higher than the figure predicted for the entire year (31.1 billion rubles compared with 26.7 billion).

Three key advisers to Gorbachev began to fear for the worst: that the Soviets would not be able to pay the army, pay the welfare payments, or run state enterprises unless something was done. Finance minister Vladimir Orlov, State Bank chairman Victor Geraschenko, and Budget chairman Victor Kucherenko were so alarmed that they sent a note to Gorbachev saying that "the economy is on the brink of a catastrophe"—by which they meant the solvency of the central Soviet government.

Why did Gorbachev insist on hailing his price hikes as market reform? First, he wanted to impress the Bush administration and the World Bank with his intentions, which could then be turned into hard currency. Second, he wanted to fool the Soviet people who wanted reform to a free market. Third, he was anxious to discredit the idea of markets; when this plan failed, he was preparing to allow the market to take the blame.

Henry Kissinger, the Nobel Prize Committee, and many others have given credit to Gorbachev for the events of 1989 in Eastern Europe, which brought down those governments. Gorbachev's real strategy in those countries, however, was to replace the old guard Stalinists (with poor images) with young men like himself who drank the same brands of brandy. He hoped he could put smoother, smarter men in power in an effort to save socialism. The situation fell out of his control, largely because the KGB had misinformed him about how deep the hatred toward socialism was in those countries. The revolutions of Eastern Europe happened in spite of Gorbachev, not because of him.

What he did in the Baltic States—authorizing the Soviet military to crack the skulls of innocent people in the Baltics—qualified him to be included among history's litany of murderous rulers, but he was never included. Even while he was heralded in the West as a great reformer, he was also running labor camps, committing human rights violations, and sending people to prison for speech crimes. As the Soviet Union came to an end, the public had been reduced to a collective of hunter gatherers, barely existing at a subsistence level.

Before the coup that removed him from power, Gorbachev told a reporter, "I've been told more than once that it is time to stop swearing allegiance to socialism." "Why should I? Socialism is my deep conviction, and I will promote it as long as I can talk and work."

Western academics and media pundits found his support for socialism charming, if a little outdated. But the people who lived under the system felt differently. They knew socialism had proven itself the most destructive ideology in human historys—responsible for untold millions of deaths. For those populations onto whom socialism had been imposed, it had impoverished them, wiped out their cultural heritage, and in many cases, resulted in massive bloodshed.

President George Bush played no small part in keeping Gorbachev in power longer than he should have been, sticking by him, and doing everything politically possible to support him. Bush lent his support to the only major world leader without a democratic mandate, a man despised by his subjects, who imposed a system antithetical to Western values. Is it an American tradition that the U.S. president should support the head of Soviet communism in time of need? Similarly, Herbert Hoover bailed out Lenin, Franklin Roosevelt bailed out Stalin, and George Bush rescued Gorbachev.[11]

For six and a half years, Gorbachev straddled the fence between reform and the status quo. As part of his effort to carve out this incoherent third way, he gathered around him a group of hard-line communists. Eventually, they became his closest advisers and the most powerful people in the country—militarily, economically, and politically. It was that same old guard that tried to slit Gorbachev's throat during the failed coup on August 19, 1991. Six of the Gang of Eight who organized the coup against him were directly appointed by himself. Before he elevated them to power, they were little more than lightweight bureaucrats. Had the coup succeeded, the structure and personnel of the coup government would have been much the same as it was before. For example, Gennadi Yanayev, president for a day, was appointed by Gorbachev as secretary of trade unions and then promoted to vice president. Prime Minister Valentin Pavlov was responsible for many of the economic blunders of the previous year that inflamed the public, including the price hikes, the ruble reform, and excessive money creation. And Anatoly Lukyanov,

[11]One historical account of such activity is Joseph Finder, *Red Carpet* (New York: Holt, Rinehart, Winston, 1983).

president of the Supreme Soviet, was a close confidant of Gorbachev's.

Gorbachev appointed and protected these six as part of his compromise strategy to placate the hardliners. They were utterly lacking in charisma, so Gorbachev assumed they could not be a threat. But they tried to be. He should have expected that communists can only be trusted to behave like communists, and for this reason, he bore primary responsibility for the coup. Had he conducted himself as he ought during his six and a half years in power, he could have spared himself and his country this harrowing experience.

Everyone in the higher reaches of power had known for some time that a coup against Gorbachev would be a snap. One evening in Moscow, I discussed the possibility with a friend of mine, a general in the Soviet Army. He told me that an actual coup would be the easy part. "We could take power in ten minutes," he said. "But then what? We have no sausages, no bread—nothing to offer the people." The Moscow junta hoped its power grab would be bolstered by Gorbachev's low popularity. But as much as the people hated their ruler, they hated the coup leaders more. The coup government achieved only a short moment of glory. Once in power, it faced a people seething with anger at the crimes of totalitarianism and the poverty of socialism. The coup leaders also faced a hard winter, a very bad harvest, and the prospect of mass starvation. The coup leaders lost their nerve and sobriety, and Boris Yeltsin thwarted their efforts.

The coup attempt, ironically, illustrated that communist economic ideology had been discredited. The Stalinist leaders of the Soviet coup never spoke of Marx or Lenin, or of resuscitating the machinery of central planning and nationalization. They spoke instead of market reforms, however insincere they may have been. Any alternative rhetoric would have brought them even more unpopularity than they already had. Note that this was despite the fact that the command system brought the people more material goods than Gorbachev's confused system of *perestroika*.

At his first news conference after the Soviet coup attempt,
Gorbachev promised: "I will struggle until the very end for the
renewal of this party. I am a true believer in socialism." He
could not have delivered a greater insult to the Soviet peoples,
who quickly resumed their demands that he resign. Conventional wisdom has long said the Russians are culturally inclined toward passivity, authoritarianism, and envy. Hendrick
Smith has made a career out of promoting this idea. The heroic
actions of the people during the coup and after told the real
truth: the Russians are like people everywhere who want
freedom from arbitrary rule. They have been the victims of a
tragic past, but their desire to be free from chains of slavery
triumphed. Once Boris Yeltsin assumed control of the government from Gorbachev, the Soviet Union fell completely apart.
And at the age of 74, on December 8, 1991, the Soviet Union
died.

Since that time, the Yeltsin government has proven another
point: Gorbachevian socialism was not the only way to ruin an
economy's wealth-creating potential. During the first wave of
Yeltsin's reforms in Russia, prices soared 20 fold instead of the
promised two fold. Production dropped 15 percent since last
year (compared with a 13 drop in 1990). New foreign and
domestic contracts in 1992 amount to only seven percent of the
1991 level. And 1991 was supposed to be a "bad" year, with only
two percent of the new contracts in 1985. To top it off, the
budget deficit exceeded 35 percent of the GDP. The outlook for
the economy continued to look worse and worse. This is not
because Yeltsin had not applied the advice from Western academics and World Bank bureaucrats. The problem was he took
them at their word when they said flexible prices, not private
property, is what the Russian economy needed.

Contrary to all the promises and beliefs of Russian Keynesi-
ans headed by the Yeltsin economic minister Yegor Gaidar, we
watched a simultaneous increase in prices and a fall-off in production. Because the essence of socialism is public ownership,
without dismantling this system, none of Yeltsin's "reforms"
will work. Like Gorbachev before him, Yeltsin's government is

directed at "restructuring the state regulatory mechanism." "We cannot link the restructuring of the regulatory mechanism to full-scale privatization," wrote his chief economist. "If we did, we simply wouldn't live long enough to see it." Meanwhile, every new announcement of impending reform causes perverse public responses and every new law passed, ostensibly to increase freedom, only increases opportunities for fines and bribes.

Former communists urgently sought a replacement for archaic Marxism-Leninism, and they found it in *"gosudarsvennichestvo,"* or the "cult of the state." Based on Max Weber's theorizing, it exalts bureaucratic, hierarchical, centralized management. A series of organizations were founded to support this ideology, including the Russian National Union, the Party of Regeneration, and the Civic Union.

The sad legacy of Marxism is the mind set of certain people, both in the East and West, who believe that the state can cure all economic ills and bring about social justice. Yet a return to central management under whatever label is not the solution, but neither is the status quo. What is needed in the former Soviet Union and Soviet-client states is a wholesale repudiation of the legacy of Marx. In the United States, too, Marx's ideas influenced a generation of reformers during the Progressive Era (out of which came modern central banking and the progressive income tax), the New Deal, the Great Society, and continues to infect departments of literature and sociology in major universities. Remarkably, even after the fall of Soviet and East European social regimes, Marxism has not lost all its academic cache.[12] "I think it's an exciting time to be a Marxist," Steve Cullenberg of the University of California at Riverside told the Associated Press. He was among the 2,000 academics that attended the University of Massachusetts at Amherst conference in November 1992 entitled "Marxism in the New World Order:

---

[12]For a refutation of neo-Marxist attempts to save the system from itself, see David Gordon, *Resurrecting Marx: The Analytical Marxists on Freedom, Exploitation, and Justice* (New Brunswick, N.J.: Transaction, 1990).

Crises and Possibilities." The mass media, moreover, pays tribute to Marx's honor every time it uses the terms "progressive" and "reactionary," demonstrating an unwitting acceptance of Marx's version of the historical inevitability of socialism.

In *Requiem for Marx*, we attempt to set the record straight on a subject clouded with economic, historical, and philosophical error. Accordingly, the essays here can be regarded as revisionist. David Gordon shows exactly how much Marx has been misunderstood in a wholesale reevaluation of Marx's philosophical basis for socialism. Hans-Hermann Hoppe recasts Marx's argument about the class struggle in line with an Austrian understanding of the state and economy, and arrives at entirely different conclusions from Marx's own. Personal history is never out of bounds at a Requiem, and Gary North piles on evidence that Marx's personal habits, financial and otherwise, strayed far from the socialist ideal. David Osterfeld demonstrates that much of Marx's view of the world rests on empirical propositions which turn out to be false and definitions which turn out to be shallow and analytically useless. The doctrine of the classes, properly understood, is a useful framework, argues Ralph Raico, but it was taken from an older and sounder classical liberal school of eighteenth century France. And finally, Murray Rothbard argues that Marx's communist views of history, property, marriage, and much else, were rooted in the bloody millinnarianism of the middle ages, thereby representing nothing uniquely evil in the history of thought.

Contra Marx, these essays offer another vision of what an economy needs: private property, defined as both autonomous ownership and control of homesteaded resources; free prices, which provide the means of calculating profits and loss, the measure of economic usefulness and waste; freedom of contract, which allows free exchange of privately owned resources; and the rule of law, which establishes institutional structures that protect the previous three conditions from third-party intervention. Until these are firmly in place, there can be no hope for getting back the road to economic prosperity.

Taken together, the essays present Marx in an entirely different light than most any literature on the subject. In short, among scholarly works, this is probably the most anti-Marxist collection ever published. We are confident that many who have lived under systems constructed in Marx's name now share this perspective.

Yuri N. Maltsev, associate professor of economics at Carthage College, is a senior fellow of the Ludwig von Mises Institute, and was a reformist member of the Institute of Economics of the Soviet Academy of Sciences until his defection in 1989.

~ 1 ~

The Marxist Case
for Socialism

David Gordon

K arl Marx believed that "with the inexorability of a law of nature" capitalism was doomed. In the past, capitalism aided the growth of production; now that system had become a "fetter on the forces of production." Since in Marx's view the forces of production must develop, the pressure on capitalism would sooner or later prove impossible to contain. Under socialism, the economic system next on the historical agenda, the forces of production will grow to unheard of heights.

Not everything that is inevitable is desirable, as death and taxes remind us. For Marx, questions of what is good and bad have no universally true answers. One can speak only of what is good or bad for an economic class. Those who have prospered under capitalism will find the demise of the old order a matter of regret: those who have done poorly will look to socialism as "a very present hope in all our troubles." The proletariat stand foremost among those who will benefit from the arrival of socialism.

Marx's position raises three questions for discussion. Will socialism replace capitalism? Is capitalism a bad system for workers? Will socialism be a better system for them? One of Marx's reasons for thinking that capitalism had neared its end was that because workers suffered from exploitation, they would rise in revolt against it. Thus, the answer to the first question in part depends on our assessment of the second, and, as we shall see, the third as well. This fact provides a natural order in which to respond to the questions.

Marx argued that capitalism exploits workers. Before one can evaluate his conclusion, a prior issue arises: what did he mean by exploitation? In the 'ordinary language' sense of the term, if capitalists exploit workers, then they act toward workers in a morally objectionable way. They 'use' those whom they exploit.

Marx meant something entirely different by exploitation. He uses the term to designate a situation in which workers do not receive the full value of the products their labor creates. The surplus is the source of rent, interest, and profit. The details of Marx's claim will be addressed immediately below. But even on the basis of this very rough sketch, it is apparent that Marx's claim does not by itself show that something is wrong with capitalism. Unless there is something objectionable about Marxist exploitation, it does not follow that workers exploited in Marx's sense will find in their circumstances a reason for change.

A more detailed account of Marxist exploitation will clarify this contention. In Marx's view, the socially necessary labor time required to produce a commodity is the basis of its exchange value. If, e.g., one house exchanges on the market for two cars, then the labor needed to produce one house will be twice the labor needed to produce two cars. By 'socially necessary,' Marx means roughly speaking, the 'average amount' of labor required to make something.[1] Marx does not maintain that prices on the capitalist market are the exact equivalent of labor values. Rather, in a complicated and disputed way, labor values underlie market prices. Fortunately, for the purposes of this essay we can avoid this arid and arcane sector of Marxist scholasticism. A 'bare bones' account of Marx's economics is all that we need.

---

[1]For an argument that Marx's concept of socially necessary labor involves him in a circular argument, see Robert Nozick, *Anarchy, State, and Utopia* (New York: Basic Books, 1974), p. 260.

The labor theory of value applies to labor. Like other commodities, the price of labor, i.e., the wages laborers receive, is determined by the labor-value of labor. This at first sounds like an impossible expression, just as the 'length in feet of one foot' has no meaning. How can the standard of value itself have a value? But, in Marx's view, appearances are deceiving. We can find a labor value for the laborer: this is the labor time required to produce him. Put more simply, the value of labor is the laborer's cost of living, determined by whatever a society regards as needed for living.

Here precisely, Marx thinks, lies the key to the riddle of profit. A capitalist employer pays labor its price, i.e., its labor value, computed in the way just explained. For this price he gets whatever the laborer can produce during the time he works. In Marx's formula, the capitalist buys labor power but pays only for labor. The difference between the two quantities is surplus value, the source of rent, interest, and profit. The rate of surplus value Marx also terms the rate of exploitation. Marx attached great value to his proof of exploitation, since he believed that with it he had laid bare the secret of capitalism. The driving force of a capitalist economy is profit; without it, the economy would grind to a halt. Yet how is profit possible, if everything exchanges for its true labor value? Precisely in the purchase of labor, as Marx conceived of it, the answer lies at hand. The capitalist does *not* pay the laborer less than his value. The laborer's wages are determined by the value of the commodities required to produce him, and in equilibrium he does not receive less than this. But because of surplus value, the capitalist can still secure his profit. In Marx's analysis, therefore, the entire capitalist system rests on the exploitation of labor. No exploitation, no surplus value; no surplus value, no profit; no profit, no capitalism.

Marx's ingenious argument has not at all withstood the test of critical analysis. Most importantly, it rests on the discredited labor theory of value. Marxists have never been adequately able to reply to the devastating analysis by Eugen von Böhm-Bawerk.

As this is well-trodden ground, a brief summary will suffice for our purpose.

Marx assumed that an exchange is an equality: in our earlier example, 1 house = 2 cars. In sharp contrast, in the Austrian view, an exchange takes place only if there is a double inequality: each person must value what he gains more than what he gives up. This view seems to me far-reaching in its importance. It exposes a pre-supposition of classical economics which, once questioned by the Austrian, appears the very reverse of obvious. *Why* is an exchange an equality? Neither Marx nor any other defender of the labor theory has given an explanation for this assumption.

Further, Marx assumed that an exchange involves a very strong sense of equality. In his view, the equality constituting an exchange must be explained by a common element on both sides of the equality. In other words, for Marx an exchange was an identity, in the same way that the two sides of an equation in mathematics designate the same quantity. If 1 house = 2 cars, then both '1 house' and '2 cars' share some common quantity. To those not enmeshed in the Marxist metaphysics of value, this step seems if anything even more wrongheaded than its predecessor, the postulate of equality. And if even, *per absurdum*, one accepted identity, Marx offers no argument for the contention that the common quantity must be labor.[2]

Still another problem arises from the fact that, as Marx well knew, market prices differ from labor values. Marx dealt with this by trying to show that labor values could somehow be transformed into price. Those interested in the technical details of this issue should consult Böhm-Bawerk, who, *pace* Thomas Sowell, understood Marx perfectly well.

It seems to me that one fact is often overlooked in the details of simple and expanded reproduction, Divisions I and II, and other elements of the Marxist architectonic. Suppose that

[2]A very critical account of the labor theory of value, summarizing the latest literature, is contained in Jon Elster, *Making Sense of Marx* (Cambridge: Cambridge University Press, 1985), pp. 127–41.

Marx *could* show that market prices can be derived from labor values, by using a formula that gives the 'correct' results. In what way would this prove that labor values are the explanation of price? Marx's assumption that labor value was 'ultimate' would remain just that—an assumption.

Given these and other difficulties, it is small wonder that most of the recent 'analytical Marxists,' a group which has attempted to revivify Marxism by applying to it the techniques of analytic philosophy and modern economics, dispense altogether with the labor theory.

But what of Marx's much vaunted explanation of profit? This too fails, even if one grants Marx the labor theory of value. Sometimes, first thoughts are best; and the phrase "the labor value of labour" is indeed unmeaning. Labor is the measure of value: if so, it cannot at the same time have a value. Marx quite correctly noted that one can on his theory obtain the labor value of a laborer. But laborers are not for sale on the capitalist market: this, on the contrary, is the situation that obtains in a slave society. The laborer sells exactly what the capitalist buys—his labor power. Marx's explanation of profit through labor exploitation goes wrong at its first step.

This brief excursion into Marxist economics enables us to grasp a principal weakness of Marx's argument that the arrival of socialism is inevitable. Part of his claim rests on showing that workers are exploited. Their exploitation in his view increases as capitalism develops. Eventually, they find conditions intolerable and revolt. "The death-knell of the old order sounds."

As we have just seen, however, Marx has failed to demonstrate that workers under capitalism are exploited at all. To the extent that his case for the collapse of capitalism depends on proletarian dissatisfaction owing to exploitation, it at once collapses.

The problems with Marx's view of exploitation go even deeper. As already mentioned, he uses a term, 'exploitation,' which suggests that something is wrong with the state of affairs so designated. But why *should* workers receive the full value of the products their labor helps to produce? Presumably workers, like everyone else, would like to increase their earnings; but why is the capitalist wage system one they will find intolerable?

Of course one can take the line that capitalists are not the rightful possessors of their capital assets: their wrongful possession enable them to obtain a share of production to which they are not properly entitled. But this is a separate problem from the one Marx attempted to solve in his exploitation theory. Marx endeavored to show that workers suffered from exploitation stemming from the manner in which the market determines wages. This argument does not work and would not show anything wrong with capitalism if its conclusion were true.

Marx thought not only that capitalism was finished but that socialism would replace it. The two predictions are connected in that, even if workers felt rebellious over exploitation, they would not rise in revolt unless they saw something better on the horizon. The question at issue then becomes: does socialism exploit workers? A response to this cannot be given with certainty, since Marx never deigns to tell us the content of the future system. But the evidence that does exist gives a reasonable basis for a response.

Marx explicitly notes in the *Critique of the Gotha Program* that funds will be set aside for those who are unable to work. In addition, there will be investment in the new socialist commonwealth: its alleged vast productive capacity depends on this. But how are these things to be done unless surplus value is extracted from the workers? (We are here assuming the Marxist analysis of profit since it is on this basis that Marx contends workers are exploited.) If so, exploitation in the Marxist sense exists under socialism. What then happens to the argument that the proletariat will become increasingly discontented and eventually overthrow capitalism? Even if they are 'exploited,' they will be unlikely to revolt unless socialism offers them a different prospect.

Marx's main line of defense to this was that workers will make decisions about investment themselves, since under the 'dictatorship of the proletariat,'[3] they control the government. Investment decisions will cease to be made by the hated capitalist class. Marx's argument, in brief, seems to be that workers will not mind exploitation because they will be exploiting themselves. This seems implausible: if exploitation is objectionable, it hardly seems to become acceptable just because the exploiters are termed 'workers.' This, however, is not the point that now concerns us. Whether or not workers will find tolerable exploitation under socialism that they reject under capitalism, Marx cannot appeal to exploitation as a reason for proletarian revolt if socialism will not eliminate it.

Suppose Marx responded that his point has been ignored. It is only capitalist exploitation that workers abominate. The problem here, besides the fact that the contention is grossly implausible, is that the reason for raising the issue of exploitation in the first place was that this allegedly explained proletarian discontent with capitalism. It is circular reasoning to add to this that it is not *any* exploitation that concerns workers—just capitalist exploitation. This leaves unanswered the question: what are workers supposed to find bad about capitalism in the first place?

An argument on which we have relied is that Marxist exploitation is not the same as 'ordinary-language' exploitation. Might not this argument be turned against us? Marx might be read as not basing most of his argument that workers find capitalism unsatisfactory on *his* sense of exploitation. He also thought that workers lived under very bad conditions: he spends a great deal of time in the first volume of *Capital* recounting 'horror stories' of the Industrial Revolution. Here lies the principal reason for thinking that the proletariat will rise against capitalism.

This argument also fails. An important factual issue, although one space limitation prevents us from discussing, is

---

[3]The phrase is used in the *Critique of the Gotha Program*. The violent suppression of the old order which Marx favored is hardly compatible with the democratic humanism some of his latter-day disciples wish to foist on him.

that Marx misrepresents the nature of the Industrial Revolution. On the whole, this improved the status of workers.[4] But even if one accepted the dire picture of the working class painted by Marx in *Capital* and Engels in *The Condition of the English Working Class in 1844*, the argument would still not work. The rigorous conditions of labor to which Marx drew attention occurred during the onset of capitalism. Many of the worst of his accounts in point of fact date from an even earlier period, when capitalism existed only in nascent form. But to make his case for proletarian revolt, Marx needs to show that bad conditions of labor are *essential characteristics* of capitalism.

This Marx was unable to do; not even he could deny that the standard of living of the workers had risen since the mid-nineteenth century. If, in fact, things are getting better, how is the argument for increased proletarian discontent supposed to proceed? One reply is that capitalism will be subject to increasingly severe crises as it develops: this view will be discussed below. Another line of reply for Marx is that because of constant struggles for profit on the part of capitalists, the workers become more and more exploited.

But 'exploited' in what sense? How can Marx claim that workers' conditions are worsening, in the face of evidence to the contrary? Evidently he has reintroduced his own sense of exploitation, i.e., workers are exploited because they produce surplus value. Yet we previously had turned aside from this, seeking in the more usual usage of exploitation a better case for Marx. He oscillates back and forth between the two senses in a way that has the effect of concealing the question-begging nature of his argument. He has shown neither that workers are 'exploited' in the sense of Marxist economics in a way they are not exploited under socialism nor that workers must be exploited in the ordinary sense of the term under capitalism. He cannot strengthen his arguments by having them take in their own washing.

[4]F. A. Hayek, ed., *Capitalism and the Historians*, is an excellent series of papers on this topic.

The analytical Marxists on the whole have abandoned Marx's claims about exploitation. John Roemer, the group's leading economist, has devised his own concept of exploitation. On his usage, practically any deviation from an initial equality of assets will lead to exploitation.[5] With the details of his account, we are not here concerned. Suffice it to say that, even more clearly than in Marx's original account, Roemer has failed to show anything is 'wrong' if his sort of exploitation is present. Unless one assumes that workers strongly desire a system of equality of wealth, this version of exploitation gives no grounds for the assumption that workers will overthrow capitalism. Roemer himself does not use it for this purpose.

Another attempt to show that capitalism disadvantages workers stems from G. A. Cohen. Most workers in a capitalist economy do not work in cooperatives; instead, they are employed by capitalists. Although some workers can avoid this by opening small businesses by themselves, most cannot. The proletariat is 'collectively unfree' to exit from its dependent position. Once again we have a case of an argument that fails to show proletarian dissatisfaction except on question-begging assumptions. Unless there is something objectionable in working for a capitalist, Cohen's argument will be of no assistance to Marx in the present context. It will not help to say that the problem is that a worker who is employed by a capitalist has sacrificed his autonomy. Why cannot a worker exercise his autonomy by choosing to work for a capitalist? Once more, one cannot in an argument designed to show why workers will find capitalism unsatisfactory assume as a given that some feature of capitalism is unsatisfactory.[6]

Both Roemer's and Cohen's arguments can be criticized over an issue that has arisen before. Neither argument suffices to show that socialism at all improves upon its respective

---

[5] John Roemer, *A General Theory of Exploitation and Class* (Cambridge, Mass.: Harvard University Press, 1982), p. 113.

[6] G. A. Cohen, "The Structure of Proletarian Unfreedom," *Philosophy and Public Affairs* 12 (1983): 3–33.

complaints against capitalism. Roemer does not show that initial assets would be equal under socialism; quite the contrary, he explicitly allows for the possibility of socialist exploitation. If it is said that inequality under socialism would be less than under capitalism, the historical record of the various Worker's Paradises hardly tells in support of this prediction. As for Cohen, it is not the case that most workers under socialism are self-employed: possibly none is. Why does a worker have more autonomy if he follows the directives of a Central Planning Board than if he works for a capitalist?

The considerations advanced so far, however, do not by themselves dispose of Marx's claim that the era of socialism would inevitably dawn. Part of his claim rests on the prediction of proletarian discontent, and this issue we have addressed. But Marx placed primary emphasis on the claim that the development of the forces of production has progressed beyond the level at which capitalism can work effectively. Now, only socialism can permit the growth of the forces to their full capacity. Not only must this argument be assessed but its bearing on the argument for proletariat discontent must also be considered.

By the 'forces of production,' Marx very roughly meant the principal technology in use in a society. The exact definition of the forces has occasioned much controversy, but for our purposes the rough definition is all we need. Nothing turns on the technicalities. The forces of production determine a society's economic system, the so-called 'relations of production'; in turn, the relations determine the various constituents of society's superstructure, including its legal and political system. As Marx states the matter in a famous statement in the *Preface to the Critique of Political Economy*: "The hand mill gives you feudal society; the sawmill, industrial society."

Marx viewed the forces as if they were an autonomous power, developing by themselves. As Ludwig von Mises noted with his characteristic surgical precision, Marx's 'forces of production' have all the properties of a human mind even though of course they are not a mind but merely an aggregate of tools of various sorts. Marx's reification of the forces is a venture in self-contradiction. Not only does it fly in the face of methodological individualism, it ascribes mental properties to non-living entities.[7]

Once the assumption of the self-developing forces is removed, the sum and substance of Marx's case that the development of the forces makes the demise of capitalism inevitable collapses utterly. There is no reason to assume that the forces *will* always continue to grow. If one adheres to the principle that only individuals act, how much the forces of production develop is a matter that cannot be settled in advance. The question will be determined by the actions of individuals, and does not seem amenable to prediction. If individuals do *not* develop the forces, they will not develop: and that is that. This result, it is clear, ruins at its first step Marx's technological argument for the demise of capitalism.

Another contribution of von Mises strikes at the Marxist argument with even greater force. Marx thinks that socialism is due to arrive because it will be vastly more productive than capitalism. But Mises's famous calculation argument shows that socialism, far from being *more* productive than capitalism, cannot work at all. An economics system must have a way of deciding how to produce things efficiently. How is an economy to choose between the various methods of production that are technologically possible? Mises contends that only a private market can answer this question; a centrally directed economy cannot. Marx, oblivious of this, relied on central planning for the increase of production he thought socialism would bring.

Marxists might protest that I have simply taken for granted the validity of Mises's argument. While it does indeed seem to me that Mises's point is incontrovertible, this is

---

[7]I have discussed Mises's argument in more detail in "Ludwig von Mises and the Philosophy of History" in *The Meaning of Ludwig von Mises: Contributions in Economics, Sociology, Epistemology, and Political Philosophy*, Jeffrey M. Herbener, ed. (Auburn, Ala.: Ludwig von Mises Institute, 1992), pp. 118–33.

obviously not the place for a discussion of the debate over this argument. But even if we turn a blind eye to Mises's demonstration, Marx's argument still does not work. Even if a socialist system *could* function, what reason is there to think it more productive than capitalism? Marx never devoted more than a few lines to socialism; unlike Moses, he could not catch sight his Promised Land even from across its borders. In the absence of argument, the assumption of the superior productivity of socialism is mere assertion.

Marx's argument can also be challenged at another place. Why does he assume that capitalism will act as a fetter upon the development of the forces of production? (Here we leave aside the point that Marx had failed to show these forces will constantly develop.)

Marx advances two main arguments, neither of which succeeds. First, he maintains that production under capitalism is constantly taking on a social character in spite of its officially private form. The argument here is rather difficult to unravel, since it is not at once apparent what Marx meant by the 'social' nature of production. As best one can make out, he had in mind two things: as capitalism develops, a constant struggle for profit will force more and more businesses to the wall. The 'winners' in the struggle will be very large businesses. Monopoly will prevail in most areas of the economy. Supplementing this process, the ever larger scale of production will demand close coordination between the various branches of production. To sum up, the social nature of production means that monopolies coordinated with one another dominate the economy.

We cannot escape a now familiar litany. Marx's argument fails. Even if production constantly rises, there is no general tendency to monopoly on the free market. In some cases, no doubt very large firms will be more efficient than smaller firms and drive them out. But there is no general law of economics to the effect that 'the bigger, the more efficient.' Quite the contrary, the size of the firm that is most efficient in an industry depends on many different factors—the production functions, the nature of the demand curve, the substitutability of the goods produced, etc.,—which by no means are always constantly increasing functions of size. Why should one assume, e.g., that returns increase constantly to scale, at least to the point at which monopoly develops?

As Murray Rothbard has noted, the calculation problem imposes limits to the size of a firm. If firms become so large that competitive markets cannot develop in all production goods, a situation will prevail akin to that of socialism. In the absence of markets, these firms will be unable to calculate, i.e., decide on efficient methods of production. To put the issue more exactly: since a market of *some* degree of development will exist if firms exist at all, firms that are 'too' large will find it difficult, though not impossible, to calculate. Rothbard's problem thus imposes an absolute limit to the growth of monopoly, since inefficient large firms will presumably be replaced by their abler rivals.

So far as the issue of the coordination of production is concerned, one must distinguish two senses of increased coordination. In the first of these, the market in an economy has wider scope as the scale of production increases. No longer, e.g., are markets confined to the small towns or even cities: they may encompass an entire nation or even become world-wide. The other sense of coordination is quite different: here the term refers to planning that takes place apart from the price system. If Columbian coffee sells in Los Angeles, this is a case of coordination in the first sense: if the government establishes a commission to oversee production in the steel industry, this is coordination in the second sense.

It is hardly disputable that as capitalism develops, coordination in the first sense will increase. This in fact comes very close to being a tautology, since one of the principal criteria of development is the wide extension of the market. It does not follow from this that non-market coordination must also increase as capitalism grows. Why must it? To say that this *is* necessary is equivalent to saying the market cannot handle development beyond a certain level of difficulty.

This in my opinion underestimates the potential of the market; and, if Mises is right, it is *only* the market that can properly coordinate economic activity. This of course assumes a view of capitalism which the Marxist will spurn; but the Marxist argument fails even if one does *not* assume any economic view he will question. Just the issue under consideration is Marx's claim that the social nature of production makes the replacement of capitalism by socialism inevitable. If 'social' here entails the direction of the economy by the government, Marx's argument transparently begs the question. The assertion taken as a premise for proving the forthcoming failure of capitalism just *is*, in part, the assertion that capitalism as a certain level of development will fail. It hardly strikes one as a very deep argument for the truth of a proposition p that if p, then p. If, however, Marx uses coordination in the non-question-begging sense, his argument also cries out for speedy interment. If the market widens in scope and complexity, this fact does not entail the failure of the market. On the contrary, it is a good indication of its success.

Even if the argument that the social nature of production will result in the overthrow of capitalism does not work, Marx still remains in the field of battle. He has another argument for the collapse of the market system. In his view, the continued growth of capitalism will produce ever more severe economic crises.

Here, for once, the difficulty is not that Marx offers no argument for his contention. He presents in *Capital* a lengthy analysis of economic depressions. It is however unnecessary for our purposes to undertake an exposition and criticism of Marx's view of depressions. We can take the 'easy way out' and avoid the topic entirely, since even if his account of depressions is right, his case for the collapse of capitalism still fails. Before endeavoring to show why this is true, it seems to me important to note that according to Austrian theory of the business cycle, especially as this has been developed by Ludwig von Mises and Murray Rothbard, depressions result from governmentally induced expansion of bank credit, not from defects intrinsic to the free market.[8] This analysis seems to me entirely persuasive; but since the limits of our topic preclude a presentation of it, nothing in the ensuing discussion will rest on the acceptance of this theory.

The claim advanced here is on the surface paradoxical. How can one accept for the purpose of argument Marx's account of depression while yet claiming that he has not proved that capitalism must collapse? The question in fact poses little difficulty. Even if Marx were right that capitalism is periodically plagued by depressions, this does not suffice to prove that the system is fatally damaged. Few people welcome depressions, but in itself they are merely a negative aspect of an economic system that suffers from them. It does not follow from the fact that depressions have bad consequences that a system which has them will collapse.

Marx does have a further argument that addresses the point just raised. He thinks that depressions will constantly worsen as capitalism develops. One could respond to this by repeating the point just made: even if depressions *do* continue to get worse, this alone is insufficient to 'sound the death knell of capitalism.' Of course, if Marx means that there will at some time be a complete collapse of the capitalist system from which it will be unable to recover, this would indeed 'prove' the inevitable end of capitalism—but only because it asserts that very thesis.

No doubt it is possible to press too hard on our claim that even very bad depressions do not show that capitalism will be replaced. If depressions are bad enough in their effects, perhaps they *would* be 'too much' for the system. But in point of fact, Marx's arguments for the worsening of depressions do not succeed.

These arguments depend crucially on the claim that developed capitalism will be dominated by monopolies. When an enormous industrial combine collapses, its effects on the

---

[8]The Austrian theory is applied to the 1930s depression by Murray Rothbard, *America's Great Depression* (Princeton: D. Van Nostrand, 1963).

economy are drastic. As we have already seen, Marx's argument that monopoly control lies inevitably in capitalism's future is implausible. The failure of this thesis undermines the argument for worsening depressions which rests on it.

Marx also tried to buttress his assertion of capitalist demise by appeal to a constantly more exacting struggle among capitalists to extract surplus value from workers. Even if our earlier claim that the proletariat has little ground for the overthrow of capitalism is true for a non-expanding capitalism, the fight for more and more surplus changes the picture. Now workers will rise in rebellion, if they are "pushed" beyond certain limits.

This argument does no better than its predecessors. The reasons for rejecting the whole surplus value analysis bag and baggage have already been given. Unless one accepts the discredited labor theory and its corollaries in Marxist political economy, there is no reason to expect constantly increasing pressure on workers.

Even if there were such pressure, there remains room for considerable doubt that socialism would replace capitalism. Marx really gives no account of how this system will operate. What reason is there to think that if capitalism does collapse, then socialism will replace it? The collapse of capitalism and the arrival of socialism are two very different things: neither one entails the other.

If this point is applied to our earlier discussion about proletarian discontent, one can readily see that our conclusion that the argument for a proletarian attempt to overthrow capitalism does not succeed requires no alteration when an expanding economy is under consideration. An expanding economy, Marx to the contrary, does not make things worse for the proletariat. It is for this reason that we need not revise our earlier examination of the nature of proletarian unrest.

If capitalism does continue to develop, and if, directly contrary to the stance taken here, one thinks the forces of production *must* grow, one could arrive at an argument exactly contradictory to Marx's. Since socialism will not work, as shown by the calculation argument, and since the forces inevitably grow, then (unless some third system is more productive than either capitalism or socialism) one has ready-to-hand an argument that capitalism is inevitably here to stay. Only in this system can the economy continue to progress.

Since grounds have been offered against the view that technology inevitably grows, no stress will be placed on the argument just given. Rather than say that capitalism *must* exist, given the constant march onwards of technology, we claim instead that if people desire the widest attainable variety of goods and services, then they ought to adopt capitalism. Nothing compels them to establish a free enterprise economy; but if they want prosperity, the course of action they must take is clear.

~ 2 ~

Marxist and Austrian Class Analysis

Hans-Hermann Hoppe

First I will present a series of theses that constitute the hard-core of the Marxist theory of history. I claim that all of them are essentially correct. Then I will show how these true theses are derived in Marxism from a false starting point. Finally, I want to demonstrate how Austrianism in the Mises-Rothbard tradition can give a correct but categorically different explanation of their validity.

Let me begin with the hard-core of the Marxist belief system:[1]

(1) "The history of mankind is the history of class struggles."[2] It is the history of struggles between a relatively small ruling class and a larger class of the exploited. The primary form of exploitation is economic: The ruling class expropriates part of the productive output of the exploited or, as Marxists say, "it appropriates a social surplus product" and uses it for its own consumptive purposes.

---

[1]See on the following Karl Marx and Friedrich Engels, *The Communist Manifesto* (1848; New York: New York Labor News, 1948); Karl Marx, *Das Kapital*, 3 vols. (1867; 1885; 1894; Hamburg: O. Meissner, 1919); as contemporary Marxists, Ernest Mandel, *Marxist Economic Theory* (London: Merlin, 1962); idem, *Late Capitalism* (London: New Left Books, 1975); Paul A. Baran and Paul M. Sweezy, *Monopoly Capital* (New York: Monthly Review Press, 1966); from a non-Marxist perspective, Leszek Kolakowski, *Main Currents of Marxism*; Gustav Wetter, *Sowjetideologie heute* vol. 1 (Frankfurt/M.: Fischer, 1962); Werner Leonhard, *Sowjetideologie heute* vol. 2 (Frankfurt/M.: Fischer, 1962).

[2]Marx, *The Communist Manifesto*, sect. 1.

(2) The ruling class is unified by its common interest in upholding its exploitative position and maximizing its exploitatively appropriated surplus product. It never deliberately gives up power or exploitation income. Instead, any loss in power or income must be wrestled away from it through struggles, whose outcome ultimately depends on the class consciousness of the exploited, i.e., on whether or not and to what extent the exploited are aware of their own status and are consciously united with other class members in common opposition to exploitation.

(3) Class rule manifests itself primarily in specific arrangements regarding the assignment of property rights or, in Marxist terminology, in specific "relations of production." In order to protect these arrangements or production relations, the ruling class forms and is in command of the state as the apparatus of compulsion and coercion. The state enforces and helps reproduce a given class structure through the administration of a system of "class justice," and it assists in the creation and the support of an ideological superstructure designed to lend legitimacy to the existence of class rule.

(4) Internally, the process of competition within the ruling class generates a tendency toward increasing concentration and centralization. A multipolar system of exploitation is gradually supplanted by an oligarchic or monopolistic one. Fewer and fewer exploitation centers remain in operation, and those that do are increasingly integrated into a hierarchical order. And externally, i.e., as regards the international system, this internal centralization process will (and more intensively the more advanced it is) lead to imperialist interstate wars and the territorial expansion of exploitative rule.

(5) Finally, with the centralization and expansion of exploitative rule gradually approaching its ultimate limit of world domination, class rule will increasingly become incompatible with the further development and improvement of "productive forces." Economic stagnation and crises become more and more characteristic and create the "objective conditions" for the emergence of a revolutionary class consciousness of the

exploited. The situation becomes ripe for the establishment of a classless society, the "withering away of the state," "the replacement of government of men over men by the administration of things"[3] and, as its result, unheard of economic prosperity.

All of these theses can be given a perfectly good justification, as I will show. Unfortunately, however, it is Marxism, which subscribes to all of them, that has done more than any other ideological system to discredit their validity in deriving them from a patently absurd exploitation theory.

What is this Marxist theory of exploitation? According to Marx, such pre-capitalist social systems as slavery and feudalism are characterized by exploitation. There is no quarrel with this. For after all, the slave is not a free laborer, and he cannot be said to gain from his being enslaved. Rather, in being enslaved his utility is reduced at the expense of an increase in wealth appropriated by the slave master. The interest of the slave and that of the slave owner are indeed antagonistic. The same is true as regards the interests of the feudal lord who extracts a land rent from a peasant who works on land homesteaded by himself (i.e., the peasant). The lord's gains are the peasant's losses. And it is also undisputed that slavery as well as feudalism indeed hamper the development of productive forces. Neither slave nor serf will be as productive as they would be without slavery or serfdom.

But the genuinely new Marxist idea is that essentially nothing is changed as regards exploitation under capitalism, i.e., if the slave becomes a free laborer, or if the peasant decides to farm land homesteaded by someone else and pays rent in exchange for doing so. To be sure, Marx, in the famous chapter 24 of the first volume of his *Kapital*, titled "The So-called Original Accumulation," gives a historical account of the emergence of

---

[3]Marx, *The Communist Manifesto*, sect. 2, last 2 paragraphs; Friedrich Engels, "Von der Autorität," in Karl Marx and Friedrich Engels, *Ausgewählte Schriften* 2 vols. (East Berlin: Dietz, 1953), vol. 1, p. 606; idem, *Die Entwicklung des Sozialismus von der Utopie zur Wissenschaft*, ibid., vol. 2, p. 139.

capitalism which makes the point that much or even most of
the initial capitalist property is the result of plunder, enclosure, and conquest. Similarly, in chapter 25, on the "Modern
Theory of Colonialism," the role of force and violence in export-
ing capitalism to the—as we would nowadays say—Third World
is heavily emphasized. Admittedly, all this is generally correct,
and insofar as it is there can be no quarrel with labeling such
capitalism exploitative. Yet one should be aware of the fact that
here Marx is engaged in a trick. In engaging in historical
investigations and arousing the reader's indignation regarding
the brutalities underlying the formation of many capitalist
fortunes, he actually side-steps the issue at hand. He distracts
from the fact that his thesis is really an entirely different one:
namely, that even if one were to have "clean" capitalism so to
speak, i.e., one in which the original appropriation of capital
were the result of nothing else but homesteading, work and
savings, the capitalist who hired labor to be employed with this
capital would nonetheless be engaged in exploitation. Indeed,
Marx considered the proof of this thesis his most important
contribution to economic analysis.

What, then, is his proof of the exploitative character of a
clean capitalism?

It consists in the observation that the factor prices, in
particular the wages paid to laborers by the capitalist, are
lower than the output prices. The laborer, for instance, is paid
a wage that represents consumption goods which can be produced in three days, but he actually works five days for his
wage and produces an output of consumption goods that exceeds what he receives as remuneration. The output of the two
extra days, the surplus value in Marxist terminology, is appropriated by the capitalist. Hence, according to Marx, there is
exploitation.[4]

---

[4]See Marx, *Das Kapital*, vol. 1; the shortest presentation is his *Lohn, Preis,
Profit* (1865). Actually, in order to prove the more specific Marxist thesis that
exclusively the owner of labor services is exploited (but not the owner of the other
originary factor of production: land), yet another argument would be needed. For
if it were true that the discrepancy between factor and output prices constitutes an

What is wrong with this analysis?[5] The answer becomes obvious, once it is asked why the laborer would possibly agree to such a deal! He agrees because his wage payment represents present goods—while his own labor services represent only future goods—and he values present goods more highly. After all, he could also decide not to sell his labor services to the capitalist and then reap the "full value" of his output himself. But this would of course imply that he would have to wait longer for any consumption goods to become available to him. In selling his labor services he demonstrates that he prefers a smaller amount of consumption goods now over a possibly larger one at some future date. On the other hand, why would the capitalist want to strike a deal with the laborer? Why would he want to advance present goods (money) to the laborer in exchange for services that bear fruit only later? Obviously, he would not want to pay out, for instance, $100 now if he were to receive the same amount in one year's time. In that case, why not simply hold on to it for one year and receive the extra benefit of having actual command over it during the entire time? Instead, he must expect to receive a larger sum than

---

exploitative relation, this would only show that the capitalist who rents labor services from an owner of labor, and land services from an owner of land would exploit either labor, or land, or labor and land simultaneously. It is the labor theory of value, of course, which is supposed to provide the missing link here by trying to establish labor as the sole source of value. I will spare myself the task of refuting this theory. Few enough remain today, even among those claiming to be Marxists, who do not recognize the faultiness of the labor theory of value. Rather, I will accept for the sake of argument the suggestion made, for instance, by the self-proclaimed "analytical Marxist" John E. Roemer (*A General Theory of Exploitation and Class* [Cambridge: Harvard University Press, 1982]; *Value, Exploitation and Class* [London: Harwood Academic Publishers, 1985]) that the theory of exploitation can be separated analytically from the labor theory of value; and that a "generalized commodity exploitation theory" can be formulated which can be justified regardless of whether or not the labor theory of value is true. I want to demonstrate that the Marxist theory of exploitation is nonsensical even if one were to absolve its proponents from having to prove the labor theory of value and, indeed, even if the labor theory of value were true. Even a generalized commodity exploitation theory provides no escape from the conclusion that the Marxist theory of exploitation is dead wrong.

[5]See on the following Eugen von Böhm-Bawerk, *The Exploitation Theory of Socialism-Communism* (South Holland, Ill.: Libertarian Press, 1975); idem, *Shorter Classics of Böhm-Bawerk* (South Holland, Ill.: Libertarian Press, 1962).

$100 in the future in order to give up $100 now in the form of wages paid to the laborer. He must expect to be able to earn a profit, or more correctly an interest return. And he is constrained by time preference, i.e., the fact that an actor invariably prefers earlier over later goods, in yet another way. For if one can obtain a larger sum in the future by sacrificing a smaller one in the present, why then is the capitalist not engaged in more saving than he actually is? Why does he not hire more laborers than he does, if each one of them promises an additional interest return? The answer again should be obvious: because the capitalist is a consumer, too, and cannot help being one. The amount of his savings and investing is restricted by the necessity that he, too, like the laborer, requires a supply of present goods "large enough to secure the satisfaction of all those wants the satisfaction of which during the waiting time is considered more urgent than the advantages which a still greater lengthening of the period of production would provide."[6]

What is wrong with Marx's theory of exploitation, then, is that he does not understand the phenomenon of time preference as a universal category of human action.[7] That the laborer does not receive his "full worth" has nothing to do with exploitation but merely reflects the fact that it is impossible for man to exchange future goods against present ones except at a discount. Contrary to the case of slave and slave master where the latter benefits at the expense of the former, the relationship between the free laborer and the capitalist is a mutually beneficial one. The laborer enters the agreement because, given his time preference, he prefers a smaller amount of present goods over a larger future one; and the capitalist enters it because, given his time preference, he has a reverse preference order

[6]Ludwig von Mises, *Human Action* (Chicago: Henry Regnery, 1966), p. 407; see also Murray N. Rothbard, *Man, Economy, and State*, 2 vols. (Los Angeles: Nash, 1970), pp. 300–1.

[7]See on the time preference theory of interest in addition to the works cited in notes 5 and 6 above, also Frank Fetter, *Capital, Interest, and Rent* (Kansas City: Sheed Andrews and McMeel, 1977).

and ranks a larger future amount of goods more highly than a smaller present one. Their interests are not antagonistic but harmonious. Without the capitalist's expectation of an interest return, the laborer would be worse off having to wait longer than he wishes to wait; and without the laborer's preference for present goods the capitalist would be worse off having to resort to less roundabout and less efficient production methods than those which he desires to adopt. Nor can the capitalist wage system be regarded as an impediment to the further development of the forces of production, as Marx claims. If the laborer were not permitted to sell his labor services and the capitalist to buy them, output would not be higher but lower because production would have to take place with relatively reduced levels of capital accumulation.

Under a system of socialized production, quite contrary to Marx's proclamations, the development of productive forces would not reach new heights but would instead sink dramatically.[8] For obviously, capital accumulation must be brought about by definite individuals at definite points in time and space through homesteading, producing and/or saving. In each case it is brought about with the expectation that it will lead to an increase in the output of future goods. The value an actor attaches to his capital reflects the value he attaches to all expected future incomes attributable to its cooperation and discounted by his rate of time preference. If, as in the case of collectively owned factors of production, an actor is no longer granted exclusive control over his accumulated capital and hence over the future income to be derived from its employment, but partial control instead is assigned to non-homesteaders, non-producers, and non-savers, the value for him of the expected income and hence that of the capital goods is reduced. His effective rate of time preference will rise. There will be less

---

[8]See on the following Hans-Hermann Hoppe, *Theory of Socialism and Capitalism* (Boston: Kluwer Academic Publishers, 1988); idem, "Why Socialism Must Fail," *Free Market* (July 1988); idem, "The Economics and Sociology of Taxation," in Llewellyn H. Rockwell, ed., *Taxation: An Austrian View* (Auburn, Ala.: Ludwig von Mises Institute, forthcoming 1993).

homesteading of resources whose scarcity is recognized, and less saving for the maintenance of existing and the production of new capital goods. The period of production, the round-aboutness of the production structure, will be shortened, and relative impoverishment will result.

If Marx's theory of capitalist exploitation and his ideas on how to end exploitation and establish universal prosperity are false to the point of being ridiculous, it is clear that any theory of history which can be derived from it must be false, too. Or if it should be correct, it must have been derived incorrectly. Instead of going through the lengthier task of explaining all of the flaws in the Marxist argument as it sets out from its theory of capitalist exploitation and ends with the theory of history which I presented earlier, I will take a shortcut here. I will now outline in the briefest possible way the correct—Austrian, Mis-esian-Rothbardian—theory of exploitation; give an explanatory sketch of how this theory makes sense out of the class theory of history; and highlight along the way some key differences be-tween this class theory and the Marxist one and also point out some intellectual affinities between Austrianism and Marxism stemming from their common conviction that there does indeed exist something like exploitation and a ruling class.[9]

[9]Mises's contributions to the theory of exploitation and class are unsystem-atic. However, throughout his writings he presents sociological and historical interpretations that are class analyses, if only implicitly. Noteworthy here is in particular his acute analysis of the collaboration between government and banking elite in destroying the gold standard in order to increase their inflationary powers as a means of fraudulent, exploitative income and wealth redistribution in their own favor. (See for instance his *Monetary Stabilization and Cyclical Policy* (1928) in idem, *On the Manipulation of Money and Credit*, Percy L. Greaves, ed. (Dobbs Ferry, N.Y.: Free Market Books, 1978); see also his *Socialism: An Economic and Sociological Analysis* (Indianapolis: Liberty Fund, 1981), chap. 20; "The Clash of Group Interests and Other Essays" in Richard M. Ebeling, ed., *Money, Method, and the Market Process: Essays by Ludwig von Mises* (Boston: Kluwer Academic Publishers, 1990.) Yet Mises does not give systematic status to class analysis and exploitation theory because he ultimately misconceives of exploitation as merely an intellectual error which correct economic reasoning can dispel. He fails to fully recognize that exploitation is also and probably even more so a moral-motivational problem that exists regardless of all economic reasoning. Rothbard adds this insight to the

The starting point for the Austrian exploitation theory is plain and simple, as it should be. Actually, it has already been established through the analysis of the Marxist theory: Exploitation characterized in fact the relationship between slave and slave master and serf and feudal lord. But no exploitation was found possible under a clean capitalism. What is the principle difference between these two cases? The answer is: the recognition or non-recognition of the homesteading principle. The peasant under feudalism is exploited because he does not have exclusive control over land that he homesteaded, and the slave because he has no exclusive control over his own homesteaded body. If, contrary to this, everyone has exclusive control over his own body (is a free laborer, that is) and acts in accordance with the homesteading principle, there can be no exploitation. It is logically absurd to claim that a person who homesteads goods not previously homesteaded by anybody else, or who employs such goods in the production of future goods, or who saves presently homesteaded or produced goods in order to increase the future supply of goods, could thereby exploit anybody. Nothing has been taken away from anybody in this process and additional goods have actually been created. And it would be equally absurd to claim that an agreement between different homesteaders, savers and producers regarding their non-exploitatively appropriated goods or services

---

Misesian structure of Austrian economics and makes the analysis of power and power elites an integral part of economic theory and historical-sociological explanations; and he systematically expands the Austrian case against exploitation to include ethics in addition to economic theory, i.e., a theory of justice next to a theory of efficiency, such that the ruling class can also be attacked as immoral. For Rothbard's theory of power, class and exploitation, see in particular his *Power and Market* (Kansas City: Sheed Andrews and McMeel, 1977); *For a New Liberty* (New York: McMillan, 1978); *The Mystery of Banking* (New York: Richardson and Snyder, 1983); *America's Great Depression* (Kansas City: Sheed and Ward, 1975). On important nineteenth century forerunners of Austrian class analysis, see Leonard P. Liggio, "Charles Dunoyer and French Classical Liberalism," *Journal of Libertarian Studies* 1, no. 3 (1977); Ralph Raico, "Classical Liberal Exploitation Theory," ibid; Mark Weinburg, "The Social Analysis of Three Early 19th Century French Liberals: Say, Comte, and Dunoyer," *Journal of Libertarian Studies* 2, no. 1 (1978); Jospeh T. Salerno, "Comment on the French Liberal School," ibid; David M. Hart, "Gustave de Molinari and the Anti-Statist Liberal Tradition," 2 parts, *Journal of Libertarian Studies* 5, nos. 3 and 4 (1981).

could possibly contain any foul play, then. Instead, exploitation takes place whenever any *deviation* from the homesteading principle occurs. It is exploitation whenever a person successfully claims partial or full control over scarce resources which he has not homesteaded, saved or produced, and which he has not acquired contractually from a previous producer-owner. Exploitation is the expropriation of homesteaders, producers and savers by late-coming non-homesteaders, non-producers, non-savers and non-contractors; it is the expropriation of people whose property claims are grounded in work and contract by people whose claims are derived from thin air and who disregard others' work and contracts.[10]

Needless to say, exploitation thus defined is in fact an integral part of human history. One can acquire and increase wealth either through homesteading, producing, saving, or contracting, or by expropriating homesteaders, producers, savers or contractors. There are no other ways. Both methods are natural to mankind. Alongside homesteading, producing and contracting, there have always been non-productive and non-contractual property acquisitions. And in the course of economic development, just as producers and contractors can form firms, enterprises and corporations, so can exploiters combine to large-scale exploitation enterprises, governments and states. The ruling class (which may again be internally stratified) is initially composed of the members of such an exploitation firm. And with a ruling class established over a given territory and engaged in the expropriation of economic resources from a class of exploited producers, the center of all history indeed becomes the struggle between exploiters and the exploited. History, then, correctly told, is essentially the history of the victories and defeats of the rulers in their attempt to maximize exploitatively appropriated income and of the ruled in their attempts to resist and reverse this tendency. It is in

---

[10]See on this also Hoppe, *Theory of Socialism and Capitalism*; idem "The Justice of Economic Efficiency," *Austrian Economics Newsletter* 1 (1988); idem, "The Ultimate Justification of the Private Property Ethics," *Liberty* (September 1988).

this assessment of history that Austrians and Marxists agree and why a notable intellectual affinity between Austrian and Marxist historical investigations exists. Both oppose a historiography which recognizes only action or interaction, economically and morally all on a par; and both oppose a historiography that instead of adopting such a value-neutral stand thinks that one's own arbitrarily introduced subjective value judgments have to provide the foil for one's historical narratives. Rather, history must be told in terms of freedom and exploitation, parasitism and economic impoverishment, private property and its destruction—otherwise it is told false.[11]

While productive enterprises come into or go out of existence because of voluntary support or its absence, a ruling class never comes to power because there is a demand for it, nor does it abdicate when abdication is demonstrably demanded. One cannot say by any stretch of the imagination that homesteaders, producers, savers, and contractors have demanded their expropriation. They must be coerced into accepting it, and this proves conclusively that the exploitation firm is not in demand at all. Nor can one say that a ruling class can be brought down by abstaining from transactions with it in the same way as one can bring down a productive enterprise. For the ruling class acquires its income through non-productive and non-contractual transactions and thus is unaffected by boycotts. Rather, what makes the rise of an exploitation firm possible, and what alone can in turn bring it down is a specific state of public opinion or, in Marxist terminology, a specific state of class consciousness.

An exploiter creates victims, and victims are potential enemies. It is possible that this resistance can be lastingly broken down by force in the case of a group of men exploiting another group of roughly the same size. However, more than force is needed to expand exploitation over a population many times its

[11]See on this theme also Lord (John) Acton, *Essays in the History of Liberty* (Indianapolis: Liberty Fund, 1985); Franz Oppenheimer, *System der Soziologie, Vol. II: Der Staat* (Stuttgart: Gustav Fischer, 1964); Alexander Rüstow, *Freedom and Domination* (Princeton: Princeton University Press, 1986).

own size. For this to happen, a firm must also have public support. A majority of the population must accept the exploitative actions as legitimate. This acceptance can range from active enthusiasm to passive resignation. But it must be acceptance in the sense that a majority must have given up the idea of actively or passively resisting any attempt to enforce non-productive and non-contractual property acquisitions. The class consciousness must be low, undeveloped and fuzzy. Only as long as this state of affairs lasts is there still room for an exploitative firm to prosper even if no actual demand for it exists. Only if and insofar as the exploited and expropriated develop a clear idea of their own situation and are united with other members of their class through an ideological movement which gives expression to the idea of a classless society where all exploitation is abolished, can the power of the ruling class be broken. Only if and insofar as a majority of the exploited public becomes consciously integrated into such a movement and accordingly displays a common outrage over all non-productive or non-contractual property acquisitions, shows a common contempt for everyone who engages in such acts, and deliberately contributes nothing to help make them successful (not to mention actively trying to obstruct them), can its power be brought to crumble.

The gradual abolishment of feudal and absolutist rule and the rise of increasingly capitalist societies in Western Europe and the United States, and along with this unheard of economic growth and rising population numbers was the result of an increasing class consciousness among the exploited, who were ideologically molded together through the doctrines of natural rights and liberalism. In this Austrians and Marxists agree.[12] They disagree, however, on the next assessment: The reversal of this liberalization process and steadily increased levels of exploitation in these societies since the last third of the nineteenth

---

[12]See on this Murray N. Rothbard, "Left and Right: The Prospects for Liberty," in idem, *Egalitarianism As a Revolt Against Nature and Other Essays* (Washington, D. C.: Libertarian Review Press, 1974).

century, and particularly pronounced since World War I, are the result of a loss in class consciousness. In fact, in the Austrian view Marxism must accept much of the blame for this development by misdirecting attention from the correct exploitation model of the homesteader-producer-saver-contractor vs. the non-homesteader-producer-saver-contractor to the fallacious model of the wage earner vs. the capitalist, thus muddling things up.[13]

The establishment of a ruling class over an exploited one many times its size by coercion and the manipulation of public opinion, i.e., a low degree of class consciousness among the exploited, finds its most basic institutional expression in the creation of a system of public law superimposed on private law. The ruling class sets itself apart and protects its position as a ruling class by adopting a constitution for their firm's operations. On the one hand, by formalizing the internal operations within the state apparatus as well as its relations vis-à-vis the exploited population, a constitution creates some degree of legal stability. The more familiar and popular private law notions are incorporated into constitutional and public law, the more conducive this will be to the creation of favorable public opinion. On the other hand, any constitution and public

---

[13]All socialist propaganda to the contrary notwithstanding, the falsehood of the Marxist description of capitalists and laborers as antagonistic classes also comes to bear in certain empirical observations: Logically speaking, people can be grouped into classes in infinitely different ways. According to orthodox positivist methodology (which I consider false but am willing to accept here for the sake of argument), that classification system is better which helps us predict better. Yet the classification of people as capitalists or laborers (or as representatives of varying degrees of capitalist- or laborer-ness) is practically useless in predicting what stand a person will take on fundamental political, social and economic issues. Contrary to this, the correct classification of people as tax producers and the regulated vs. tax consumers and the regulators (or as representatives of varying degrees of tax producer- or consumer-ness) is indeed also a powerful predictor. Sociologists have largely overlooked this because of almost universally shared Marxist preconceptions. But everyday experience overwhelmingly corroborates my thesis: Find out whether or not somebody is a public employee (and his rank and salary), and whether or not and to what extent the income and wealth of a person outside of the public sector is determined by public sector purchases and/or regulatory actions—people will systematically differ in their response to fundamental political issues depending on whether they are classified as direct or indirect tax consumers, or as tax producers!

law also formalizes the exemptory status of the ruling class as regards the homesteading principle. It formalizes the right of the state's representatives to engage in non-productive and non-contractual property acquisitions and the ultimate subordination of private to public law. Class justice, i.e., a dualism of one set of laws for the rulers and another for the ruled, comes to bear in this dualism of public and private law and in the domination and infiltration of public law over and into private law. It is not because private property rights are recognized by law, as Marxists think, that class justice is established. Rather, class justice comes into being precisely whenever a legal distinction exists between a class of persons acting under and being protected by public law and another class acting under and being protected instead by some subordinate private law. More specifically then, the basic proposition of the Marxist theory of the state in particular is false. The state is not exploitative because it protects the capitalists' property rights, but because it itself is exempt from the restriction of having to acquire property productively and contractually.[14]

---

[14]Oppenheimer, *System der Soziologie*, vol. 2, pp. 322–23, presents the matter thus: "The basic norm of the state is power. That is, seen from the side of its origin: violence transformed into might. Violence is one of the most powerful forces shaping society, but is not itself a form of social interaction. It must become law in the positive sense of this term, that is, sociologically speaking, it must permit the development of a system of 'subjective reciprocity': and this is only possible through a system of self-imposed restrictions on the use of violence and the assumption of certain obligations in exchange for its arrogated rights. In this way violence is turned into might, and a relationship of domination emerges which is accepted not only by the rulers, but under not too severely oppressive circumstances by their subjects as well, as expressing a 'just reciprocity.' Out of this basic norm secondary and tertiary norms now emerge as implied in it: norms of private law, of inheritance, criminal, obligational and constitutional law, which all bear the mark of the basic norm of power and domination, and which are all designed to influence the structure of the state in such a way as to increase economic exploitation to the maximum level which is compatible with the continuation of legally regulated domination." The insight is fundamental that "law grows out of two essentially different roots . . . : on the one hand, out of the law of the association of equals, which can be called a 'natural' right, even if it is no 'natural right,' and on the other hand, out of the law of violence transformed into regulated might, the law of unequals."

On the relation between private and public law, see also Friedrich A. Hayek, *Law, Legislation and Liberty*, 3 vols. (Chicago: University of Chicago Press, 1973–79), esp. vol. 1, chap. 6 and vol. 2, pp. 85–88.

In spite of this fundamental misconception, however, Marxism, because it correctly interprets the state as exploitative (contrary, for instance to the public choice school, which sees it as a normal firm among others),[15] is on to some important insights regarding the logic of state operations. For one thing, it recognizes the strategic function of redistributionist state policies. As an exploitative firm, the state must at all times be interested in a low degree of class consciousness among the ruled. The redistribution of property and income—a policy of *divide et impera*—is the state's means with which it can create divisiveness among the public and destroy the formation of a unifying class consciousness of the exploited. Furthermore, the redistribution of state power itself through democratizing the state constitution and opening up every ruling position to everyone and granting everyone the right to participate in the determination of state personnel and policy is a means for reducing the resistance against exploitation as such. Secondly, the state is indeed, as Marxists see it, the great center of ideological propaganda and mystification: Exploitation is really freedom; taxes are really voluntary contributions; non-contractual relations are really "conceptually" contractual ones; no one is ruled by anyone but we all rule ourselves; without the state neither law nor security would exist; and the poor would perish, etc. All of this is part of the ideological superstructure designed to legitimize an underlying basis of economic exploitation.[16] And finally, Marxists are also correct in noticing the close association between the state and business, especially the banking elite—even though their explanation for it is faulty. The reason is not that the bourgeois establishment sees and supports the state as the guarantor of private property rights and contractualism. On the contrary, the establishment correctly perceives the state as the very antithesis to private

---

[15]See James M. Buchanan and Gordon Tullock, *The Calculus of Consent* (Ann Arbor: University of Michigan Press, 1965), p. 19.

[16]See Hans-Hermann Hoppe, *Eigentum, Anarchie und Staat* (Opladen: Westdeutscher Verlag, 1987); idem, *Theory of Socialism and Capitalism*.

property that it is and takes a close interest in it for this reason. The more successful a business, the larger the potential danger of governmental exploitation, but the larger also the potential gains that can be achieved if it can come under government's special protection and is exempt from the full weight of capitalist competition. This is why the business establishment is interested in the state and its infiltration. The ruling elite in turn is interested in close cooperation with the business establishment because of its financial powers. In particular, the banking elite is of interest because as an exploitative firm the state naturally wishes to possess complete autonomy for counterfeiting. By offering to cut the banking elite in on its own counterfeiting machinations and allowing them to counterfeit on top of its own counterfeited notes under a regime of fractional reserve banking, the state can easily reach this goal and establish a system of state monopolized money and cartelized banking controlled by the central bank. And through this direct counterfeiting connection with the banking system and by extension the banks' major clients, the ruling class in fact extends far beyond the state apparatus to the very nervous centers of civil society—not that much different, at least in appearance, from the picture that Marxists like to paint of the cooperation between banking, business elites and the state.[17]

Competition within the ruling class and among different ruling classes brings about a tendency toward increasing concentration. Marxism is right in this. However, its faulty theory of exploitation again leads it to locate the cause for this tendency in the wrong place. Marxism sees such a tendency as inherent in capitalist competition. Yet it is precisely so long as people are engaged in a clean capitalism that competition is *not* a form of zero-sum interaction. The homesteader, the producer, saver and contractor do not gain at another's expense. Their gains either leave another's physical possessions completely

---

[17]See Hans-Hermann Hoppe, "Banking, Nation States and International Politics," *Review of Austrian Economics* 4 (1989); Rothbard, *The Mystery of Banking*, chaps. 15–16.

unaffected or they actually imply mutual gains (as in the case of all contractual exchanges). Capitalism thus can account for increases in absolute wealth. But under its regime no systematic tendency toward relative concentration can be said to exist.[18] Instead, zero-sum interactions characterize not only the relationship between the ruler and the ruled, but also between competing rulers. Exploitation defined as non-productive and non-contractual property acquisitions is only possible as long as there is anything that can be appropriated. Yet if there were free competition in the business of exploitation, there would obviously be nothing left to expropriate. Thus, exploitation requires monopoly over some given territory and population; and the competition between exploiters is by its very nature eliminative and must bring about a tendency toward relative concentration of exploitative firms as well as a tendency toward centralization within each exploitative firm. The development of *states* rather than capitalist firms provides the foremost illustration of this tendency: There are now a significantly smaller number of states with exploitative control over much larger territories than in previous centuries. And within each state apparatus there has in fact been a constant tendency toward increasing the powers of the central government at the expense of its regional and local subdivisions. Yet outside the state apparatus a tendency toward relative concentration has also become apparent for the same reason. Not, as should be clear by now, because of any trait inherent in capitalism, but because the ruling class has expanded its rule into the midst of civil society through the creation of a state-banking-business alliance and in particular the establishment of a system of central banking. If a concentration and centralization of state power then takes place, it is only natural that this be accompanied by a parallel process of relative concentration and cartelization of banking and industry. Along with increased state powers, the associated banking and business establishment's powers of eliminating or

---

[18]See on this in particular Rothbard, *Man, Economy, and State*, chap. 10, esp. the section "The Problem of One Big Cartel"; also Mises, *Socialism*, chaps. 22–26.

putting economic competitors at a disadvantage by means of non-productive and/or non-contractual expropriations increase. Business concentration is the reflection of a "state-ization" of economic life.[19]

The primary means for the expansion of state power and the elimination of rival exploitation centers is war and military domination. Interstate competition implies a tendency toward war and imperialism. As centers of exploitation their interests are by nature antagonistic. Moreover, with each of them—internally—in command of the instrument of taxation and absolute counterfeiting powers, it is possible for the ruling classes to let others pay for their wars. Naturally, if one does not have to pay for one's risky ventures oneself, but can force others to do so, one tends to be a greater risk taker and more trigger happy than one would otherwise be.[20] Marxism, contrary to much of the so-called bourgeois social sciences, gets the facts right: there is indeed a tendency toward imperialism operative in history; and the foremost imperialist powers are indeed the most advanced capitalist nations. Yet the explanation is once again faulty. It is the *state* as an institution exempt from the capitalist rules of property acquisitions that is by nature aggressive. And the historical evidence of a close correlation between capitalism and imperialism only seemingly contradicts this. It finds its explanation, easily enough, in the fact that in order to come out successfully from interstate wars, a state must be in command of sufficient (in relative terms) economic resources. *Ceteris paribus*, the state with more ample resources will win the war. As an exploitative firm, a state is by nature

---

[19]See on this Gabriel Kolko, *The Triumph of Conservatism* (Chicago: Free Press, 1967); James Weinstein, *The Corporate Ideal in the Liberal State* (Boston: Beacon Press, 1968); Ronald Radosh and Murray N. Rothbard, eds., *A New History of Leviathan* (New York: Dutton, 1972); Leonard P. Liggio and James J. Martin, eds., *Watershed of Empire* (Colorado Springs, Colo.: Ralph Myles, 1976).

[20]On the relationship between state and war see Ekkehart Krippendorff, *Staat und Krieg* (Frankfurt/M.: Suhrkamp, 1985); Charles Tilly, "War Making and State Making as Organized Crime," in Peter B. Evans, et al., eds., *Bringing the State Back In* (Cambridge: Cambridge University Press, 1985); also Robert Higgs, *Crisis and Leviathan* (New York: Oxford University Press, 1987).

destructive of wealth and capital accumulation. Wealth is produced exclusively by civil society; and the weaker the state's exploitative powers, the more wealth and capital society accumulates. Thus, paradoxical as it may sound at first, the weaker or the more liberal a state is internally, the further developed capitalism is; a developed capitalist economy to extract from makes the state richer; and a richer state then makes for more and more successful expansionist wars.

It is this relationship that explains why initially the states of Western Europe, and in particular Great Britain, were the leading imperialist powers, and why in the twentieth century this role has been assumed by the United States.

And a similarly straightforward yet once again entirely non-Marxist explanation exists for the observation always pointed out by Marxists, that the banking and business establishment is usually among the most ardent supporters of military strength and imperial expansionism. It is not because the expansion of capitalist markets requires exploitation, but because the expansion of state protected and privileged business requires that such protection be extended also to foreign countries and that foreign competitors be hampered through non-contractual and non-productive property acquisitions in the same way or more so than internal competition. Specifically, it supports imperialism if this promises to lead to a position of military domination of one's own allied state over another. For then, from a position of military strength, it becomes possible to establish a system of—as one may call it—*monetary imperialism*. The dominating state will use its superior power to enforce a policy of internationally coordinated inflation. Its own central bank sets the pace in the process of counterfeiting, and the central banks of the dominated states are ordered to use its currency as their own reserves and inflate on top of them. This way, along with the dominating state and as the earliest receivers of the counterfeit reserve currency its associated banking and business establishment can engage in an almost costless expropriation of foreign property owners and income producers. A double layer of exploitation of a foreign state and a foreign elite on top of a national state and elite is imposed on the exploited class in the dominated territories, causing prolonged economic dependency and relative economic stagnation vis-à-vis the dominant nation. It is this—very uncapitalist—situation that characterizes the status of the United States and the United States dollar and that gives rise to the—correct—charge of United States economic exploitation and dollar imperialism.[21]

Finally, the increasing concentration and centralization of exploitative powers leads to economic stagnation and thereby creates the objective conditions for their ultimate demise and the establishment of a classless society capable of producing unheard of economic prosperity.

Contrary to Marxist claims, this is not the result of any historical laws, however. In fact, no such things as inexorable historical laws as Marxists conceive of them exist.[22] Nor is it the result of a tendency for the rate of profit to fall with an increased organic composition of capital (an increase in the proportion of constant to variable capital, that is), as Marx thinks. Just as the labor theory of value is false beyond repair, so is the law of the tendential fall of the profit rate, which is based on it. The source of value, interest and profit is not exclusively the expenditure of labor, but much more general: acting, i.e., the employment of scarce means in the pursuit of goals by agents who are constrained by time preference and uncertainty (imperfect knowledge). There is no reason to suppose, then, that changes in the organic composition of capital should have any systematic relation to changes in interest and profit.

Instead, the likelihood of crises which stimulate the development of a higher degree of class consciousness (i.e., the subjective conditions for the overthrow of the ruling class)

---

[21]On a further elaborated version of this theory of military and monetary imperialism see H. H. Hoppe, "Banking, Nation States and International Politics."

[22]See on this in particular Ludwig von Mises, *Theory and History* (Auburn, Ala.: Ludwig von Mises Institute, 1985), esp. part 2.

increases because—to use one of Marx's favorite terms—of the "dialectics" of exploitation which I have already touched on earlier: Exploitation is destructive of wealth formation. Hence, in the competition of exploitative firms, i.e., of states, less exploitative or more liberal ones tend to outcompete more exploitative ones because they are in command of more ample resources. The process of imperialism initially has a relatively liberating effect on societies coming under its control. A relatively more capitalist social model is exported to relatively less capitalist (more exploitative) societies. The development of productive forces is stimulated, economic integration is furthered, division of labor extended, and a genuine world market established. Population figures go up in response, and expectations as regards the economic future rise to unprecedented heights.[23] With exploitative domination taking hold, and interstate competition reduced or even eliminated in a process of imperialist expansionism, however, the external constraints on the dominating state's power of internal exploitation and expropriation gradually disappear. Internal exploitation, taxation and regulation begin to increase the closer the ruling class comes to its ultimate goal of world domination. Economic stagnation sets in and the—worldwide—higher expectations become frustrated. And this—high expectations and an economic reality increasingly falling behind these expectations—is the classical situation for the emergence of a

---

[23]It may be noted here that Marx and Engels, foremost in their *Communist Manifesto*, championed the historically progressive character of capitalism and were full of praise for its unprecedented accomplishments. Indeed, reviewing the relevant passages of the *Manifesto* concludes Joseph A. Schumpeter, "Never, I repeat, and in particular by no modern defender of the bourgeois civilization has anything like this been penned, never has a brief been composed on behalf of the business class from so profound and so wide a comprehension of what its achievement is and what it means to humanity." "The *Communist Manifesto* in Sociology and Economics," in Richard Clemence, *Essays of J. A. Schumpeter* (Port Washington, N. Y.: Kennikat Press, 1951), p. 293. Given this view of capitalism, Marx went so far as to defend the British conquest of India, for example, as a historically progressive development. See Marx's contributions to the *New York Daily Tribune* (June 25, 1853; July 11, 1853; August 8, 1853 in Karl Marx and Friedrich Engels, *Werke* vol. 9 (East Berlin: Dietz, 1960). As a contemporary Marxist taking a similar stand on imperialism see Bill Warren, *Imperialism: Pioneer of Capitalism* (London: New Left Books, 1981).

revolutionary potential.[24] A desperate need for ideological solutions to the emerging crises arises, along with a more widespread recognition of the fact that state rule, taxation and regulation—far from offering such a solution—actually constitute the very problem that must be overcome. If in this situation of economic stagnation, crises, and ideological disillusion[25] a positive solution is offered in the form of a systematic and comprehensive libertarian philosophy coupled with its economic counterpart: Austrian economics, and if this ideology is propagated by an activist movement, then the prospects of igniting the revolutionary potential to activism become overwhelmingly positive and promising. Anti-statist pressures will mount and bring about an irresistible tendency toward dismantling the power of the ruling class and the state as its instrument of exploitation.[26]

If and insofar as this occurs, however, this will not mean—contrary to the Marxist model—social ownership of means of production. In fact, social ownership is not only economically inefficient as has already been explained; moreover, it is incompatible with the idea that the state is "withering away."[27] For if means of production are owned collectively, and if it is realistically assumed that not everyone's ideas as to how to employ

---

[24]See on the theory of revolution in particular Charles Tilly, *From Mobilization to Revolution* (Reading, Mass.: Addison-Wesley, 1978); idem, *As Sociology Meets History* (New York: Academic Press, 1981).

[25]For a neo-Marxist assessment of the present era of "late capitalism" as characterized by "a new ideological disorientation" born out of permanent economic stagnation and the exhaustion of the legitimatory powers of conservatism and social-democratism (i.e., "liberalism" in American terminology) see Jürgen Habermas, *Die Neue Unübersichtlichkeit* (Frankfurt/M.: Suhrkamp, 1985); also idem, *Legitimation Crisis* (Boston: Beacon Press, 1975); Claus Offe, *Strukturprobleme des kapitalistischen Staates* (Frankfurt/M.: Suhrkamp, 1972).

[26]For an Austrian-libertarian assessment of the crisis-character of late capitalism and on the prospects for the rise of a revolutionary libertarian class consciousness see Murray Rothbard, "Left and Right"; idem, *For a New Liberty*, chap. 15; idem. *Ethics of Liberty* (Atlantic Highlands, N.J.: Humanities Press, 1982), part 5.

[27]On the internal inconsistencies of the Marxist theory of the state see also Hans Kelsen, *Sozialismus und Staat* (Vienna: Verlag der Wiener Volksbuchhandlung, 1965).

these means of production happen to coincide (as if by miracle), then it is precisely socially owned factors of production which require continued state actions, i.e., an institution coercively imposing one person's will on another disagreeing one's. Instead, the withering away of the state, and with this the end of exploitation and the beginning of liberty and unheard of economic prosperity, means the establishment of a pure private property society regulated by nothing but private law.

~ 3 ~

The Marx Nobody Knows

Gary North

Much of my immediate motivation to investigate the life and teachings of Marx came when I read a seminal essay on Marx by Louis J. Halle. I came across "Marx's Religious Drama" shortly after it was published in October of 1965. Halle asked a very important question at the beginning of the essay: Why did Marx become so important? His answer: Marx's religious vision.

> What did this man have that made him, at last, such a powerful influence in history? As a revolutionary, organizing revolutionary action, he was no better than others of his day. He was to go in for economics later, basing his thought on the classical and rather naïve labor theory of value, but it was not as an economist that he would achieve the topmost heights of distinction. As a political analyst he was surely not as good as his contemporary of lesser fame, Walter Bagehot; as a social philosopher he was inferior to Alexis de Tocqueville. His development of the sociological view that men's concepts reflect the material circumstances of their productive lives—this certainly would entitle him to an important place in the history of human thought. But it is hardly commensurate with the magnitude of his influence.

> Marx was extraordinary, I conclude, not as a man of action or as an academic thinker, but as one of the great visionaries of history. It was the Karl Marx who saw an immense and enthralling vision of human society, the Karl Marx who on the basis of that vision created a compelling myth of human society—this is the Marx who was extraordinary

among his contemporaries. He had more of St. Paul in him
than of the social scientist or the empirical scholar. His mission, too, began with a vision on the Road to Damascus.[1]

I asked myself: Is Halle correct? Concerning Marx's intellectual attainments, he is generally correct: Marx was not a
distinguished scholar. Concerning the influence of Marx's religious vision, he is also correct, although I am unaware of any
Damascus-type experience. He did lose his youthful commitment to liberal Christianity almost overnight, in between his
graduation from the *gymnasium* and his early years as a college student. Shortly before his graduation from the *gymnasium*, Marx wrote an essay called "Reflections of a Young Man
on the Choice of a Profession," in which he exhibited such
liberal and bourgeois sentiments as this one: "But the chief
guide which must direct us in the choice of a profession is the
welfare of mankind and our own perfection."[2] How did the
young man who could write these words in 1835 become the
philosopher of class revolution a decade later? One thing is certain, as we shall see: his "conversion" to revolutionary communism was not the product of any grinding personal poverty.

His radically anti-Christian unpublished one-act play, "Ou-
lanem," is undated, but it was an early effort.[3] Oulanem, writes
Payne, is an anagram: oulanem = Manuelo = Immanuel = God.
Immanuel is the New Testament word meaning "God with us"
(Matt. 1:23).[4] Marx's 1841 poem, "The Player," published in the
Berlin literary magazine, *Athenaeum*, reveals the extent of his
conversion to anti-Christianity. Payne reprints it.[5]

---

[1]Louis J. Halle, "Marx's Religious Drama," *Encounter* 25 (October, 1965): 29.

[2]Marx, "Reflections of a Young Man on the Choice of a Profession" (August 1835) in Karl Marx and Frederick Engels, *Collected Works* (New York: International Publishers, 1975), vol. 1, p. 8.

[3]This poem was made available in English in Robert Payne's 1971 collection, *The Unknown Karl Marx* (New York: New York University Press, 1971), p. 63.

[4]"Oulanem" appears in volume 1 of *Collected Works*, pp. 588–607. Contrast this with his 1835 schoolboy essay, "The Union of Believers with Christ," pp. 636–39.

[5]Payne, *The Unknown Karl Marx*, p. 59. It is this poem and the seemingly overnight loss of Marx's faith that led Pastor Richard Wurmbrand, a victim of much

Look now, my blood-dark sword shall stab
Unerringly within thy soul.
God neither knows nor honors art.
The hellish vapors rise and fill the brain.

Till I go mad and my heart is utterly changed.
See this sword—the Prince of Darkness sold it to me.
For he beats the time and gives the signs.
Ever more boldly I play the dance of death.

But what about Halle's equating of Marx with St. Paul? That was what bothered me most in Halle's essay. That Karl Marx offered mankind a religious drama is certain; that it had anything in common with the experience or theology of St. Paul is a misreading of Marx's religion, for his was a modernized version of ancient paganism's religion of revolution.[6]

The point I want to make in this brief biographical survey is that Marx from the beginning of his career was subsidized, and for the most part, subsidized well. He lived his entire life on the dole, though at least the various doles were private rather than public. The image of Marx the Promethean figure struggling against overwhelming odds continues to this day, but this legend is as mythical as Prometheus was. It was the product of Marx's own skills as a self-promoter.

The Subsidies Begin

Karl Marx, the self-appointed philosopher, economist, and social theorist for the nineteenth-century industrial proletariat,

---

torture in Communist prisons, to conclude that Marx made some sort of pact with the devil: *Marx and Satan* (Westchester, Ill.: Crossway, 1985), chap. 2. Wurmbrand cites Albert Camus, *The Rebel*, who claimed that some 30 volumes of Marx materials are as yet unpublished by Moscow. Wurmbrand wrote to the Marx Institute, and received a reply from M. Mtchedlov, who insisted that Camus was lying, and then went on to explain that over 85 volumes are still unpublished, due to the effects of World War II. He wrote this in 1980, 35 years after the War ended. Wurmbrand speculates that there may be evidence of Marx's satanism in these unpublished volumes. *Marx and Satan*, pp. 31–32.

[6]Gary North, *Marx's Religion of Revolution* (Nutley, N.J.: Craig Press, 1968). Reprinted in 1988 with additional material by the Institute for Christian Economics in Tyler, Texas.

was the bourgeois son of a bourgeois father. Born in Trier, in
what is today Rhineland Germany, Marx found himself in a
highly privileged position. In 1816, two years before his birth,
his father had renounced his Jewish origins and had joined the
official state Protestant church, enabling his family to enter
the ranks of bourgeois society. It was only to be expected that
Heinrich (Herschel) Marx, a relatively successful lawyer, would
want his son to do well in the world of "affairs." He provided for
young Karl a thoroughly liberal humanistic education, first in
the Trier gymnasium, then at the University of Bonn, and then
at the University of Berlin.

He began at the University of Bonn, but his time had been
spent more in drinking and dueling than in study, a situation
which was typical for those young men who had aspirations of
entering the state's official bureaucracies upon graduation.[7]
Marx's father therefore insisted that Marx transfer to the more
academically rigorous University of Berlin; Marx did so at the
beginning of his second year of college. Ludwig Feuerbach once
remarked of the University of Berlin that "Other universities
are positively Bacchanalian compared with this workhouse,"[8]
and Heinrich Marx could do no more than to send his son to
such an institution. Nevertheless, his strategy failed.

We know relatively little about the life of Karl Marx over
the succeeding five years. He piled up many bills, received
continual financial support from his parents (his father died in
1838), and spent much of his time in the so-called Professors'
Club or Doctors' Club, a group of about thirty youthful members which met in the Cafe Stehely. It was here and in his
extracurricular reading, not in the classroom, that he received
most of his education.[9]

[7]Cf. Max Weber, "National Character and the Junkers" (1917), in H. H. Gerth
and C. Wright Mills, eds., *From Max Weber: Essays in Sociology* (New York: Oxford
University Press, 1946), chap. 15.
  [8]Cited in Franz Mehring, *Karl Marx: The Story of His Life*, Edward Fitzgerald,
trans. (1933; Ann Arbor: University of Michigan Press, 1962), p. 9.
  [9]This, however, is generally the case when very bright young men enter
college. Textbooks bore them. Classroom lectures bore them. European lectures are

As a student at the Universities of Bonn and then Berlin, he spent prodigious quantities of his father's money. It was a habit he was never to break: spending other people's money. It required the adoption of a lifetime strategy of begging. In late December, 1837, a few months before his death, his father wrote a long, despairing, and critical letter to him. It is obvious that the father knew his son only too well. He described in detail his son's personal habits—habits that remained with him for a lifetime:

> God's grief!!! Disorderliness, musty excursions into all departments of knowledge, musty brooding under a gloomy oil-lamp; running wild in a scholar's dressing-gown and with unkempt hair instead of running wild over a glass of beer; unsociable withdrawal with neglect of all decorum and even of all consideration for the *father*. . . . And is it here, in this workshop of senseless and inexpedient erudition, that the fruits are to ripen which will refresh you and your beloved [Jenny von Westphalen], and the harvest garnered which will serve to fulfil your sacred obligations!?[10]

The desperate dying man then resorted to sarcasm, only too well deserved, regarding his son's capacity for spending money:

> As if we were men of wealth, my Herr Son disposed in one year of almost 700 talers contrary to all agreement, contrary to all usage, whereas the richest spend less than 500. And why? I do him the justice of saying that he is no rake, no squanderer. But how can a man who every week or two discovers a new system and has to tear up old works laboriously arrived at, how can he, I ask, worry about trifles? How can he submit to the pettiness of order? Everyone dips a hand in his pocket, and everyone cheats him, so long as he doesn't disturb

---

notoriously boring, and nineteenth-century German university lectures may have established the modern international world record in the production of student boredom. Oxford's lectures were boring, Adam Smith insisted. But at least they were not in German.

[10]Herschel Marx to Karl Marx, 9 December 1837; Marx and Engels, *Collected Works* 1, p. 688.

him in his studies, and a new money order is soon written again, of course.[11]

Poor deceived Heinrich! He had read his son's letters that described in detail the voluminous amount of reading that the young man had covered, unaware that the young man was spending endless nights drinking in the local pub with other "young Hegelians" in the "Doctors' Club." Recalling his experience in Bonn—a parental-enforced transfer—Karl had not written of these familiar collegiate uses of his father's funds. And so, the old man concluded that "my hard-working talented Karl spends wretched nights awake, weakens his mind and his body by serious study, denies himself all pleasure, in order in fact to pursue lofty abstract studies, but what he builds today he destroys tomorrow, and in the end he has destroyed his own work and not assimilated the work of others."[12]

What had "busy beaver" Karl actually accomplished in the winter term of 1837–38? Attendance at a single course, criminal legal procedure. (Too bad for him that he did not learn enough to keep him out of future trouble with the legal authorities of several nations, 1842–49.) The son had been running a year's "confidence game" with his father's money. He had taken only seven courses in his three terms at the University of Berlin. Over the next four years, he took only six more.[13] He did not graduate from Berlin. He could never work up the courage to face his examinations. In 1841, Marx graduated from the University of Jena with a doctorate in philosophy (not in law, as his father had hoped). Due to the procedures of the German university system in Marx's day, he had never actually attended Jena, although his doctoral dissertation entitled him to full honors.

His dissertation was titled, "Difference Between the Democritean and Epicurean Philosophy of Nature," an appropriately

---

[11]Ibid. 1, p. 690.
[12]Idem.
[13]The courses are listed in ibid., 1, pp. 703–4.

narrow topic for a dissertation. It is even less interesting than its title indicates.[14] The reader should note how far removed its subject matter was from anything Marx subsequently wrote. He later paid to have it printed as a book. The English-language version is 72 pages long. It has never played an important role in Marxism or anything else, but the final sentence of the foreword to the printed version is important, for it reveals Marx's hatred of both God and authority: "Prometheus is the most eminent saint and martyr in the philosophical calendar." Immediately preceding this, he had quoted in Greek from Aeschylus's *Prometheus Bound*: "Be sure of this, I would not change my state of evil fortune for your servitude. Better to be the servant of this rock than to be faithful boy to Father Zeus."[15] Best of all, pretend to be the servant of the rock, and then get your father and friends to finance the illusion.

The Subsidies Continue

He took his first job with the newly established *Rheinische Zeitung* in 1842. He became a regular contributor in April of 1842, and within a few months the editorship was given to him. Charges had been leveled at the paper that it was communist in its orientation. On the day that he took over as editor (October 15, 1842), Marx wrote an editorial denying the charge. Not only was he against communism, he claimed, but he was equally opposed to the panacea of revolution, noting that for all Germany's problems there was no single remedy, "no great deed that should absolve us from all these sins!"[16] Communism, whether revolutionary or evolutionary, was not the goal of Karl Marx in 1842. As he put it: "The *Rheinische Zeitung*, which does not admit that communist ideas in their present form possess

---

[14]For a mercifully brief summary of Marx's insufferably dull dissertation, see Henry F. Mins, "Marx's Doctoral Dissertation," *Science and Society* 12 (1948): 157–69.

[15]*Collected Works*, 1, p. 31 n.

[16]Marx, "Communism and the Augsburg *Allgemeine Zeitung*" (16 October 1842); ibid., 1, p. 219.

even *theoretical reality*, and therefore can still less desire their *practical realization*, or even consider it possible, will subject these ideas to thoroughgoing criticism."[17]

Despite the denials, what happened to the *Rheinische Zeitung* would also happen to two other publishing ventures Marx was associated with in the next few years: it became so radical that the authorities shut it down.[18] The history of this newspaper is illuminating. Originally, this Cologne paper had been started by the Prussian government, which had recently annexed the western German provinces in which Cologne was located. The government, fearing the possibility of a militant Catholicism that might succeed in agitating against Protestant control, had hoped to counter a successful Catholic newspaper in Cologne. The government venture, like so many governmental intellectual ventures, failed.

Several wealthy Cologne industrialists who had liberal sympathies were encouraged to take it over. One of those doing the encouraging was Moses Hess, a young man who was heir to a large fortune, and who was the first of the "young Hegelians" to be converted to communism. His associates were not yet aware of his radicalism, however, and even as his beliefs became more obvious his industrialist friends continued to accept at least some of his suggestions. One of his suggestions was to hire Karl Marx as editor of the paper. Isaiah Berlin, one of Marx's biographers, describes what took place: "From a mildly liberal paper it rapidly became a vehemently radical one; more violently hostile to the Government than any other German newspaper. . . . The shareholders were, indeed, scarcely less surprised than the authorities. . . ."[19]

The authorities, while censoring the newspaper constantly, were at first afraid to close it, probably because they did not

---

[17]Ibid., 1, p. 220.

[18]The two other papers were *Deutsch-Französischen Jahrbücher* (1844) and the *Neue Rheinische Zeitung* (1848).

[19]Isaiah Berlin, *Karl Marx: His Life and Environment*, 3rd ed. (New York: Oxford University Press, 1963), p. 74.

wish to alienate the prominent owners. It was only when Emperor Nicholas I of Russia happened to read one of Marx's anti-Russian diatribes that the authorities acted. The Emperor complained to the Prussian government, and the government responded, unwilling to anger the Emperor and endanger the Russo-Prussian alliance which was in effect at the time.

Another opportunity to enter into the world of journalism presented itself shortly thereafter. Marx took his young bride, Jenny von Westphalen, to Paris, where he and his old "Young Hegelian" associate, Arnold Ruge, set out to edit *Deutsch-Französischen Jahrbücher (German-French Yearbooks)*. The first edition was published in February of 1844; it was also to be the last edition. The two men quarrelled, and the breach was never healed. Many of the copies were confiscated by the Prussian government when issues were sent into Prussia. In the *Yearbooks*, two of Marx's important early essays appeared: the "Introduction to a Critique of the Hegelian Philosophy of Law," and his reply to Bruno Bauer, "On the Jewish Question," so, from the historian's viewpoint, the endeavor was not totally useless. But given the era in which he lived, Marx was not really the best man to have as an editor, as the radicals in Prussia and France were beginning to learn. Nevertheless, he continued to write for another radical publication, *Vorwärts! (Forward!)*.[20]

The Indispensable Partner

In 1844, Marx and Engels began a long friendship which was to last as long as both were alive. Engels was the son of a wealthy German industrialist, and he himself did not break off relations with the business until late in his career. He was a man of expensive tastes who enjoyed an evening at the opera or the ballet. He was hardly the man one would expect to find as the collaborator of Karl Marx, the founder of Marxist revolutionary thought. Engels's own work, *The Condition of the Working*

---

[20]On Marx's early journalism, See Mehring, *Karl Marx*, pp. 32–87.

Class in England in 1844, was to have a profound effect on Marx; from 1845 on, Marx was to have far more respect for economic research and investigation than he had ever imagined possible in his early "philosophical" days.

The greatest irony regarding the massive amount of published attention that is squandered on Karl Marx is this: *Engels was the indispensable partner in the history of Communism, not Marx.*[21] Engels was ahead of Marx conceptually from the beginning, although he was two years younger. He became a communist a year before Marx did. He became interested in the economic conditions of industrial civilization before Marx did; his *Condition of the Working Class in England* was the book that in 1845 converted Marx to the theory of the economic foundations of the revolution. There is at least a reasonable suspicion that he and Marx together worked out the idea of the materialist conception of history, although Marx is usually given credit for the discovery.[22] Joseph Schumpeter, after dutifully doffing his intellectual cap to Marx's greater "depth of comprehension and analytic power," then observes that "In those years Engels was certainly farther along, as an economist, than was Marx."[23] Engels co-authored *The German Ideology* (1845–46). He co-authored the *Communist Manifesto* (1848). He ghost wrote many of Marx's journalism pieces to help earn him some extra money.[24] He had a lively writing style and the ability to turn a phrase. He also knew how to make and keep money. Marx possessed neither skill. Alvin Gouldner has attempted to

---

[21]I had not come to this conclusion in 1968, when my book on Marx first appeared, although I fully recognized that Engels had been the more effective literary stylist.

[22]There is no evidence in his published and unpublished manuscripts prior to *The German Ideology* (1845) that Marx had devised any such conception of history. Engels was the co-author of *The German Ideology.* See Oscar J. Hammen, *The Red '48ers: Karl Marx and Friedrich Engels* (New York: Scribner's, 1969), pp. 116–17.

[23]Joseph A. Schumpeter, "The *Communist Manifesto* in Sociology and Economics," *Journal of Political Economy* 57 (1949): 200.

[24]The most notable examples were the articles Engels wrote on the revolution of 1848 in Germany for the *New York Daily Tribune* (1851–52) which were later assembled into a book, *Revolution and Counter-Revolution, or Germany in 1848.* I own a version published by Charles H. Kerr & Company, no publication date, with Marx's name on it. Presumably, it was published around the turn of the century.

rehabilitate Engels's reputation, but in my view, he did not go far enough.[25]

Engels thoroughly enjoyed the trappings of the wealth he possessed, while Marx spent many years of his life in hock to pawn brokers. He financed Marx throughout their long relationship.[26] He outlived Marx by over a decade, corresponding with many revolutionaries throughout Europe, keeping the Marxist flame burning. He edited and published reprints of Marx's books and his many unpublished manuscripts. The arguments in his *Socialism: Utopian and Scientific*[27] have had far more impact in bringing men to Communism than *Das Kapital* has ever had. He was not a pedant. He was not an anti-Semite, either, at least not in his writings; Marx was, and all the hedging and squirming of contemporary liberal and Marxist scholars regarding "the hidden underlying meaning" of

---

The Kerr edition of volume 1 of *Capital* was published in 1906. The book contains an 1896 "Note by the Editor," Marx's daughter, Eleanor Marx-Aveling, who says that Marx was paid one British pound per article (p. 9). She did not admit what she must have known, that Engels had written them. In volume 11 of the *Collected Works*, the essays are reproduced under Engels's name. The editors discretely fail to mention that for at least half a century, Marx had been given credit for having written them.

In 1848, Charles A. Dana (1819–97), visited Europe for the *Tribune* to meet with various revolutionaries, where he met Karl Marx. Dana later became the *Tribune's* managing editor. He was later to serve as Assistant Secretary of War in Lincoln's administration when Horace Greeley fired him from the newspaper in 1861: William Harlan Hale, *Horace Greeley: Voice of the People* (1950; New York: Collier, 1961), p. 261. Dana in 1840 had been a founder and financier of Brook Farm, an early writers' colony farm (Ibid., p. 110). He and Greeley were followers of Charles Fourier, and were also members of a secret society known as the Columbians (founded in New York City in 1795): David Tame, "Secret Societies in the Life of Karl Marx," *Critique* 25 (1987): 95. They built the *Tribune* into a highly successful newspaper. The paper ceased publishing Marx's essays in 1861. The association had lasted a decade.

[25]Alvin Gouldner, *The Two Marxisms: Contradictions and Anomalies in the Development of Theory* (New York: Seabury Press, 1980), chap. 9. He believes that there are two Marxisms, critical Marxism and scientific Marxism.

[26]Edgar Longuet, Marx's grandson through his daughter Jenny, remarked in 1949: "There is no doubt that without Engels Marx and his family would have starved." Edgar Longuet, "Some Aspects of Karl Marx's Family Life," in *Marx and Engels Through the Eyes of Their Contemporaries* (Moscow: Progress Publishers, 1972), p. 172.

[27]An extract from the less readable *Herr Eugen Dühring's Revolution in Science* (1878).

Marx's vicious essay, "On the Jewish Question" (1843), will not erase the fact.[28]

Engels was not a Ph.D-holding drudge. Those who *are* Ph.D-holding drudges have a distinct tendency to identify with Marx rather than Engels. They pretend to suffer with Marx, who was, like themselves, a heavily subsidized "victim" of the hated capitalist system. They share his alienation. Many of them also share his literary style, which is best described as Germanic verbal constipation coupled with a bad case of hemorrhoids. (The shouts! The groans! The outrage! The vows of revenge!)[29] They write fat, unreadable books on Marxism, and they attribute to Marx rather than Engels almost everything of intellectual importance in Marxism. They attribute far greater importance to Marx's academic drudgery than to Engels's original insights. In one sense, however, this assessment may be valid, because Marxism has always been a movement that owes its success to its appeal to envy-driven intellectuals and academics who have revolutionary pretensions. This explanation of Marxism's success is seldom discussed by Marxists and academic humanists. Marxism has not united the workers of the world, but it certainly has united tens of thousands of well-fed bourgeois academics, at least until the Marxist revolution actually comes and sweeps them into the Gulag or its regional equivalents.

---

[28]Nethaniel Weyl, *Karl Marx: Racist* (New Rochelle, New York: Arlington House, 1979). Cf. Julius Carlebach, *Karl Marx and the Radical Critique of Judaism* (London: Routledge and Kegan Paul, 1978). Fritz J. Raddatz, who is typical of modern Marx scholars in this regard, explains away the essay's clear language: "The context, however, shows that Marx was using the words 'Jew' and 'Judaism' in a 'quasi-non-Jewish' sense." Raddatz, *Karl Marx: A Political Biography*, Richard Barry, trans. (1975; Boston: Little, Brown, 1978), p. 41. Anti-Semitic language is not normally tolerated by intellectuals in the West, but Marx was a Jew and even more important, he was a Communist, so his anti-Semitism is treated as if it were something else.

[29]A modern expositor of Marxism who is similarly afflicted is George Lichtheim, whose ponderous *Marxism: An Historical and Critical Study* (1961) is matched by his *Origins of Socialism* (1969), which has been highly recommended by Steven Marcus, "in spite of the fact that he buries about half of what he has to say in footnotes of unendurable length. . . ." Marcus, *Engels, Manchester, and the Working Class* (New York: Random House, 1974), p. 88 n.

Marx's Aura of Authority

This academic emphasis on Marx over Engels is made much easier by the fact that Marx maintained an aura of authority and self-confidence (except when he was begging for money) regarding his position as the primary leader of the European revolutionary movement, and loyal historians have accepted Marx's self-assessment at face value, unlike the pawn brokers who wisely discounted everything Marx brought to them. This view of Marx as the key figure is also a lasting testimony to Marx's own machinations and maneuverings in the narrow, German-speaking circles of the European revolutionary movement. He took all the credit from Engels, in both senses. The pattern never changed: Engels gave; Marx spent.

Engels was a humble man. In his 1893 letter to Franz Mehring, he insisted that "you attribute more credit to me than I deserve, even if I count in everything which I might possibly have found out for myself—in time—but which Marx with his more rapid *coup d'oeil* (grasp) and wider vision discovered much more quickly."[30] He had lived in the shadow of Marx's footnotes all his life, and his traditional Germanic awe of the academic drudge colored his own self-evaluation right up until his death. His own admission of a manufactured false front of self-confidence reveals a great deal about his own sense of inferiority: "Here in Paris I have come to adopt a very insolent manner, for bluster is all in the day's work, and it works well with the female sex."[31] The latter concern was always high on his list of priorities.

Moses Hess: The Forgotten Co-Founder

When writing *Marx's Religion of Revolution*, I became familiar with the major writings of these two intellectual founders of

---

[30]Engels to Mehring, 14 July 1893, in Karl Marx and Friedrich Engels, *Correspondence, 1846–1895*, Dona Torr, ed. (New York: International Publishers, 1935), p. 510.

[31]Engels to Marx, 15 January 1847; Marx and Engels, *Collected Works*, 38, p. 108.

the most important secular religion of the modern world. By reading Sidney Hook's *From Hegel to Marx*, I also stumbled onto the existence of the shadowy figure who converted Frederick Engels to communism in 1842, Moses Hess (1812-1875).[32] He was the son of a successful Jewish businessman. As an adolescent, he had wanted to join his father in the family business, but his father insisted that the young man devote his life to the study of traditional Judaism's holy books, the Babylonian Talmud, which young Moses hated. He fell into bad company, young Jews who were rebelling against their parents' religion. Hess lost his faith in Judaism[33] about a decade prior to Engels's loss of faith in Christianity.[34] By 1836, Hess was a communist, as reflected in his anonymously published book, *Holy History of Mankind*.[35] Hess's second book, *The European Triarchy* (1841), predicted that a fusion of French revolutionary socialist political theory, German revolutionary philosophy, and English social revolution would produce a new society.

Engels read the second book and was greatly influenced by it.[36] He met with Hess in late 1842. Seven months later, Hess described this meeting with Engels: "We talked of questions of the day. Engels, who was revolutionary to the core when he met me, left as a passionate Communist."[37] Engels also met Marx briefly at this time, but the two did not get along.[38] For one thing, Marx was not yet a Marxist. Sidney Hook dates Marx's first appearance as a Marxist—an expositor

---

[32]Sidney Hook, *From Hegel to Marx: Studies in the Intellectual Development of Karl Marx* (1950; Ann Arbor: University of Michigan Press, 1962), chap. 6.

[33]Shlomo Avineri, *Moses Hess: Prophet of Communism and Zionism* (New York: New York University Press, 1985), pp. 10–11.

[34]Wurmbrand, *Marx and Satan*, chap. 3.

[35]Avineri, *Moses Hess*, p. 13.

[36]Marcus, *Engels, Manchester, and the Working Class*, p. 87.

[37]Cited by David McLellan, *Friedrich Engels* (New York: Viking, 1977), p. 21. This statement was made the following summer (19 June 1843), cited in Hammen, *Red '48ers*, p. 39.

[38]Terrell Carver, *Engels* (New York: Hill and Wang, 1981), p. 20.

of historical materialism—with *The German Ideology* (1845), an unpublished manuscript co-authored with Engels.[39] Part of this manuscript actually appears in Hess's handwriting.[40]

Marx had read essays by Engels in 1843, which the latter submitted to Marx as editor of the latter's two short-lived radical newspapers. By 1844, Marx had also been converted to communism, though not the "scientific" Marxist version, which began to take shape only in 1845. It was in 1844 that the long collaboration between Marx and Engels began. Hess had been the catalyst.

In the widely read, notoriously pro-Marx biography by Franz Mehring, Hess's influence is downplayed; Mehring even goes so far as to write: "Both Marx and Engels co-operated with Hess on numerous occasions during the Brussels period, and at one time it appeared as though Hess had completely adopted their ideas."[41] He makes it appear as though they were Hess's teachers, when in fact it had been the other way around, at least in the early stages (1842–44). This Marxist rewriting of history is understandable, since Marx and Engels concentrated their fire on Hess's ideas in the section on "True Socialism" in the *Communist Manifesto* (1848), despite the fact that Hess had adopted many of their views on political economy.[42] This attack on a former friend and teacher was typical of Marx and Engels from the very beginning. His early associates had been warned. Biographer Fritz Raddatz writes: "One of the scenes of that Köln period, vividly pictured by Heinzen, is both revealing and sinister. The chief editor [of the *Rheinische Zeitung*] and his colleagues often sat over a glass of wine in the evenings, and if the row of empty glasses was becoming noticeably long, Marx would look round the company with the angry

---

[39]Sidney Hook, *Revolution, Reform, and Social Justice: Studies in the Theory and Practice of Marxism* (1975; Oxford: Basil Blackwell, 1976), p. 58.

[40]Hook, *From Hegel to Marx*, p. 186.

[41]Mehring, *Karl Marx*, p. 112.

[42]Hook, *From Hegel to Marx*, p. 186. For details of Engels's attack on Hess at the October 23, 1847 meeting of the executive committee of Paris Communist League's District Authority, see Hammen, *Red '48ers*, pp. 163–64.

flashing eye of the aristocrat. One of his friends would be taken
aback by a finger suddenly pointed at him, accompanied by the
words 'I will destroy you.'"[43] Hess was shortly to be repaid in
full in traditional Marxist currency for his extravagant praise
of Marx in 1841.[44]

Hess has remained a forgotten historical figure. He was
ridiculed by Marx as the "Communist rabbi."[45] He was later to
become the spiritual founder of Zionism. That one man served
as the intellectual father of both of these important ideological
movements is remarkable; even more remarkable is the fact
that his name seldom appears in textbooks on modern European history. This was equally true a century ago. When the
founder of political Zionism Theodore Herzl wrote *The Jewish
State*, he had never heard of Hess. Shown a copy of Hess's 1862
book, *Rome and Jerusalem*, over thirty years after its publication, he said that if he had known of it earlier, he would not
have written *The Jewish State*, since Hess's book had so thoroughly prefigured his own writing.[46]

One fact is generally de-emphasized by students of early
Marxism: neither Marx nor Engels, and certainly not Hess,
suffered from dire poverty as young men. All three were bourgeois intellectuals. All three came from comfortable, if not
wealthy, backgrounds. Of the three, only Engels had any close
contact with the industrial proletariat, and he was the son of
the proletariat's employer, working as an executive of the

---

[43]Raddatz, *Karl Marx*, p. 35.

[44]Hess had written: "Here is a phenomenon who has made an enormous
impression on me although I work in the same field. In short prepare to meet the
greatest, perhaps the *only genuine philosopher* now living who will soon have the
eyes of all Germany upon him wherever he may appear in public, whether in print
or on the rostrum. Dr. Marx, as my idol is called, is still quite a young man (aged
about 24 at most) and it is he who will give medieval religion and politics their *coup
de grace*; he combines a biting wit with deeply serious philosophical thinking.
Imagine Rousseau, Voltaire, Holbach, Lessing, Heine and Hegel combined into one
person—and I say *combined*, not blended—and there you have Dr. Marx." Cited by
Raddatz, *Karl Marx*, pp. 25–26; also cited by Robert Payne, *Marx* (New York: Simon
& Schuster, 1968), p. 82; and by Avineri, *Moses Hess*, pp. 14–15.

[45]Hammen, *Red '48ers*, p. 39.

[46]Avineri, *Moses Hess*, pp. 243–44.

company almost all of his adult life. He hated it, but he refused to quit until he was middle aged.[47]

Marx's Income: 1844–48

In March of 1843 Marx lost his job, yet got married in June— not to some proletarian, but to Jenny von Westphalen, his old sweetheart, the daughter of a high and respected Prussian official. Their long honeymoon was spent on a tour through Switzerland where, Jenny later related, they literally gave money away. Jenny's mother had given the couple a small legacy for the trip. Marx spent the next few months reading and writing articles. (The journal for which he was writing went through one issue, and was immediately confiscated by the authorities, never to be revived.) At the end of the year he and his new bride went to Paris. These are hardly the activities of some starving proletarian philosopher.[48]

There are a handful of accounts of Marx's financial status during the years 1844–48. All of them point to the same fact: he lived high on the hog. I have pieced together the fragmentary

---

[47]Eleanor Marx-Aveling, Marx's daughter, described the situation: "For twenty years Engels was doomed to the forced labor of business life. . . . But I was with Engels when he reached the end of this forced labor and I saw what he must have gone through all those years. I shall never forget the triumph with which he exclaimed: 'For the last time!' as he put on his boots in the morning to go to the office for the last time. A few hours later we were standing at the gate waiting for him. We saw him coming over the little field opposite the house where he lived. He was swinging his stick in the air and singing, his face beaming. Then we set the table for a celebration and drank champagne and were happy. I was then too young to understand all that and when I think of it now the tears come to my eyes." *Marx and Engels Through the Eyes of Their Contemporaries*, p. 163. How touching!

Eleanor committed suicide in 1898. (Her sister Laura died the same way in 1911.) It is notable that Eleanor's estate was valued at £1,909, which was a small fortune in 1898. She had inherited Marx's estate, mainly his books' royalties. Her bankrupt communist husband then inherited everything. Payne, *Marx*, p. 530. Not a bad windfall for a bigamist who had secretly and illegally married the year before to another woman, a 22-year-old actress, to whom he immediately returned (Ibid., pp. 525, 530–31).

The Revolution consumes its own. But not soon enough.

[48]Payne, *Marx*, p. 92.

and sometimes conflicting data as best I can. In March of 1844, while he was living in Paris for about fourteen months, Marx's friends in Germany had collected 1,000 talers for him,[49] which was the equivalent of three years' income for a Silesian weaver working 14 to 16 hours a day.[50] Shortly thereafter, Raddatz says, another 800 talers arrived.[51] To this was added the money he earned from his 1,800 franc annual salary from *Vorwärts*,[52] plus the 4,000 francs he had received from the "Köln Circle" of liberals who had funded the short-lived newspaper, the *Rheinische Zeitung*.[53] To this, Raddatz says, should be added another 2,000 francs that Marx received for the sale of proof sets of the *Deutsche-Französische Jahrbücher*.[54] I have not found any confirmation of this additional 2,000 francs, however, so I do not count it. In any case, his total income, as Raddatz correctly observes, "should have been enough for several years."[55] Arnold Ruge had sarcastically remarked in a letter of 1844: "His wife gave him for his birthday a riding switch costing 100 francs and the poor devil cannot ride nor has he a horse. Everything he sees he wants to 'have'—a carriage, smart clothes, a flower garden, new furniture from the Exhibition, in fact the moon."[56]

---

[49]Hal Draper, *The Marx-Engels Chronicle: A Day-by-Day Chronology of Marx & Engels' Life & Activity* (New York: Schocken, 1985), p. 29. This is an exhaustive and indispensable volume.

[50]According to an estimate—perhaps exaggerated—by Wilhelm Wolff in 1844. Less than one taler a day was a net working wage for a weaver in Silesia in 1844. See the extract from his 1844 essay in Frank Eyck, ed., *The Revolutions of 1848-49* (New York: Barnes & Noble, 1972), p. 22. Wolff complained that retired high army officers received pensions of 1,000 talers a year. Wolff was Marx's benefactor who left him a small fortune in 1864: See below.

[51]Raddatz, *Karl Marx*, p. 46.

[52]Ibid., p. 283, 20 n.

[53]Ibid., p. 61.

[54]For the life of me, I cannot imagine anyone paying this much for proof copies of a journal that survived only one issue.

[55]Ibid., p. 58.

[56]Cited in ibid., p. 47.

Marx in Belgium

Marx was expelled from Paris in early 1845. He fled to Belgium. He was begging for money within a few months. Predictably, during the next three years in Brussels, he did not earn a penny.[57] But the money still rolled in. In December of 1844, he received 1,000 francs for the publication of *The Holy Family*.[58] Engels also gave him the advance he had received in May for *The Condition of the Working Class in England*.[59] Köln sent him another 750 francs. He also took advance payment of 1,500 francs for a book he never got around to writing. The publisher made a serious financially fatal mistake. After signing an initial contract with Marx that promised a payment of 1,500 francs upon completion of the manuscript, and another 1,500 at the time of publication,[60] he relented for some reason and sent Marx the initial 1,500 a few months later. He would spend the next few years demanding the manuscript or the return of his money, all to no avail. (As a publisher who has also been sucked in on several occasions by the pleas and promises of initially enthusiastic, boldly self-confident, perpetually indebted, and "ideologically pure" authors, I can sympathize with him. The surest way to bury any book publishing project is to pay the prospective author in advance.) He also borrowed 150 francs from his brother-in-law in November of 1847.[61] There is no record of any repayment. In an 1847 letter to Engels, Marx brings up the life-long theme of themes in his correspondence with Engels: "money."[62]

We know that Marx received 6,000 francs from his father's estate in March of 1848. His father had died in 1838; Marx could not persuade his mother and his Uncle Lion Philips to

---

[57]Ibid., p. 61.

[58]Draper, *Chronicle*, p. 16.

[59]Raddatz, *Karl Marx*, p. 61. I may be double counting here: Raddatz and Draper do not mention each other's data on Marx's book income. Maybe they are referring to the same payment.

[60]"Contract," February 1, 1845, in Marx and Engels, *Collected Works*, 4, p. 675.

[61]Draper, *Chronicle*, p. 28.

[62]Marx to Engels, 15 May 1847, *Collected Works*, 38, p. 116.

give him the money until 1848.[63] Robert Payne claims, without offering any substantiating evidence, that Marx immediately spent 5,000 to fund the purchase of weapons for Belgian workmen.[64] I have found no evidence of this, nor does any of the standard biographies of Marx refer to such a thing. If he did this, it was the least Marx-like act of his entire career. What we do know is that he was expelled from Belgium a few weeks later, after the publication of the *Communist Manifesto*, and by then he apparently had no money. We may never know for certain what happened to this legacy from his father.

If we add up his income, 1844 to early 1848, it comes to over 15,000 francs, plus the 1,800 talers, plus whatever money Engels received for *Condition of the Working Class*. Not bad for a generally unemployed Ph.D!

Lifestyle

The obvious question arises: How much money was this in purchasing power? A lot. Statistical data from this period are not highly reliable, but we can make usable estimates. A survey made in February of 1848, as the revolution was breaking out, indicated that the average wage of a Parisian male worker was slightly under four francs per day,[65] or around 1,250 francs per year, if he worked continually, six days a week, 52 weeks per year. Thus, during his brief stay of less than a year in Paris, Marx pulled in about 6,800 francs, plus 1,800 talers, or about *six times the average Parisian worker's salary* (even if we do not count the 2,000 francs for the supposed sale of proof sets), and he was not required to work 52 weeks to earn it.

What did it cost to live in Paris? One survey in 1845 indicated that the minimum expenses for a childless family in Paris were in the range of 750 francs per year.[66] Marx had only one

---

[63]Hammen, *Red '48ers*, p. 190.

[64]Payne, *Marx*, p. 176.

[65]Donald Cope McKay, *The National Workshops: A Study in the French Revolution of 1848* (Cambridge, Mass.: Harvard University Press, 1933), p. xv.

[66]Ibid., p. xvi.

child in 1844, so even if expenses were twice this, he could have survived. His income that year was ten or eleven times the Parisian family's minimum expenditure. (I have not pursued the question of the cost of living in Brussels. It is unlikely to have been drastically different. There was an international gold standard at the time, free mobility of population, and growing business competition. All these factors would have tended to equalize the costs of living the major cities.)

Consider these ratios in terms of today's income in the United States. First, recall that there were no income taxes in 1844. Taxes were quite low, way under double-digit levels. If today's family of three reached the poverty level at about $8,500 per year in 1985,[67] and if we assume that the average poor family spends all that it pulls in, then the Marx family was spending the equivalent of $85,000 *after-tax* 1985 dollars, or at least $125,000 of pre-tax income. This would put him at least in the upper two percent of U.S. income earners. This poverty-level figure does not include food stamps, free education, health care services, or other modern welfare benefits. If these are added to the base level income of $8,500, then the poverty line for American families in 1985 was considerably above $10,000 a year, meaning that Marx was pulling in the equivalent of over $100,000 a year after taxes.

Another way of looking at the figures is to assume that the average black family in the United States is at the lower end of the income level. The mean average after-tax income level of black families in 1985 was $16,000.[68] At six times the average Parisian worker's family, after taxes, the Marx family was doing well. Six times the average U.S. black family after taxes would have placed the Marx family's income 1985 income at $96,000. The average married couple with two children pulled in $28,000 after taxes. If you compute six times this income, the Marx family pulled in $168,000.

---

[67]*Statistical Abstract of the United States, 1988* (Washington, D.C.: Department of Commerce, 1988), p. 406.

[68]Ibid., table 695.

Marx, in short, was no starving proletarian. By anyone's standards in 1844, he was a rich man.

As far as I know, I seem to be the first investigator to search out even this minimal data on wage levels and the cost of living in Paris during the 1840s in order to compare Marx's income with the average workers. I am surely not the only person bright enough to do this. What we are suffering from is a combination of laziness on the part of scholars of Marx's life, plus an element of dignified silence: to discuss such matters would lead to the overthrow of the myth of Marx's poverty. It throws serious doubt on Marx's lifelong self-posturing as the Prometheus figure of the European proletariat. Only if someone finally turns up evidence that he really did donate 5,000 francs to the Belgian workers in early 1848 should we find reserves of compassion for poor Karl (unless, of course, the money was given to finance arms purchases so that they, rather than Marx, could get killed storming the barricades).

His years of serious financial hardship began in 1848, but by this time his philosophy of dialectical materialism and economic communism had already crystallized in his mind. In short, his philosophy of life had been developed in his years of remarkable prosperity. He became the self-appointed "voice of the proletarians" before he suffered the self-inflicted financial hardships of proletarianism. Unlike proletarians, he never held a steady job after 1844, and that job in Paris had lasted less than a year.

Marx returned to Cologne in 1848, and in June he began publication of still another paper, the *Neue Rheinische Zeitung*. The following February saw him brought to trial and subsequently acquitted of the charge of subversion. In May he published the inflammatory "red issue"—literally printed in red ink—since he was about to be expelled anyway. He left for France, but was expelled three months later (August 1849). From there he traveled to London, which, along with Switzerland, was the home of most nineteenth-century radicals after the revolutions of 1848–1850. He was to spend most of his remaining life in London, the city of exiles.

Self-Imposed Poverty, 1848–1863

It was in the fifteen-year period from 1848 to 1863 that Marx gained his reputation for poverty, a reputation he earned by his unwillingness to go out and earn a living. He lost three of his children, lived in indescribable squalor, and struggled along on handouts from Engels and whatever income he could gain from the articles he wrote (or which Engels wrote under Marx's name) for Horace Greeley's *New York Daily Tribune*.

In 1861, things became desperate for Marx. The Civil War in the United States had begun to cause havoc in the English cotton market, for the South placed an embargo on its cotton exports to England in the hope (which proved illusionary) that such an act would force English industrialists and workers to pressure the English government into official recognition of Southern independence. What money Engels possessed came from his employment in his father's mills, and Engels was employed in the Manchester branch of his father's industrial holdings. His income dropped as a result of the depressed conditions, and he was, for three years, unable to aid Marx very much. Simultaneously, the *Tribune* canceled Marx's column on European affairs in order to make more room for news concerning the war. Thus, Marx's two chief sources of financial support were cut off. He went deeply into debt.

Things grew so bad in these years that Karl Marx was driven into the ultimate breaking point: he actually had to go out and look for a job! He applied for a post at a local railway office. His explanation to his Hanoverian correspondent, Dr. Kugelmann, was straightforward: "I did not get the post because of my bad handwriting."[69] Anyone who has ever seen Marx's handwriting can sympathize with both the railway officials and Dr. Kugelmann.[70] He never went looking again.

[69]Marx to Kugelmann, 28 December 1862, in *Letters To Kugelmann* (New York: International Publishers, 1934), p. 24. Marx and Engels, *Collected Works*, 41, p. 436.

[70]Samples can be found in Mehring, *Karl Marx*, p. 283, and Payne, *Marx*, pp. 35, 153, 405.

There is no denying that the Marx family lived in abject poverty in these years. But the textbooks seldom mention that the cause of this self-imposed poverty was that Marx never bothered to go out and get a job. "Nothing human is foreign to me," he once wrote, citing the Roman Republic's playwright Terence, thereby proclaiming his personal commitment to radical humanism. Nothing human was foreign to Marx, one is tempted to add, except steady employment. In 1864, he had squandered a fortune. The money had been advanced (given) to him by Engels, plus what he inherited from his mother's estate, plus a huge inheritance from Wilhelm Wolff. In 1865, broke again, he was offered the opportunity to write a column each month on the movements of the money-market. He refused to accept the job, never bothering to so much as offer an explanation.[71]

Karl and Jenny Marx were simply not capable of handling money with any degree of success. Three things served to alleviate their economic hardship in this bleak period of their lives. First there was Helene (Lenchen) Demuth, the Marx's housekeeper. She had grown up as a servant in the von Westphalen home, and Jenny's mother sent her to be with the Marxes in 1846. She remained with the family until the death of Karl Marx in 1883. As Payne's biography of Marx demonstrates, she was the keeper of the family purse, and she kept it as solvent as possible. She also bore Marx an illegitimate son in 1851—a son Marx was never willing to acknowledge for fear of embarrassment in London's revolutionary circles—another hitherto ignored fact which Payne's book brought to light.

The Inheritances

A second factor was the advance on his inheritance from his mother (who had not yet died) which he received in early 1861.

Karl's mother paid off his old debts, and through the executor of her estate, her immensely successful industrialist

---

[71]Mehring, *Karl Marx*, pp. 342–43. This took place in 1865, the year following Marx's massive inheritance.

brother-in-law Lion Philips.[72] Marx received £160, part of which he spent on a whirlwind European tour.[73]

Finally, in 1863, Engels was able to scrape together £125, and possibly more—the record is unclear—for Marx's relief.[74] It was on this occasion that Engels criticized Marx openly, the only time he ever did so. In January, Engels's "wife" died, and he wrote to Marx in despair. Marx replied with two brief sentences of regret and then launched into a description of his own financial woes. Engels was infuriated, told Marx so, and Marx apologized—possibly the only time in his adult life that he apologized to anyone outside his immediate family. So, Engels sent him the money, and the two partners were reconciled.

In late 1863, Marx's mother died. His share of the inheritance, minus the advance, came to something less than £100.[75] He collected this early in 1864. It was enough, as one biography puts it, to mitigate "at least the worst of Marx's distress."[76] Then came the deluge. An obscure German follower, Wilhelm Wolff, one of the original eighteen conspirators of the 1846 League of the Just, died and left Marx the staggering (by 1864 standards) sum of £824.[77] Marx later dedicated *Das Kapital* to Wolff.[78] In September, Engels was made a full partner in his father's firm, and may have been less resentful than usual when Marx demanded an additional £40, which he insisted was owed to him by Engels (who was executor of Wolff's estate).[79]

---

[72]Lion Philips, Marx's uncle by marriage, became the founder of one of Europe's most powerful companies, the Philips Electrical Company, of which the North American Philips Company (Norelco) is a subsidiary. See Payne, *Marx*, p. 330.

[73]Ibid., p. 330.

[74]Ibid., pp. 339–40. The Nicolaievsky biography reports that Engels actually paid Marx £350 in 1863, although I am inclined to doubt this figure. Nicolaievsky and Maenchen-Helfen, *Karl Marx: Man and Fighter* (London: Methuen, 1936), p. 253.

[75]Ibid., p. 346.

[76]Nicolaievsky and Maenchen-Helfen, *Karl Marx*, p. 253.

[77]Payne, *Marx*, p. 354.

[78]Berlin, *Karl Marx*, pp. 247–48.

[79]Payne, *Marx*, p. 354.

Thus, in one year Marx was the recipient of almost £1000.

When I first began looking into Marx's finances (prior to the publication of Payne's revealing biography), I began to wonder just how much this money amounted to in terms of purchasing power. Not one biography prior to Payne's asked this fundamental question. Professor Bowley has estimated that in 1860, the income of an agricultural laborer in the lowest ten percent of the British population was something like £30 annually. An average income for a worker would have been about £45 per year. For those in the upper ten percent of the population, a 70-pound figure would have been typical.[80] The income of the Marx family in 1863 would have put them in the upper five percent of the British population! That was the sum sent by Engels to mitigate "at least the worst of Marx's distress." His income during the next year, 1864, would have been equivalent to the wages paid to over twenty "average" British proletarians.

Easy Come, Easy Go

Incredible as it may seem, in May of 1865 the Marx family was penniless again. On July 31 of that year he wrote to Engels for more money, claiming that he had been in hock to a pawnshop for two months.[81] Dr. Kugelmann received a letter in October which contained these words: "My economic position has become so bad as a result of my long illness and the many expenses which it entailed, that I am faced with a financial crisis in the *immediate future*, a thing which, apart from the direct effects on me and my family, would also be disastrous for me politically, particularly here in London, where one must 'keep up appearances.' "[82]

It would seem that either London's radical society had been infected with a severe case of "bourgeois affectations," or else

---

[80]A. L. Bowley, *Wages and Income in the United Kingdom Since 1860* (Cambridge University Press, 1937), p. 46.

[81]Mehring, *Karl Marx*, p. 341.

[82]Marx to Kugelmann, 13 October 1866 in *Letters to Kugelmann*, p. 42.

Dr. Marx was now associating with those of very high class standings. Marx then went on to ask Kugelmann if he knew of anyone who would loan him money at a rate of five to six percent interest, since, as he announced, "I am now paying 20 to 30 percent interest for the small sums which I borrow, but even so I cannot put off my creditors much longer. . . ."[83] Marx, the economist of the proletarian class, was hardly what we could call a sound financial administrator.

Where did the money go? Payne's biography supplies a key clue. In a letter to his uncle Lion Philips, Marx announced (June 1864) that he had made £400 on the stock exchange. On July 4th, he wrote to Engels asking for the final settlement of the Wolff legacy: "If I had had the money during the last ten days, I would have been able to make a good deal on the stock exchange. The time has now come when my wit and very little money one can really make a killing in London."[84] Unfortunately, Marx forgot that when some people are making killings on the stock exchange, others frequently are getting killed. We cannot be certain, but Marx's gambling instincts may have been the cause, at least in part, of his financial downfall.

Non-Proletarian Quarters

Expenditures, as we all know, tend to rise as income rises. With his mother's small legacy in hand, Marx had moved his family into a new home in March of 1864, shortly before the news of the legacy from Wolff arrived. This represented a leap into the upper middle class. Payne's description of Marx's home (and the photograph of it in his book) is revealing: "No one arriving at the new house on Maitland Park Road would mistake it for a workman's lodging. It was spacious and handsome, with cornices over the windows and elegant Corinthian columns at the head of the steps, with a small garden in front and a larger one at the back. Like nearly all the columned houses in London, this house gave an impression of subdued affluence. A

---

[83]Idem.

[84]Payne, *Marx*, p. 354. Marx and Engels, *Collected Works*, 41, p. 546.

doctor, a local magistrate, or a businessman who worked in the city would not have been out of place in it."[85]

Karl Marx remained in this home until 1875, at which time he moved into one which was apparently close to being identical with the Maitland Park home (this final residence was destroyed during the World War II). Jenny, his wife, gave a fancy ball in October 1864, another drain on Marx's finances, and she gave others as the years rolled on.[86] No doubt they served the Marx family as reminders of their affluent youth. His housing preferences certainly confirms the observation of Logan Pearsal Smith: "All reformers, however strict their social conscience, live in houses just as big as they can pay for."[87]

The Pension from Engels

When Engels decided to sell his interest in the family firm in 1869, he wrote to Marx and asked him how much money it would take to clear up all of his debts. Marx replied by return mail that he was £210 in arrears, "of which about 75 are for pawnshop and interest."[88] In July 1869, Engels settled his accounts with the firm, and was able to pay off Marx's debts, while putting him on an annual pension of £350. Yet Marx claimed that even this large sum was not enough for him to live comfortably. A year before, in a letter to Kugelmann, he had written this astounding message: "You may be sure that I have often discussed leaving London for Geneva, not only with myself and my family, but with Engels. Here I have to spend from 400 to £500 annually; in Geneva I could live on £200."[89]

Marx's income, using Professor Bowley's estimates, was some five times greater than the upper ten percent of the

---

[85]Ibid., p. 377.

[86]Ibid., p. 355.

[87]*The Portable Curmudgeon*, Jon Winokur, ed. (New York: New American Library, 1987), p. 232.

[88]Quoted by Otto Rühle, *Karl Marx: His Life and Work* (New York: New Home Library, 1942), p. 360.

[89]Marx to Kugelmann, 17 March 1868, in *Letters to Kugelmann*, p. 65.

British laboring classes. Using the 1867 figures presented in that year by R. Dudley Baxter to the Statistical Society of London, we find that Marx's income placed his family in the top 120,000 families in England and Wales. Some 5.1 million families lived below Marx's "poverty line." After 1869, Marx's regular annual pension placed him in the *upper two percent* of the British population in terms of income.

Marx, in short, felt he was unable to live comfortably on an income greater than that enjoyed by ninety-eight percent of his countrymen—in a nation which, per capita, was the wealthiest in the world.[90] Incredibly, one biography puts it this way: "But his anxieties only really ended in 1869, when Engels sold his share in the cotton mill and was able to make Marx a definite, if moderate, yearly allowance."[91] That is how history gets rewritten.

The Legend Lives On

We can now place the myth of Marx's poverty in its proper perspective. He was poor during only fifteen years of his sixty-five-year career, in large part due to his unwillingness to use his doctorate and go out to get a job. His economic opinions had been formed, at least in their essentials, before this poverty set in, and the final culmination of his system, *Das Kapital*, published in 1867, was completed in the years of high income. His own life seems to stand as a testimony against the validity of his doctrine of economic determinism. The philosopher-economist of class revolution—the "Red Doctor of Soho" who spent only six years in that run-down neighborhood—was one of England's wealthier citizens during the last two decades of his life. But he could not make ends meet.[92]

---

[90]Baxter's figures appear in *Economic History Review* 21 (April 1968): 21.

[91]Nicolaievsky and Maenchen-Helfen, *Karl Marx*, p. 254.

[92]At his death, Marx's estate was valued at about £250, consisting primarily of his books and furniture. Payne, *Marx*, p. 500. Payne's comment is only too accurate: "In spite of Engels' generosity he was continually in debt. Although he spent most of his waking hours thinking about money, he had very little

In one respect, at least, things have not changed very much since the middle years of the nineteenth century. You can still find far more self-proclaimed Marxists on the bourgeois college campus than you can find in the "proletarian" workshops of Detroit or Chicago. The well-fed bourgeois intellectuals have far more of an affinity for the ideas of Marx and Engels than today's industrial proletariat does. Marx's ideas were born in the university and its intellectual underground, nurtured during years of voluntary withdrawal from economic production, and flowered in declining years of luxury, far removed from the environment of the displaced proletariat.

The "tragedy" of Marx's "poverty-stricken" life consisted only in the fact that if he had lived in the mid-twentieth century, he could have avoided those fifteen years of self-imposed trouble. There are today plenty of tax-exempt foundations that make a point of supporting such revolutionary conspirators in the high style which he experienced throughout most of his life.

Karl Marx set the pattern, both intellectually and financially, for the present generation of well-fed, well-subsidized, bourgeois intellectuals. An economist who could not economize, a revolutionary organizer whose organizations invariably fell apart, a secular prophet whose prophecies did not come true, a self-proclaimed autonomous man who spent his life on Engels's dole and in hock to the pawnbrokers, the self-proclaimed spokesman of the working class who never did an hour's manual labor in his life, the inventor of a theory of inevitable industrial revolutions that have in fact only occurred in backward rural societies, the man who predicted the withering away of the State whose ideas revived the ancient quest for world empire, Karl Marx's life serves as testimony to the failure of bad ideas. The only people who still take his ideas seriously are bourgeois intellectuals, heretical middle-class pastors, and power-seekers who want to

---

understanding of the risk attached to borrowing. He would sign bills of exchange at high interest and wonder how he had brought himself to such a pass when the bills fell due. He was improvident and oddly childlike in financial matters. He had no gift for making money and none for spending it" (p. 342).

become tyrants for life—the kind of people Marx despised, that is, people very much like himself.

On the bourgeois dole for his entire life, he spent his days criticizing the very economic structure which permitted him his leisure time: capitalism. He attacked "Bourgeois Liberalism," yet it was that system of liberal attitudes and broadmindedness which produced an atmosphere of intellectual freedom, without which he would have been imprisoned and his books burned as a lesson for others. Had bourgeois London not given him a place to hide and work—analogous to the Old Testament's cities of refuge (Numbers 35:6-32)—we would never have heard of this third-rate materialist philosopher and fourth-rate classical economist. In short, Marx did his best to undercut the very foundations of his own existence. By 1998, in those nations that were officially Marxist, anti-Communist ideas had become the coin of the realm. Nothing remains of Marxism except its quest for power. Paraphrasing bourgeois intellectual Lincoln Steffans, the Communists have seen the future at close range, and it does not work.

Critically Critical Criticism

Fritz Raddatz correctly notes that Marx's doctoral dissertation on Epicurus and Democritus was a work of criticism. "Even in this very first work Marx showed himself as an 'anti' writer, an author who defined his own position as a result of polemic and criticism. His most important productions have as their title or subtitle the word 'Critique'; his less important polemical writings are attempts to pick a quarrel or to counterattack."[93] Alvin Gouldner makes a similar observation.[94] Look at the titles and subtitles of his essays and books: "Contribution to the Critique of Hegel's Philosophy of Law" (1843), *The Holy Family, or Critique of Critical Criticism* (1844), *A Contribution to the Critique of Political Economy* (1859),

---

[93]Raddatz, *Karl Marx*, p. 28.
[94]Gouldner, *The Two Marxisms*, p. 11

Capital: A Critique of Political Economy (1867); *Critique of the Gotha Program* (1875). As was the case in so many other aspects of the origin of Marxism, Engels was the originator of the tradition. He started this "critique" mania with his early titles, *Schelling and Revelation: Critique of the Latest Attempt of Reaction Against the Free Philosophy* (1841),[95] and "On the Critique of the Prussian Press Laws" (1842).[96]

What Marx was, from beginning to end, was an uncompromising critic of others. He criticized everything and everyone except himself, especially those people who had befriended him earlier. Only Engels escaped his wrath, because Engels always offered public obeisance to him, and because he subsidized Marx handsomely, decade after decade. (In their only known dispute, Marx backed down—apparently the only time he ever backed down in any dispute.[97]) Karl Marx was the foremost hater and most incessant whiner in the history of Western Civilization. He was a spoiled, overeducated brat who never grew up; he just grew more shrill as he grew older. His lifelong hatred and whining have led to the deaths (so far) of perhaps a hundred million people, depending on how many people perished under Mao's tyranny. We will probably never know.

Whiners, if given power, readily become tyrants. Marx was seen by his contemporaries as a potential tyrant. Giuseppe Mazzini (1805–72), the Italian revolutionary, and a rival of Marx's in the International Workingmen's Association in the mid-1860s,[98] once described Marx as "a destructive spirit

---

[95]Marx and Engels, *Collected Works*, 1, pp. 192–240.

[96]Ibid., 1, pp. 304–11.

[97]It took place when Engel's mistress Mary Burns died in January of 1863. Engels wrote to Marx, telling of his loss on January 7. The next day—the letter went from Manchester to London in one day!—Marx wrote two sentences of condolences and then begged for more money in two long paragraphs. On January 13, Engels replied, indicating that he was displeased with Marx's "frosty reaction." On January 24, Marx sent a letter apologizing for his behavior. Karl Marx and Friedrich Engels, *Selected Letters: The Personal Correspondence, 1844–1877*, Fritz J. Raddatz, ed. (Boston: Little, Brown, 1980), pp. 104–6.

[98]"Record of Marx's Speech on Mazzini's Attitude to the International Working Men's Association" (1866), in Marx and Engels, *Collected Works*, 20, p. 401.

whose heart was filled with hatred rather than love of mankind ... extraordinarily sly, shifty and taciturn. Marx is very jealous of his authority as leader of the Party; against his political rivals and opponents he is vindictive and implacable; he does not rest until he has beaten them down; his overriding characteristic is boundless ambition and thirst for power. Despite the communist egalitarianism which he preaches he is the absolute ruler of his party; admittedly he does everything himself but he is also the only one to give orders and he tolerates no opposition."[99] This is the essence of Marxism, despite Marx's claims to the contrary: a system of bureaucratic control that attempts to overcome the leader's lack of omniscience and omnipresence by means of top-down centralized power. It has been the characteristic feature of Lenin, Stalin, Mao, and subsequent Communist dictators. It is inherent in the Communist system.

Bakunin's Warning

Michael Bakunin, the revolutionary anarchist and rival of Marx in their battle for control over the International Workingmen's Association,[100] accurately prophesied in 1869 what would be the legacy of Marx's theory of Communism: statism.

> The reasoning of Marx ends in absolute contradiction. Taking into account only the economic question, he insists that only the most advanced countries, those in which capitalist production has attained greatest development, are the most capable of making social revolution. These civilized countries, to the exclusion of all others, are the only ones destined to initiate and carry through this revolution. This revolution will expropriate either by peaceful, gradual, or by violent means, the present property owners and capitalists. To appropriate all the landed property and capital, and to carry out its extensive economic and political programs, the revolutionary State will have to be very powerful and highly centralized. The State will administer and direct

[99]Cited by Raddatz, *Karl Marx*, p. 66.

[100]Paul Thomas, *Karl Marx and the Anarchists* (London: Routledge and Kegan Paul, 1980), pp. 249–340.

the cultivation of the land, by means of its salaried officials commanding armies of rural workers organized and disciplined for this purpose. At the same time, on the ruins of the existing banks, it will establish a single state bank which will finance all labor and national commerce.

It is readily apparent how such a seemingly simple plan of organization can excite the imagination of the workers, who are as eager for justice as they are for freedom; and who foolishly imagine that the one can exist without the other; as if, in order to conquer and consolidate justice and equality, one could depend on the efforts of others, particularly on governments, regardless of how they may be elected or controlled, to speak and act for the people! For the proletariat this will, in reality, be nothing but a barracks: a regime, where regimented workingmen and women will sleep, wake, work, and live to the beat of a drum; where the shrewd and educated will be granted government privileges; and where the mercenary-minded, attracted by the immensity of the international speculations of the state bank, will find a vast field for lucrative, underhanded dealings.[101]

Insufficiently Self-Critical

How critical is "critical?" In testing the truth or falsehood of any world-and-life view, we need to ask ourselves: "Does the theorist who is proposing this comprehensive explanation of cause and effect actually apply it to his own life and work?" Almost no modern social theorist is willing to do this. Allan Bloom has commented on this carefully ignored problem: "It is Nietzsche's merit that he was aware that to philosophize is radically problematic in the cultural, historicist dispensation. He recognized the terrible intellectual and moral risks involved. At the center of his every thought was the question 'How is it possible to do what I am doing?' He tried to apply to his own thought the teachings of cultural relativism. This practically nobody else does. For example, Freud says that men are

---

[101]*Bakunin on Anarchy: Selected Works by the Activist-Founder of World Anarchism*, Sam Dolgoff, ed. (New York: Knopf, 1972), pp. 283–84.

motivated by desire for sex and power, but he did not apply those motives to explain his own science or his own scientific activity. But if he can be a true scientist, i.e., motivated by love of the truth, so can other men, and his description of their motives is thus mortally flawed. Or if he is motivated by sex or power, he is not a scientist, and his science is only one means among many possible to attain those ends. This contradiction runs throughout the natural and social sciences. They give an account of things that cannot possibly explain the conduct of their practitioners. The highly ethical economist who speaks only about gain, the public-spirited political scientist who sees only group interest, the physicist who signs petitions in favor of freedom while recognizing only unfreedom—mathematical law governing moved matter—in the universe are symptomatic of the difficulty of providing a self-explanation for science and a ground for the theoretical life, which has dogged the life of the mind since early modernity but has become particularly acute with cultural relativism."[102]

Consider the theories of Marx and Engels. These men preached the gospel of inevitable proletarian revolution. But who were they? Two bourgeois writers who were converted to revolutionary socialism in their mid-twenties. Both were sons of successful bourgeois fathers, and Engels grew steadily richer over the years because of his skills in managing his father's industrial textile mills. It never seemed to bother Lenin that he had no consistent Marxist explanation for the historical fact regarding the workers that he could not deny: the Social-Democratic consciousness of proletarians does not develop by itself. "This consciousness could only be brought to them from without. The history of all countries shows that the working class, exclusively by its own effort, is able to develop only trade-union consciousness. . . . The theory of Socialism, however, grew out of the philosophic, historical and economic theories that were

---

[102]Allan Bloom, *The Closing of the American Mind* (New York: Simon & Schuster, 1987), pp. 203–4.

elaborated by the educated representatives of the propertied classes, the intellectuals. The founders of modern scientific Socialism, Marx and Engels, themselves belonged to the bourgeois intelligentsia."[103] The obvious question is: Why? It has no obvious Marxist answer.

Marx and Engels also predicted the initial successes of this proletarian revolution in nations that had adopted modern industrial capitalism. So, where have the only successful indigenous Communist revolutions taken place? In rural Third World nations and in nations that were only in the very early stages of industrialism (e.g., Russia). Who have their ideological recruits been? First and foremost, intellectuals in industrial countries who have themselves recruited no proletarian followers but who have strongly influenced a small army of other intellectuals who are basically favorable to Marxist humanism, or who are at least unfavorable to the efforts of the enemies of Marxist tyrannies.[104] Second, highly educated bourgeois intellectual activists in rural nations who have succeeded in recruiting dedicated peasant followers. In short, nowhere have the theories of Marx and Engels been less applicable or their prophecies less accurate than in the history of Communism. This is seldom discussed by Communists. The critical attitude fostered by Marxism has not been sufficiently self-critical. Marxists apply Marxism's comprehensive theories only to non-Marxist theories and societies. This has been true from the very beginning of Marxism.

Marx Short-Circuits at Age 49

Socialist economics eventually proved to be no solution to Marx's intellectual problems. The fact that Marx refused to publish the second and third volumes of *Capital* and his "Theories

---

[103]Vladimir I. Lenin, *What Is To Be Done? Burning Questions of Our Movement* (1902; New York: International Publishers, 1943), pp. 32–33.

[104]Jean Francois Revel, *How Democracies Perish* (Garden City, New York: Doubleday, 1984).

of Surplus Value" is at least circumstantial evidence of the "dead end" character of his economic system, since he had plenty of money from Engels at this stage of his career; he could have afforded to get them published. If he was willing to publish his doctoral dissertation as a young man when he had much less money, why not his post-1867 *magna opera*? It was not what he wrote early in his career and did not bother to publish in uncompleted form that is most important, for he later submitted what he regarded as superior manuscripts to his publishers. The one major exception is *The German Ideology* [1845], which he and Engels tried unsuccessfully to get published, and which was never put into final form.[105] What he labored on for a decade, 1857–67, and then refused to publish is what is most significant, for it reveals the breakdown of his system. This breakdown produced a kind of mental breakdown in Marx.

As I mentioned in *Marx's Religion* in 1968, the fact that he got to the end of volume 3 of *Capital* without defining "class" is significant. He started to define that crucial term, but the manuscript ends two paragraphs later. The manuscript then sat on his shelves for well over a decade, gathering dust. Mises is correct: "Significantly the third volume breaks off after a few sentences in the chapter headed 'The Classes.' In treating the problem of class Marx got only as far as setting up a dogma without proof, and no further."[106]

The dead ends of his system finally overwhelmed him. Marx's economic analysis was visibly dead in 1867; Marx was smart enough to know that it was dead, so he wisely stopped writing economic analysis. The most accurate thing Marx ever wrote was his 1858 assessment of his notes for the manuscript that later became *Das Kapital*, notes which today are hailed as crucial in the development of Marx's later thought, published as the *Grundrisse*. Marx called this material

[105]"Preface," in Marx and Engels, *Collected Works*, 5, pp. xv, xxv.

[106]Ludwig von Mises, *Socialism: An Economic and Sociological Analysis* (1922; New Haven, Conn.: Yale University Press, 1951), p. 328 n.

Scheisse.[107] He saw clearly after 1867 that there is little use spending your "golden years" writing even more *Scheisse.*

What few scholars have admitted in print is that Marx short-circuited after age 49. It is rarely mentioned that after the publication of what later became known as volume 1 of *Capital*, Marx never had another full-length book published during his lifetime. Instead, he confined his intellectual activities to working frantically on a wide, unstructured range of unpublished projects, plus writing the usual refutations of his enemies. These tirades lacked both the venom and volume of the enormous pile of tirades published earlier in his career. It was as if he was going through the motions out of habit more than anything else, like an old dog who still chases an occasional car for a hundred feet instead of three blocks down the street. A few barks, and then he trots back to his rug on the front porch. Except for citations from *The Civil War in France* (1871) and an occasional reference to the *Critique of the Gotha Program* (1875), you will hardly see anything written by Marx referred to in anyone's book on Marx. Almost everything of significance to the Communist movement after 1867 was written by Engels. The Moscow-published, three-volume *Selected Works* of Marx and Engels has more Engels in it than Marx, and after *The Civil War in France* (the middle of volume 2), almost all of the set is written by Engels.

Frantic Reading

Raddatz has summarized Marx's later years quite well:

> As it subsequently proved, however, for the last fifteen years of his life following publication of Volume I Marx hardly, if at all, worked on *Capital*. The information given by Engels in his prefaces to Volumes 2 and 3 was almost sensational: the manuscripts he found among Marx's papers had clearly been written between 1864 and 1867, in other words *before* Volume I had been published. Moreover, Marx had not been prevented from completing his book by illness or debility. . . . Letters show that Marx

---

[107]Marx to Engels, 2 April 1858 in Marx and Engels, *Correspondence, 1846–1895*, p. 105.

actually ran away from this book, that he definitely looked for excuses. . . . He delved into such problems as the chemistry of nitrogen fertilizers, agriculture, physics, and mathematics. His book of excerpts of 1878 is full of tables and sketches, on atmospheric temperature for instance, or drawings of sea shells and fossils; whole pages are covered with chemical formulae; on page after page whole lines are carefully erased with a ruler. Methodical labor for no good purpose. This time-wasting in senseless and extreme precision was a method of evasion; even in the early days Engels had warned him: "As long as you have some book you think important lying in front of you unread, you will never get down to writing."[108] And there were always sufficient books lying unread to satisfy the appetite of this gargantuan devourer of paper—studies on differential calculus, a Danish theory of the state, or Russian grammar. Marx immediately wrote a treatise on differential calculus and various other mathematical manuscripts; he learned Danish; he learned Russian. Among his papers Engels, who knew only too well the defenses behind which Marx barricaded himself, found "over two cubic meters of books on Russian statistics alone."[109] The word 'excuse' appears even in a letter from Marx himself to the Russian translator of *Capital*; in it he counts himself lucky that publication in Germany is prevented by anti-socialist legislation and that fortunately fresh material from Russia and the United States provides him with the excuse he is looking for to continue with his research instead of finishing the book and publishing it.[110]

Raddatz then reveals that even this excuse was a lame one; the Prussian censors regarded Marx's books as social-democratic or non-revolutionary communism (which boggles the imagination), and so there was no legal excuse for prohibiting their importation.[111] What I argue is that this was not Marx's mid-life crisis; this was his inconsistent-system crisis.

There is true irony here. In constructing his critique of

---

[108]Engels to Marx, 3 April 1851, in Marx and Engels, *Collected Works*, 38, p. 330.

[109]Engels to Friederich Adolph Sorge, 29 June 1883.

[110]Marx to Nicolai F. Danielson, 10 April 1879. All cited in Raddatz, *Karl Marx*, pp. 236–37.

capitalism, Marx explicitly adopted the classical economists' erroneous intellectual legacy, the labor theory of value. The classical economists argued that the source of all economic value is human labor. One error that results from the labor theory of value is the idea that activity is a meaningful economic substitute for production. The obvious nature of the error should have warned economists that something was fundamentally wrong with the labor theory of value. Yet Marx lived out the labor theory of value during the final sixteen years of his life. He substituted frantic intellectual activity for meaningful intellectual production.

Raddatz has recognized the fragmented nature of Marx's legacy: "The fact that Marx's life's work remained fragmentary, therefore, cannot be laid at the door of external circumstances. Since, apart from his great polemics or works of criticism and shorter inflammatory writings, everything remained uncompleted, the question arises whether this was due to some fundamental tendency."[112] Marx was endlessly rewriting pieces that were more than a month old. His son-in-law Paul Lafargue records that Marx could not bear to publish anything that was less than perfect. Yet he left behind a mountain of notebooks and jumbled papers.[113] And out of this jumble many academic reputations have been constructed!

Youthful Habits Revisited

His biographer (or more accurately, his hagiographer) Franz Mehring recognized Marx's life-long problem with getting anything written in final form, from his doctoral dissertation onward. "It was characteristic of Marx, and it remained so until the end of his days, that his insatiable urge to knowledge permitted him to master difficult problems quickly, whilst his merciless self-criticism prevented him from having done with them equally quickly."[114] Merciless self-criticism was never

---

[112]Idem.
[113]Idem.
[114]Mehring, *Karl Marx*, p. 25.

one of Marx's visible personality traits, but his overwhelming desire to avoid making a mistake in print was increasingly a problem for Engels as Marx grew older. He could not get Marx to finish anything.

Arnold Ruge, one of Marx's early radical associates, had lived at the same address in Paris during one of Marx's numerous exiles.[115] Ruge had recommended in 1842 that Marx be made co-editor of the short-lived *Rheinische Zeitung*, and who within two years became an early target of his invective, once described Marx as follows: "He is a strange character with a pronounced bent towards scholarship and authorship but totally incompetent as a journalist. He reads a great deal; he works at extraordinary pressure and has a talent for criticism which sometimes develops into presumptuous and discourteous dialectics; he never completes anything, is always breaking off and plunging back again into an endless welter of books."[116] It could be said of Marx that he was the perpetual sophomore, learning new material rapidly and superficially, but inevitably becoming bogged down with details of analysis when they proved to be inconvenient with his presuppositions and initial hypotheses, as they invariably proved to be.

(Marx later got even with Ruge, as he did with all his former colleagues except Engels, who never stopped sending him money. He became a paid informant for the Austrian police, spying on his revolutionary associates. Ruge was one of them. He was paid the equivalent of $25 for each bit of information he turned up. This is not one of the biographical details heralded in the dozens of conventional histories of Marx, although the story has been known since 1960.)[117]

Perhaps it really was self-criticism that at last destroyed

---

[115]Raddatz, *Karl Marx*, p. 43.

[116]Cited by Raddatz, ibid., p. 43.

[117]The German Newspaper *Reichshruf* (January 9, 1960) reported that Chancellor Raabe of Austria gave Nikita Khrushchev an original letter from Marx that had been found accidentally in the Austrian archives. The letter gave details on this unique financial arrangement. Premier Khrushchev was not amused. Wurmbrand, *Marx and Satan*, p. 33.

him. He had criticized everything mercilessly all his life. Perhaps he did criticize himself into partial intellectual paralysis after 1867. If so, this was a fitting end to a life of endless rebuttals, detailed nit-picking of others, and continual self-justification. What I suspect, however, was that he was too arrogant to admit publicly that the economic analysis found in volume 1 of *Capital* was self-contradictory, and he was also too arrogant to admit publicly, by failing to publish volume 1, that more than a decade of struggling with economics had been a major malinvestment of his life's resources. He therefore allowed volume 1 to be published, but then refused to finish the other explanatory manuscripts for publication, knowing full well that their appearance in print would only visibly compound his problem, as indeed they did.

Endless Excommunications

Another feature of Marx's personality was his inability to co-operate with his fellow revolutionaries. Throughout his career, he found himself bickering with former associates and present workers who were, in Marx's mind, rivals. With Engels alone he remained on friendly terms, and Engels was careful always to give Marx the two things which he required: unfailing subservience and money. Otto Rühle, by no means an unfavorable biographer, has not exaggerated when he writes that "Marx was one of those persons who are overpowered by a perpetual urge towards the highest, the purest, the most ideal. It was not merely his ambition to be the most famous among those who have studied socialist literature, and the most learned of all the critics of economic science; he also wanted to be the most efficient revolutionist, and pre-eminent among the advocates of revolution. He wanted to expound the purest theory, to establish the most complete system of communism. As a preliminary to the demonstration of this superiority, he must prove that the socialist theories of all his predecessors were worthless, false, contemptible, or ludicrous. He had to show that the socialism of the utopists was a crazy-quilt of outworn and questionable ideas. That Proudhon was a suspect intruder into the realm of socialist thought. That Lassalle, Bakunin, and [Johann] Schweitzer were tainted with bourgeois ideology, and had probably sold themselves to the enemy. He, Marx alone, was in possession of the true doctrine. His was the crystal-clear knowledge; his was the philosopher's stone; his the immaculate conception of socialism; his the divine truth. With contemptuous wrath, with bitter mockery and profound hostility, he rejected all other opinions, fought against all other convictions, than his own, persecuted all ideas that had not originated in his own brain. For him, there was no wisdom except his own, no socialism other than the socialism he proclaimed, no true gospel outside the limits of his own doctrine. His work was the essence of intellectual purity and scientific integrity. His system was Allah, and he was its prophet."[118]

Marx's unwillingness to tolerate anything which he regarded as insubordination was the cause of numerous splits within the ranks of the proletarian revolutionary movement in Europe, some of which were avoidable. Even Franz Mehring, the author of the semi-official biography of Marx, has to admit that during the dispute with Lassalle, the founder of the Marxist German Social Democratic Party, Marx was excessively bitter. "In his letters to Engels Marx condemns Lassalle's activities with a severity which occasionally develops into bitter injustice."[119] Marx's references to him as "a little kike" or as a "Jewish nigger" are certainly not in the best spirit of his own self-proclaimed neutrality.[120]

Marx's Anti-Semitism

This brings up the whole question of Marx's supposed anti-Semitism. The question is extremely difficult to deal with, if for no other reason than the fact that it involves a post-mortem

---

[118]Otto Rühle, *Karl Marx*, pp. 38–83; cf. 101, 238.

[119]Mehring, *Karl Marx*, p. 308.

[120]For a list of these vitriolic references, see Leopold Schwartzschild, *Karl Marx: The Red Prussian* (New York: Grosset & Dunlap, 1947), p. 251.

psycho-analysis, a questionable academic endeavor at best. How can we know what he thought in an area where his writings are so ambiguous? Those who claim that he was an anti-Semite invariably point to the letters that he wrote to Engels which contained nasty statements about Lassalle. Why would he use the word "Jew" as the ultimate form of contempt? In his essay published in 1844, "On the Jewish Question," what was he attacking, his critics ask, if not the Jewish faith and culture? The answer, at least in part, is that he was attacking bourgeois life in general, using the famous stereotype of the European Jewish financier as his representative type of the bourgeois man. He saw the Jewish community as an infected, diseased culture—totally bourgeois, and always seeking after money. But the critic's question still remains: why did he single out the Jews?[121] Sidney Hook has tried to defend Marx on this point: "Although Marx was free of anti-Semitic prejudice, he unfortunately was not over-sensitive to using the term 'Jew,' often with unsavory adjectives, as an epithet of abuse."[122] But the fact remains that "Jew" was the word which Marx chose.

Marx: Graduate Student for Life

Writing a negative critical book is a good post-Ph.D exercise for a newly certified scholar, but it is a sign of immaturity when a scholar spends his whole life criticizing the ideas of others, never putting together a positive alternative. It is evidence that he has no positive alternative. What I have just described is the intellectual career of Karl Marx. Marx never stopped writing long-winded critical refutations of his opponents. His books' targets were almost always the writings of his socialist rivals, and usually very obscure rivals at that, not Adam Smith, David

---

[121]Jewish conservatives are especially fond of pointing out these apparently anti-Semetic statements. Cf. Max Geltman, "A Little Known Chapter in American History," *National Review* (October 5, 1965), pp. 865–67.

[122]Hook, *From Hegel to Marx*, p. 278 n. Hook's defense is of a mild sort; he challenged L. Rudas for defending Marx's practice in using the word "Jew." But what is Hook's rationale for saying that Marx was free of anti-Semitic prejudice?

Ricardo, John Stuart Mill, or other important advocates of classical economics. Marx never provided any blueprints regarding the operation of the communist society to come. He offered no program for building a new society after the revolution, except for the famous ten points of the *Communist Manifesto* (1848). He never again brought up the subject of the transition from capitalist to socialist to Communist society. Ten points in a pamphlet do not a civilization build. Almost three decades later, he wrote: "From each according to his ability, to each according to his needs!"[123] This is a slogan, not a program. Lenin played the same game when he wrote that a Communist society is simply one which combines political power and electricity,[124] one which gives equal pay to all workers and can be run by simple bookkeepers,[125] one in which gold will be used for public lavatories.[126] Marx and Lenin could produce slogans but no blueprints. They could tear down; they could not build up.

The Lenin Factor

My view regarding the importance of Karl Marx's thought in intellectual history is tied closely to my view of the political importance of Lenin. Had Lenin not successfully pulled off the October Revolution in 1917, the name Karl Marx would be

---

[123]Marx, *Critique of the Gotha Program* (1875), in Marx and Engels, *Selected Works*, 3 vols. (Moscow: Progress Publishers, 1969), 3, p. 19.

[124]"*Communism is Soviet power plus the electrification of the whole country.*" V. I. Lenin, "Communism and Electrification," (1920), in *The Lenin Anthology*, Robert C. Tucker, ed. (New York: Norton, 1975), p. 494.

[125]"Accounting and control—these are the *chief* things necessary for the organizing and correct functioning of the *first phase* of Communist society. *All* citizens are here transformed into hired employees of the state, which is made up of the armed workers. *All* citizens become employees and workers of *one* national state 'syndicate.' All that is required is that they should work equally, should regularly do their share of work, and should receive equal pay. The accounting and control necessary for this have been *simplified* by capitalism to the utmost, till they have become extraordinarily simple operations of watching, recording and issuing receipts, within the reach of anybody who can read and write and knows the first four rules of arithmetic." Lenin, *State and Revolution* (1918; New York: International Publishers, 1932), pp. 83–84.

[126]"When we are victorious on a world scale I think we shall use gold for the purpose of building public lavatories in the streets of some of the largest cities in the world." Lenin, "The Importance of Gold Now and After the Complete Victory of Socialism" (1921), in *The Lenin Anthology*, p. 515.

known only to specialists in the history of sociology,[127] to a handful of specialists in late-nineteenth-century trade union history and Russian intellectual history, and to an even smaller group of specialists in the history of mid-nineteenth-century materialist Hegelian philosophy. Wilhelm Windelband, for example, devoted only two brief bibliographical entries and part of one paragraph to Marx and Engels in his 1901 *History of Philosophy*.[128] The fact is, Marx had very little influence prior to 1917, especially in the United States.[129] Had it not been for Lenin, references to Marx would be limited to a series of obscure footnotes, rather than a library of books.

But Lenin and his colleagues did pull off the Russian Revolution, much to the surprise of Europe. I am reminded of the comment by Herr Schober, the petty police official who later became Chancellor of Austria. Ludwig von Mises records this about him: "Toward the end of 1915 he reported to his superiors that he doubted the possibility of a Russian revolution. 'Who, then, could make this revolution? Surely not this Mr. Trotsky, who used to read newspapers in Café Central.'"[130]

Modern intellectuals, always respectful of those who win major wars and also respectful of any radical group that conducts a bloody revolution against traditional, religion-supported authority, have resurrected Marx's intellectual reputation posthumously. In short, had it not been for Lenin, you would never had heard about Marx. The library shelves devoted to Marxism would be devoted to some other topic. (If the

[127]Bottomore and Rubel, "The Influence of Marx's Sociological Thought," in *Karl Marx: Selected Writings in Sociology and Social Philosophy*, T. B. Bottomore and Maximilien Rubel, eds. (1956; New York: McGraw-Hill, 1964).

[128]Wilhelm Windelband, *History of Philosophy*, 2 vols. (New York: Harper Torchbooks, 1958), 2, pp. 632, 655.

[129]Solomon Bloom writes: "Specifically, it was the Bolshevik Revolution of November, 1917, that brought the United States rather suddenly face to face with Marxism. . . ." Bloom, "Man of His Century: A Reconsideration of the Historical Significance of Karl Marx," *Journal of Political Economy* 51 (December, 1943); reprinted in Shepard B. Clough, Peter Gay, and Charles K. Warner eds., *The European Past* (New York: Macmillan, 1964), vol. 2, p. 143.

[130]Ludwig von Mises, *Notes and Recollections* (South Holland, Ill.: Libertarian Press, 1978), p. 5. (Libertarian Press is now located in Spring Mills, Pennsylvania.)

Germans had won World War II, rest assured that many of these shelves would today be filled with books praising the creative humanist vision and the rational economic planning of the Nazis. The fascination that Nazism had for Western scholars and politicians during the 1930s, including John Maynard Keynes,[131] not to mention U.S. businessmen who traded extensively with the Nazi State,[132] is a story not found in today's textbooks. Why not? Because Hitler lost.)

Conclusion

How can we hope to summarize the life and thought of a man whose words posthumously transformed the world? How can we hope to understand what motivated him? Historian Donald Treadgold has raised the question, has admitted that there is no simple answer, but then pointed to a forgotten primary source document that he believes throws light on Marx's view of his life.[133] In 1865, two years before the publication of *Das Kapital*, Marx entered these words into the guest book of some relatives:

[131]Keynes wrote these words in the Foreword to the 1936 German-language edition of his *General Theory of Employment, Interest, and Money*: "The theory of aggregate production, which is the point of the following book, nevertheless can be much easier adapted to the conditions of a totalitarian state [*eines totalen Staates*] than the theory of production and distribution put forth under conditions of free competition and a large degree of laissez-faire. This is one of the reasons that justifies the fact that I call my theory a *general* theory." Translated with the German original by James J. Martin, *Revisionist Viewpoints* (Boulder, Colo.: Ralph Myles Press, 1971), pp. 203, 205. The citation also appears in *The Collected Writings of John Maynard Keynes*, vol. 7 (New York: St. Martin's, 1973), p. xxvi.

[132]Charles Higham, *Trading With the Enemy: An Expose of the Nazi-American Money Plot, 1933–1949* (New York: Delacorte, 1983); Antony C. Sutton, *Wall Street and the Rise of Hitler* (Suffolk, England: Bloomfield, 1976), originally published by '76 Press, Seal Beach, California. On George Bush's father's work for the Harrimans in this regard, see Webster Griffin Tarpley and Anton Chaitkin, *George Bush: The Unauthorized Biography* (Washington, D.C.: Executive Intelligence Review, 1992), chap. 2.

[133]Donald W. Treadgold, Introduction to Sergei Bulgakov, *Karl Marx as A Relgious Type: His Relation to the Religion of Anthropotheism of L. Feuerbach* (Belmont, Mass.: Nordland [1907] 1979), p. 14.

Your idea of happiness: "to fight"
Your idea of misery: "to submit"
Your chief characteristic: "singleness of purpose"

Does this tell us what Marx was? Only insofar as it reveals
life-long self-deception. Did he fight? He did indeed fight all his
life, rarely against specific leading intellectual defenders of
capitalism, but instead against unknown (then and now) and
undistinguished German intellectual enemies, socialists and
atheists all. Proudhon was one of his few competent victims.

Did he submit? He submitted all his life to Engels's benevolent charity. Economically, he was Engels's "kept man," who
fathered an illegitimate son by his wife's kept woman, their
lifetime family housekeeper Helene Demuth, and who then refused to acknowledge his fatherhood or even allow the mother
to keep the baby in his home, for fear of the scandal within the
then-publicly prim socialist community, and also for fear of his
wife's jealousy.[134] He forced the mother to give the baby to poverty-stricken foster parents.[135] (Staunch Prometheus!) From
1883, at Marx's death, until her own death in 1890, Helene
Demuth became Engels's housekeeper, and it was widely assumed that Engels had been the father of her son.[136]

Did he retain his singleness of purpose? After age 49, he
never again wrote a book, but instead buried himself in a
self-imposed program of frantic undirected and voluminous
reading—a return to the pattern of his youth, when he read day
and night (in between all-night sessions at the local pub),[137] but
could never bring himself to face the rigors (the "final judgment") of a doctoral examination at the University of Berlin.
In short, in his arrogance he was utterly self-deceived. He
also succeeded in deceiving the vast majority of his bourgeois

---

[134]Payne, *Marx*, pp. 265–66, 532–38.

[135]Raddatz, *Karl Marx*, p. 134.

[136]Ibid., p. 135.

[137]He continued his "pub crawls" with friends and even enemies during his
years in London. After one of these, at 2 a.m., Marx and his friends started smashing
street lamps with stones, outrunning the local police: Payne, *Marx*, p. 282.

academic commentators. They have taken his verbal strutting at face value.

His chosen public mask was the image of Prometheus, the fire-bringer. He hated the "authoritarian" religion of Christianity. He was self-consciously in revolt against the god of bourgeois civilization, all in the name of proletarian man and the eschatology of the imminent and immanent Communist millennial paradise. Like Prometheus, he brought fire to the society of man—or as Billington has put it, Marx and his revolutionary colleagues brought fire to the minds of men.[138] That fire still rages.

Marx is important for the religion he preached, not the footnotes he assembled. He is important because he provided what appeared to be scientific proof for demonic revolution. By capturing the minds of several generations of bloody revolutionaries and ideological gangsters, Marx and Engels changed the history of the world. It was Marx's vision of an eschatological apocalypse, not his turgid scholarship, that won the day. He provided generations of intellectuals with what they have sought above all: attachment to political victors, either vicariously or directly in their service. It has also been emotionally convenient for them that Marx was a member of their own social class rather than a proletarian. Karl Marx, like Lenin, served as an inspired prophet, not of proletarian victory, which never took place, but of bourgeois victory cleverly masquerading as a proletarian victory. He served as a sort of nineteenth-century intellectual rag peddler, selling proletarian designer jeans for the costume parties of the alienated middle class. To add authenticity before they are shipped to fashion-conscious buyers, Marx-Engels designer jeans are bleached. So are the bones of a hundred million of their victims.

Father Knew Best

In the last analysis, it was Marx's father who best described his son's life, yet he did so in 1837, when his son was only 19

---

[138]James Billington, *Fire in the Minds of Men: Origins of the Revolutionary Faith* (New York: Basic Books, 1980).

years old. He did not live to see his prophetic speculations come true; he died in 1838. The opening paragraph of the letter should be reprinted in every biography of Karl Marx; I have never seen it reprinted in any.

> It is remarkable that I, who am by nature a lazy writer, become quite inexhaustible when I have to write to you. I will not and cannot conceal my weakness for you. At times my heart delights in thinking of you and your future. And yet at times I cannot rid myself of ideas which arouse in me sad forebodings and fear when I am struck as if by lightning by the thought: is your heart in accord with your head, your talents? Has it room for the earthly but gentler sentiments which in this vale of sorrow are so essentially consoling for a man of feeling? And since that heart is obviously animated and governed by a demon not granted to all men, is that demon heavenly or Faustian? Will you ever—and that is not the least painful doubt of my heart—will you ever be capable of truly human, domestic happiness? Will—and this doubt has no less tortured me recently since I have come to love a certain person like my own child [Jenny von Westphalen]—will you ever be capable of imparting happiness to those immediately around you?[139]

Eleven years later, Karl published *The Manifesto of the Community Party*. Thirty years later, he published *Das Kapital*. By then it was clear that his demon was not heavenly. His father had suspected as much. Karl Marx's true personal model—as distinguished from his ideological model—was not Prometheus, the fire-bringer, but Faust, the maker of the incomparably bad bargain.

---

[139]Heinrich Marx to Karl Marx, 2 March 1837, in *Collected Works*, 1, p. 670.

~ 4 ~

Marxism, Method, and Mercantilism

David Osterfeld

Scientific truth is always a paradox, if judged by every-day experience, which catches only the delusive appearance of things.

Karl Marx (1973b, p. 42)

Part I
Exposition

A unifying theme throughout the work of Karl Marx is the concern for penetrating to the nature or essence of things. In fact science, as defined by Marx, is precisely the method, or tool, which enables one to distinguish between form and reality, to separate the superstructural "veil" from the "hidden social essence" of the economic base (see, e.g., Marx 1970, pp. 205–217; McMurtry 1978, pp. 75 and 81; and Sowell 1985, pp. 18–21).

It would not be too much to say that, directly or indirectly, the entire corpus of Marx's wide-ranging work had but a single goal: understanding the nature or essence of the capitalist system. As E. J. Hobsbawm (p. 20) has put it, "Marx concentrated his energies on the study of capitalism, and he dealt with the rest of history in varying degrees of detail, but mainly in so far as it bore on the origins and development of capitalism." (See, also, Mandel 1971, p. 21; and Lowenthal 1984, pp. 32–33.) It is the thesis of this paper that even though it constituted the principle focus of his work, it is precisely in his analysis of capitalism, or the bourgeois mode of production, that Marx here more than anywhere else failed to distinguish appearance from reality. That is, it is precisely in his analysis of capitalism that Marx's failure to follow his own definition of science is most conspicuous. It will also be argued that it is because of this failure that his analysis of the capitalist mode of production is laced with confusions and that his critique of capitalism is fundamentally misdirected.

Marx's Taxonomy
of Socio-Economic Systems

In order to appreciate the magnitude of Marx's misdiagnosis a brief sketch of his taxonomy of socio-economic systems is necessary.

In his now famous statement in the "Preface" to his *Contribution to a Critique of Political Economy* (1970, p. 21) Marx wrote that "In broad outline, the Asiatic, ancient, feudal and modern bourgeois modes of production may be designated as marking progress in the economic development of society. The bourgeois mode of production," he adds, "is the last antagonistic form of the social process of production." This is a seemingly clear-cut statement of the universal historical succession of four socio-economic epochs, and many, including both supporters (e.g., Lenin 1967, vol. 1, pp. 42, 54–90; Leontyev 1968, pp. 24–52. And see Kiernan 1983, p. 459.) and critics (e.g., Popper 1966, pp. 81–88; Hook 1955, pp. 36–39; and Bober 1948) have interpreted it as such. In fact, in *Pre-Capitalist Economic Formations* (or the *Formen*), the work which, as Hobsbawm observes (p. 10), constitutes Marx's "most systematic attempt to grapple with the problem of historical evolution," it is clear that Marx is *not* referring to historically necessary or even to chronologically successive periods but to analytically distinct economic systems. Marx presented what is primarily a *typology* of socio-economic systems, based not so much on any theory as on his historical observations, and in which some are "higher" or more "progressive" not in the sense that they are necessarily later, historically, but that they are further removed from the primitive or original state of man "as a generic being, a tribal being, a herd animal" (Marx 1964, p. 96). Or, to state the same thing in reverse order, socio-economic systems are, to Marx, more or less progressive to the extent that they emancipate the human species from the grip of nature, thereby permitting the increasing individualization of man (Marx 1964, pp. 96–97; Hobsbawm 1964, pp. 36–37; McMurtry 1978, pp. 19–53). "Exchange itself," says Marx, "is a major agent of this individualization. It makes the herd animal superfluous and dissolves it" (Marx 1964, p. 96). Since capitalism is defined by Marx in terms of "commodity production," i.e., a system in which production and consumption of goods are separated by an intervening exchange, "capitalism" is the most "extreme case" of individualization and therefore the most "progressive" of all historical systems. The problem, however, is that because of the "dehumanized social mechanism" embedded in the nature of this mode of production, the process of individualization under capitalism is "outside and hostile to the individual" (Hobsbawm 1964, pp. 14–15), and appears as "total alienation" (Marx 1964, p. 85).

The number of socio-economic formations underwent almost continuous revision in the work of Marx and Engels. These revisions were a product both of the particular task at hand as well as Marx and Engels' evaluations and re-evaluations of their on-going historical investigations. Thus, while the "Preface" lists four "antagonistic" historical epochs, *The Communist Manifesto* mentions only three, omitting the Asiatic. The primary reason for the omission appears to be that between 1848 when *The Communist Manifesto* was first published, and the publication of the "Preface" in 1859, the historical work of Marx and Engels led them to the discovery of an additional historical socio-economic system. And in the 1857 *Pre-Capitalist Economic Formations* Marx presents in varying degrees of detail six modes of production. One, primitive communism or the Archaic mode, is harmonious, and five, the Asiatic, the Germanic, the Slavonic, the ancient and the feudal systems, are antagonistic. And finally, in the *Critique of the Gotha Programme* (1972a, pp. 14–18) in 1874 Marx presents two non-historical or future economic formations: the Socialist or lower phase of what Marx terms the modern form of the Archaic type (in *Marx, Engels and Lenin on Scientific Communism* 1967, p. 66,) and the higher or Communistic phase.

The result is that over a span of 25 years Marx and Engels present a total of nine different socio-economic systems or formations, three of which, the Archaic, the Socialist and the Communistic systems, are harmonious, and six, the Asiatic, the Germanic, the Slavonic, the ancient, the feudal and the capitalistic, are antagonistic. Since in *The Communist Manifesto* (1969, p. 57) Marx and Engels define history in terms of the presence of class struggles, it follows that the Archaic formation would represent pre-history while Socialism and Communism would fall into the post-historical phase. All except two, Socialism and Communism, are historically extant modes. The presentation of two, the Germanic and the Slavonic, and particularly the latter, are highly abstract and sketchy and there is some question whether Marx regarded them as fully distinct economic formations. It is worthy of note that in his *Anti-Dühring* (1972a) and *The Origin of the Family, Private Property and the State* (1942), Engels omits any reference to the Asiatic mode, which would thereby return the taxonomy to the three "antagonistic" systems enunciated in *The Communist Manifesto*.

These formations are summarized as follows:

1. *Primitive Communism or the Archaic Mode.* Marx believes that this formation dominates "at the dawn of all civilized races" (Bober 1948, p. 47). Since the "form of ownership is tribal ownership" there is as yet neither private property nor class differences. It is a primitive hunting, gathering and fishing economy, and its division of labor, therefore, is "still

very elementary" (Bober 1947, pp. 7–13). Its production is so meager that its members live on the verge of starvation and the principle of distribution is highly egalitarian. Man at this stage is "a tribal being, a herd being" (1964, p. 96). He identifies completely with the community. He "had not yet severed the umbilical cord that unites him with his fellow men in a primitive tribal community" (Marx 1906 p. 91). Individualization, as already noted, is a product of history.

2. *The Asiatic Mode.* In this mode the self-sufficient village communes remain and thus there is no buying and selling or market relationships. However, due to conquest or agreement made in order to secure such economic necessities as irrigation, there emerges "the despotic government suspended above the small communities." The state or despot is the "landlord," the "sole proprietor," the real owner, while the actual communities are merely the "hereditary possessors" (Marx 1964, p. 69). A result of this merger of the economic and political functions is that ground-rents and taxes coincide (Lichtheim 1973b, p. 153). A major difference between the Asiatic and the later ancient systems is that the former is characterized by "general slavery" while "private slavery" prevails in the latter. Finally, Marx believes that "the Asiatic form necessarily survives longest and most stubbornly" precisely because of the absence of private property and thus of internal conflict (Marx 1964, p. 83; Turner 1983, p. 33; Hobsbawm 1964, p. 34).

3. *The Ancient Mode.* This form is characterized by "slaveholding," i.e., the private ownership of slaves, and the emergence of cities during Greco-Roman times. Since the exploitation endemic in slavery allows the ruling elite the leisure to indulge in philosophy, art and other pursuits Engels characterizes it as an enormous step forward. Without slavery, he writes (1972a, p. 200), there would be "no Greek state, no Greek art, and science; without slavery, no Roman Empire. But without Hellenism and the Roman Empire as a basis, no modern Europe." And ultimately, therefore, "we are entitled to say: Without the slavery of antiquity, no modern socialism."

With the emergence of private property and exchange, class antagonisms begin to develop.

4. *The Germanic and Slavonic Modes.* Neither of these forms were very well developed by Marx. The locus of the Germanic mode is neither the commune nor the city but the "household." It is predominately agricultural and highly individualistic. Each "individual household contains an entire economy, forming as it does an independent center of production." Since each household is "separated by long distances" "the *community* therefore appears as an *association*, not as any *union*, as an agreement, whose independent subjects are landowners, and not as a unity" (Marx 1964, pp. 77–80). While the Germanic mode is individualistic, the self-sufficiency of the household keeps exchange to a minimum. The Slavonic mode is communal. Marx merely refers to it as "communal production" which "had been introduced and transmitted by conquering tribes." It apparently has affinities with the Asiatic or Oriental mode since Marx refers to "the oriental form, modified by the Slavs," although the modifications are not specified (Marx 1964, pp. 88, 97). It seems likely, however, that the chief difference is that the Slavonic mode lacks the "stubbornness" or resistance to change of the Asiatic, but the reasons for this are not made clear. Unfortunately, it is not developed further either in the *Formen* or in Marx's other writings. In something of an understatement Hobsbawm refers to the "somewhat shadowy" (p. 32) state in which Marx left it.

5. *The Feudal Mode.* While "antiquity started out from the town" says Marx, the feudal system of the Middle Ages "started out from the country. The different starting-point was determined by the sparseness of the population at that time, which was scattered over a large area" mainly as a result of invading conquerors (Marx 1964, p. 125). The new rulers distributed land to their retinue and these new landowners, or lords, then parcelled land out to the dispossessed and desperate peasants who in turn fell under the legal domination of the lords, i.e., they were enslaved. What emerged were self-sufficient manors or fiefdoms. The remaining independent peasants according to

Leontyev (pp. 37–38), "produced predominantly for their own consumption and exchange was only accidental. The feudal lord also rarely resorted to trade: almost everything he needed for his upkeep and that of his family and retinue was produced by the labor of the serfs." The serf would usually work three days a week on his lord's estate; the rest of the time he was "free" to work his own plot. "The hierarchical system of land ownership, and the armed bodies of retainers associated with it, gave the nobility power over the serfs." The result was the non-working owning class, the lords, "standing over [and] against . . . the enserfed small peasantry" (Marx 1964, p. 125). Exploitation and class antagonisms were clear for all to see.

6. *The Capitalist Mode.* In volume 3 of *Capital* Marx describes capitalism as "distinguished from the outset by two characteristic features. First it produces its products as commodities. . . . The second distinctive feature of the capitalist mode of production is the production of surplus value [profit] as the direct aim and determining motive of production" (Roberts and Stephenson 1973, p. 10). Commodity production, as noted earlier, is characterized by the separation of production and consumption by an intervening exchange. In *Capital* (1906, p. 94) Marx writes that capitalism is that "mode of production in which the product takes the form of a commodity, or is produced directly for exchange." And in the *Grundrisse* he says that a commodity, "is a pure element of exchange" (Marx 1971, p. 59. Also see Marx 1970, p. 27). Capitalism is therefore characterized as that mode of production in which goods are produced for sale on the market with the aim of making a profit. Commodity production implies both private property and a division of labor. Another significant characteristic of capitalism is that while the worker is "free" or "nominally free" his survival depends on him selling his "labor power," i.e., his capacity or time for work, to the owners of the means of production. Thus, under capitalism labor itself, or "labor power," becomes a commodity. This is unique to capitalism. In previous societies products were bought and sold; only under capitalism is labor power bought and sold (see, e.g., Marx 1971, pp. 111–12).

Consequently, while in more primitive modes of production "exploitation [was] veiled by religious and political illusions" under capitalism it is "naked, shameless, direct brutal exploitation" (Marx 1964, p. 62). Although exchange was present in varying degrees in more primitive modes of production, it is only under capitalism that the commodity form becomes dominant (Marx 1909, p. 94; Leontyev 1968, pp. 45–46). Finally, it is with capitalism, with its giant factories and immense productive capacities, that the material conditions indispensable for the transition to Socialism are developed.

7. *The Socialist and Communist Modes.* Although Marx used the terms Socialism and Communism interchangeably and referred to the lower and higher stages of the Post-Historical mode of production, it has become conventional to refer to the lower stage as socialism and the higher as communism. The defining characteristic of both socialism and communism is the absence of commodity production. Marx writes (1972a, p. 14) that "with the cooperative society based on common ownership of the means of production producers do not exchange their products." And Engels says (1972b, pp. 72–75) that "With the seizing of the means of production production of commodities is done away with. . . . Socialized production upon a predetermined plan becomes henceforth possible." The principle difference between socialism and communism is that during the process of reorganizing the economic structure of society some shortages will remain. Thus, the principle of distribution under socialism must be to each according to his work. Some will therefore be richer than others. However, once the reorganization has been completed, and labor has become not drudgery but "life's prime want," all shortages will have been overcome, at which point "society inscribes on its banners: From each according to his ability, to each according to his needs" (Marx 1972a, pp. 15–17).

According to Marx's taxonomy (see figure 1), primitive communism is the universal original stage of mankind. It is characterized by the absence of private property and class conflict. There are at least four possible routes out of primitive communism, the Asiatic, the ancient, the Germanic and the Slavonic. In each of these one can see the seeds of class antagonisms. They appear to be more obvious in the ancient than the other three, however. Private property, commodity production and, thus, class antagonisms are more developed in the feudal mode than the ancient and they reach their apex in the capitalist mode where even "labor power" becomes a commodity. Socialism and communism are modes of production characterized by the absence of commodity production, private property and thus class antagonisms.

The point is that Marx was primarily an organizational theorist (Roberts and Stephenson 1973). As such he was concerned with distinguishing between and cataloguing different socio-economic systems or organizations. According to Marx,

Figure 1
Marx's Taxonomy

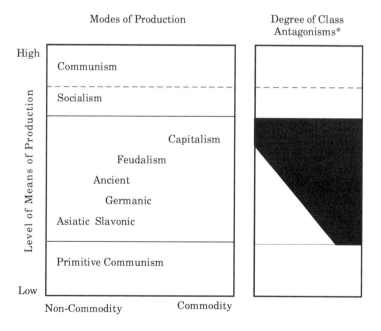

*Shaded area = class antagonisms

this could not be done by relying on some "abstract formula" or "the universal passport of a general historico-philosophical theory," (Selsam 1970, p. 71) but only by immersing oneself in the details of history. The question is whether the economic organization of a given society is sufficiently distinct to charac-terize it as a separate socio-economic system. Thus, the various economic formations are a product not so much of any elaborate abstract theory but of historical investigation, analysis and comparison. His conclusions in this area were always open, tentative and subject to modification, to addition and subtrac-tion, in light of new historical evidence. As V. G. Kiernan has phrased it (p. 458), Marx

> was seeking to identify *all possible types of productive systems*, rather than to arrange them in order, or to explain how one had been supplemented by another. [emphasis added]

Marx's Theories of History

Karl Marx had three interrelated but distinguishable theories of history: the theory of historical materialism, what I will call the theory of historical progressivity, and the theory of histori-cal inevitability. Each will be dealt with in turn.

The Theory of Historical Materialism

The theory of historical materialism posits two things: (1) that the ideological superstructure is determined by the eco-nomic base and (2) that within the economic base the relations of production are determined by the level of the forces or means of production. Thus, any change in the level of the forces of production will create tension or conflict between the forces and relations of production. The result will be "an era of social revolution" leading to "the transformation of the whole im-mense superstructure," i.e., the emergence of a new mode of production (see Marx 1970, pp. 20–21; Marx 1906, p. 96 n). It should be clear that the general theory of historical material-ism is in no way affected by Marx's revisions of his socio-eco-nomic taxonomy. The number of socio-economic systems is irrelevant to the process by which changes in the mode of production occur.

There is, however, a great deal of controversy regarding the exact status of the theory of historical materialism. Some have argued that it is an empirical theory which can be verified by recourse to historical data, while others have denied that the theory makes claims about specific historical events and cannot, therefore, be either confirmed or falsified by the use the historical data. And it must be acknowledged that the writings of Marx and Engels seem to leave room for either interpretation.

Taking the latter position, Hobsbawm argues that the theory, "requires only that there should be a succession of modes of production, though not necessarily any particular modes, and perhaps not in any particular predetermined order." Marx thought, he continues, "that he could distinguish a certain number of socio-economic formations and a certain succession. But if he had been mistaken in his observations, or if these had been based on partial and therefore misleading information, the general theory of historical materialism would remain unaffected" (pp. 19–20. Also see Dunn 1982, p. 5; Sowell 1985, pp. 56–58; and Shaw 1983, pp. 206–10, esp., pp. 209–10). That is, the theory is trying to explain the basic or essential cause of the "succession of modes of production." As such, it is actually *ahistorical* since it posits a relationship between the forces and relations of production, in particular, and the base and the superstructure, in general, but does not necessitate any particular order in the secession of periods or modes of production. One must distinguish, therefore, between the theory, on the one hand, and the historical data on the other. Both Marx and Engels were fully aware of the complexity of history. History, they tell us, rarely repeats itself and "when repetitions occur they never arise under exactly the same circumstances" (Engels 1972a, p. 99). History contains no "eternal," "final and ultimate truths," and "anyone who sets out in this field to hunt down . . . truths which are pure or absolutely immutable, will bring home but little, apart from platitudes and commonplaces of the sorriest kind" (Engels 1972a, p. 100). The materialist conception of history "is above all a guide to study," Engels said, "not a lever for construction" (Selsam 1970, p. 71). In a 1877 letter Marx objected to interpreting his work as "a historico-philosophical theory of the general path imposed by fate on all peoples regardless of their historical circumstances" (Bober 1948, p. 41). And in his 1890 letter to Joseph Bloch (Selsam 1970, pp. 76–79), Engels, in particular, warned against viewing "the economic element as the *only* determining one." That, he says, is "meaningless, abstract and absurd." "There are," he continues, "innumerable intersecting forces, an infinite series of parallelograms of forces which give rise to one resultant—the historical event." "The economic situation is the basis," he writes,

> but the various elements in the superstructure—political forms of the class struggle and its consequences, constitutions established by the victorious class after successful battle, etc.—forms of law—and then even the reflexes of all these actual struggles in the brains of the combatants: political, legal, philosophical theories, religious ideas and their further development into systems of dogma—also exercise their influence upon the course of the historical struggles and in many cases preponderate in determining their *form*. There is an interaction of all these elements in which, amid all the endless *host* of accidents (i.e., of things and events, whose inner connection is so remote or so impossible to prove that we regard it as absent and can neglect it) the economic movement finally asserts itself as necessary.

Given that any historical event is the product of an "infinite" number of conflicting forces including such things as wars and such accidents of nature as earthquakes, droughts, and even plagues, all of which may seriously affect the level of the means of production, and since it is also possible for the superstructure not only to interact with but actually dominate, at least for a time, the economic base, it follows that (1) one should not expect to find a "mechanistic" or unilinear succession of historical epochs characterized by such things as increasing complexity and productivity and the potential for increasingly greater genuine freedom and individualization, and (2) the validity of the general theory of historical materialism can be neither confirmed nor falsified by recourse to the historical data.

On the other hand, beginning with *The German Ideology* in 1846, both Marx and Engels repeatedly emphasized that the theory of historical materialism was an "empirical theory." "The premises from which we begin are not arbitrary ones, not dogmas, but real premises. . . . These premises can thus be verified in a purely empirical way" (1947, p. 6). Marx and Engels do not deny that man thinks and acts. In fact, they believed that ideas can have tremendous consequences. Their argument is that the source of all thought and action lies in the material base, and in particular, in each individual's relationship to the means of production. "The production of ideas, of conceptions, of consciousness," they write, (1947, pp. 13–16)

> is at first directly interwoven with the material activity and the material intercourse of men, the language of real life. Conceiving, thinking, the mental intercourse of men, appear at this stage as the direct efflux of their material behavior. The same applies to mental production as expressed in the language of the politics, laws, morality, religion, metaphysics of a people. Men are producers of their conceptions, ideas, etc.—real, active men, as they are conditioned by a definite development of their productive forces and of the intercourse corresponding to these, up to its furthest forms. . . . That is to say, we do not set out from what men say, imagine, conceive, nor from men as narrated, thought of, imagined, conceived, in order to arrive at men in the flesh. We set out from real, active men, and on the basis of their real life process we demonstrate the development of the ideological reflexes and echoes of this life process. The phantoms formed in the human brain are also, necessarily, sublimates of their material life process, which is empirically verifiable and bound to material premises. Morality, religion, metaphysics, all the rest of ideology and their corresponding forms of consciousness, thus no longer retain the semblance of independence.

The contradiction between the claim that historical materialism is an empirically verifiable or at least testable theory on the one hand and the denial that it can ever be either confirmed or falsified by historical data on the other is, I believe, only apparent, and stems from a confusion between two related but distinct aspects of the theory: the process by which ideas emerge, on the one hand, and the particular succession of the modes of production, on the other. Marx and Engels believed not merely that the former was empirically verifiable but that they had, in fact, verified it. It is sometimes accorded in their writing the status of a "law." But they seem to regard the latter—the succession of the modes of production—as so complicated by other, accidental factors, as to preclude empirical testability.

While ideas are accorded a certain independence, Marxism holds that "ultimately," or in the "final" analysis, they are traceable to the material base. Thus, thought Y may occur to individual A because of his relationship to the means of production. But thought Y may, in turn, cause individual B to think thought Z, which, in its turn, may "react back on" the economic base. Thus, the material base is, "ultimately," the *sole* source of all ideas. It follows that with detailed historical analysis one should be able to trace the history of any idea back to the material base. Consequently, one should also find a definite correspondence between the thought and action occurring in a particular historical period and its mode of production. Marx and Engels, as already noted, claimed that this "law of human development" had been empirically verified (Selsam 1970, p. 30). Similarly, the argument that the relations of production are "ultimately" determined by the level of the means of production, though far more complex, is also, at least in principle, "empirically testable."

It is this general derivation of ideas and the "ultimate" correspondence of the means to the relations of production that, I believe, Marx and Engels generally meant when referring to historical materialism. And if that is the case, then they regarded the theory of historical materialism as an empirically testable theory.

The Theory of Historical Progressivity

It is true, of course, that Marx viewed his general theory as having a vitally important role in enabling him to understand and predict the general course of history. But this "historical determinism" should not be confused with the theory of historical materialism. That is, even if the economic base "determines" ideas, it does not follow that the course of history is likewise determined. Historical determinism is not part of the theory of historical materialism, itself, but is derivable from the theory when an additional premise—that over time new machinery and methods of production will be introduced—is included. Since these would not be employed unless they expanded output, it follows that, *other things remaining equal*, the productivity of the means of production *must* continually increase over time. Thus, each successive mode of production must be more productive than its predecessor. And that means that historical evolution *must* be the story of the increasing control of man over nature, and thus the increasing potential for genuine freedom and individualization. The result is a unilinear or "mechanistic" view of history, and there are passages in the writings of Marx and Engels that lend support to this interpretation. For example, in the *Poverty of Philosophy* Marx writes (Sowell 1985 p. 56) that "the hand-mill gives you society with the feudal lords, the steam-mill, the industrial capitalist."

This quotation, and others like it, are a result of Marx's penchant for summarizing lengthy and complex analyses with what Sowell (1985, p. 56) calls "epigrammatic expressions." Since it is impossible to condense such complex analyses into single sentences these epigrams too often distort rather than accurately depict Marx's positions. Although Engels' statements were less "epigrammatic" than Marx's, there are passages which, when taken out of context, can be quite misleading. For example, in his "Afterword" to *Soziales aus Russland,*" he writes (*Marx, Engels and Lenin* 1967, pp. 217–19) that "It is historically impossible for a lower stage of economic development to resolve the riddles and conflicts that have sprung up, in a much higher stage." Taken by itself this gives the impression that Engels' view of history was mechanistic. However, two pages prior to this he refers to the possibility of some countries "skipping the whole capitalist period," and in the page following the quotation he states that it is possible for some countries to "undertake a shortened process of development." Elsewhere, Marx and Engels acknowledge the possibility of at least temporary regressions of some societies as well as more or less permanent stagnation of others.

But however one accounts for their more "mechanistic" statements, it is clear that neither Marx nor Engels subscribed to a unilinear or "mechanistic" view of history. For example, in 1853 Marx wrote (Selsam 1970, pp. 138–43) that Indian society had stagnated for centuries. It was, he said, "based on a sort of equilibrium." The real question was "not whether the English had a right to conquer India" but which country would conquer it. Marx clearly preferred the English. England "has to fulfill a double mission in India: one destructive, and the other regenerative—the annihilation of old Asiatic society, and the laying the material foundations of Western society in Asia." By breaking up the "self-sufficient *inertia* of the villages," and linking them together through transportation and trade, the English bourgeoisie, according to Marx, will enable India to move directly from an Asiatic to a capitalist society.

And Marx writes that because of the "permanent condition" of war in Spain the "towns lost their medieval power without gaining modern importance." They "have vegetated in a state of continuous decay." The result is that Spain had regressed from a feudal to an "Asiatic form of government." Moreover, Marx seems to imply that it is possible for a new revolution to propel Spain directly to socialism (Selsam 1970, pp. 146–48).

While originally believing that it was feudal, as early as 1853 Marx and Engels began describing Russia as "Asiatic," "Semi-Asiatic" or "Oriental." And in a letter to Vera Zasulich in 1885 (Selsam 1970, pp. 175-76) Engels describes Russia as a society "where every stage of social development is represented, from the primitive commune to modern large-scale industry and high finance. . . ." Karl Wittfogel (p. 492) summarizes Marx's position as follows:

> The Mongol conquest destroyed Russia's proto-feudal society by compelling the Muscovite Tsars to *"tartarize"* Muscovy. The Tatar Khans and their Russian agents combined the ruthless expansion of despotic power with an internal system of "enslavement." According to this interpretation, the Mongols introduced the two-pronged policy; the early Tsars implemented it in Muscovy; Peter the Great "generalized" it. And in Marx's time Russia's political attitude was in substance what it had been at the end of the Mongol period.

In short, the Mongol conquest forced Russia to regress from a feudal to an Asiatic or semi-Asiatic status. It is noteworthy that, despite its Asiatic status, both Marx and Engels believed that late-nineteenth century Russia was on the brink of a socialist revolution. In 1877 Marx wrote that Russia is "on the threshold of an upheaval," and in 1875 Engels wrote that "There is no doubt that Russia is on the eve of a revolution." There is also no doubt that the revolution they were referring to was the socialist revolution (see, e.g., Bober 1948, pp. 41–43).

The theory of historical progressivity is clearly not an empirical theory. It is what may be called a "pure" or "axiomatic theory," i.e., a theory of what would happen if other things remained equal. But, as Marx and Engels make abundantly clear, other things rarely, if ever, remain equal. There are simply too many other factors—"accidents"—that can affect the means of production for any empirical predictions to be derived from the theory. Thus, while the theory may indicate a *trend* toward progress it clearly does not rule out either periods of stagnation or actual regressions. Nor does it require that any society must go through all the various socio-economic stages or to go through them in any particular order.

The Theory of Historical Inevitability

Finally, there is what may be termed the theory of historical inevitability. While neither Marx nor Engels appear to have subscribed to a mechanistic, unilinear view of the course of history, it is abundantly clear that both thought that history had a predetermined goal. Although one could not predict the exact time or place of its arrival, the triumph of socialism was "inevitable." In *Capital* (1906, p. 897) Marx says that socialism must come "with the inexorability of a law of nature." And in the *Communist Manifesto* (1969, p. 79) Marx and Engels write that "Its [the bourgeoisie's] fall and the victory of the proletariat are equally inevitable." And their writings contain many other, similar, statements regarding the inevitable triumph of socialism (see, e.g., Engels 1972a, pp. 311–25; and 1972b, pp. 54–75.)

While these statements may well represent the triumph of desire over common sense, there is a certain logic to them. Capitalism, which was the dominant mode of production in Europe, had an innate tendency to become universal. And since capitalism was beset by insoluble internal contradictions its demise, including that of the ruling bourgeois class, was inevitable. Since the only remaining class would be the proletariat, which Marx assumed was naturally predisposed to socialism, it follows that the triumph of socialism was "inevitable." This conclusion, it is worth noting, was derived from neither the theory of historical materialism nor the theory of historical progressivity, but was, rather, a questionable deduction from Marx's detailed *economic* analysis of the capitalist mode of production.

It is important to point out that there can be no historical regression from socialism since, (1) socialism is a harmonious mode of production and would therefore eliminate the incentives for war and (2) productivity under this mode of production would be so vast that it would be able to weather any natural catastrophe. Thus, the triumph of socialism is not only inevitable, it is also irreversible.

Conclusions

Marx's historical outlook has been presented in some detail. It is both complex and sophisticated. First, Marx was intent upon presenting a taxonomy which would include "all possible" socio-economic systems. His list in the "Preface" is best interpreted not as a list of necessary, chronological stages but as part of his on-going work on this taxonomy. Second, Marx's historical work can actually be broken down into three distinct theories. The theory of historical materialism, which claims (1) that all ideas are derived, at least "ultimately," from the economic base, and (2) that the relations of production are determined by the level of the means of production, is an empirical theory. The theory of historical progressivity, which claims that what may be called the "natural course of history" is for each successive mode of production to be more productive than its predecessor, is an example of a "pure" or "axiomatic" theory which can be neither confirmed nor falsified by the historical data since there are too many "accidental" factors which cannot be taken into account and may, at least temporarily, override the natural course of events. And finally, there is the theory of historical inevitability which claims that capitalism must, "with the inexorability of a law of nature" collapse and that socialism is its inevitable successor.

Part II
Analysis

The second part of this paper will analyze both Marx's taxonomy and his method of analyzing history. The latter will be dealt with first.

Method of Historical Analysis

Empirical Theory

Marx claims that his theory of historical materialism is an empirical theory. "The phantoms of the human brain," he says in his *Economic and Philosophical Manuscripts* (Bottomore and Rubel 1961, p. 75) "are necessary sublimates of men's material life-process, which can be empirically established, and which is bound to material preconditions." "The production of ideas, conceptions and consciousness" he says, "is a direct emanation of their [men's] material behavior." And in his "Preface" (1970, pp. 20–21) he says that the "relations of production correspond to a definite stage of development of their material productive forces"; that "definite forms of social consciousness," i.e., the superstructure, "correspond" to "the economic structure of society": that "with the change in the economic foundation the entire immense superstructure is more or less rapidly transformed." And in *The German Ideology* (1947, p. 6) Marx and Engels write that what individuals are "coincides with their production . . . The nature of individuals thus depends on the material conditions determining their production."

This theory has, they claim, been empirically confirmed. Marx, says Engels, "had proved" it and he calls it a "law of human development" (Selsam 1970, p. 30). Lenin refers to it is a law that is "without exception" and claims that "the latest discoveries of natural science . . . have been a remarkable confirmation" of it. The numerous attempts by its "enemies" to "refute" it, he says have invariably failed (Lenin 1967, vol 1., pp. 13, 41–42).

a. *The Problem of Definition.* Terms such as "correspond," and "coincide" imply a precise, perhaps even quantifiable, relationship between the base and superstructure. This, in turn, demands a precise understanding of the elements or components to which the relationship corresponds. It is, after all, impossible to determine the empirical validity of a relationship if one is unsure of such things as the meaning and scope of the principle factors constituting that relationship. But Marx, as even his most ardent supporters acknowledge, never provided a definition of such terms as "economic" "material productive forces," "economic base," "superstructure," "class," etc. As the Marxist writer, McMurtry observes (p. 72),

> Although this category of relations of production/economic structure seems thus the theoretical linchpin of all Marx's analysis, its precise meaning has been a matter of unresolved

controversy for more than a century. Marx, himself, as with
all the basic categories of his *Weltanschauung*, never proffers
a definition.

Interestingly, McMurtry defends this imprecision on the
grounds that Marx's "usage is so rich and elliptical" (p. 72).
Moreover, he argues that this does not undermine its claim to
scientific status. For example, Marx's argument that the superstructure must correspond to the economic base means that
those superstructural or ideological phenomena that are not
"fit," i.e., do not correspond to the base, will, in Darwinian
fashion, be eliminated. This means that for Marx, as for Darwin, "empirical enquiry into the relevant concrete circumstances is required to generate a judgement of what in fact will
be selected, or selected out, in the 'struggle for life'" (pp. 163–
64). Whether or not "Marx's theory of social selection" is "ho-
mologous" to Darwin's "theory of natural selection" is debat-
able. It is also irrelevant. For even if Darwin's concepts are, as
imprecise as Marx's, this does not thereby render Marx's theories scientific. It merely calls into question the scientific status
of Darwin's theory.[1]

In fact, McMurtry confuses universal laws with specific
conditions. A causal explanation or prediction of the type Marx
makes regarding such things as the relationship between the
base and superstructure, requires two premises: (1) a universal
law and (2) a statement of specific conditions. The universal
law must be clearly formulated and the formulation must include the conditions under which the law would hold. Thus,
"empirical enquiry into the concrete circumstances" cannot be
used to establish the scope of the law. On the contrary it is the
law which determines what the "relevant concrete circumstances" are. If one doesn't know the scope of the law then there
is no way to ascertain what the "relevant concrete circumstances are." The problem here has less to do with Darwin's
theory of natural selection than with Toynbee's theory of the

---

[1] A very different interpretation of Darwin's *Theory of Natural Selection* can
be found in Hayek, pp. 31–33.

life cycle of civilizations. As Popper (1956, p. 27n) points out, "of nearly every theory it can be said that it agrees with many facts." In "Professor Toynbee's allegedly empirical investigations of what he calls 'species civilization' . . . he seems to overlook the fact that he classifies as civilizations only such entities as conform to his *a priori* belief in life cycles." He then finds that he has provided empirical confirmation for his theory that all societies follow a particular "life cycle." That is, instead of testing the theory by reference to the facts, the facts are "selected in light of the very theories they are supposed to test." It is similar for Marx. Since one does not know the scope or domain of any of his relevant concepts, McMurtry's claim that "reliable predictions or explanations can be deduced" from "empirical enquiry into the relevant concrete circumstances" can only mean that those superstructural elements that "survive" must correspond to the current level of the base; those that are eliminated, it follows, do not correspond. The lack of conceptual rigor renders the theory non-falsifiable and thus empirically non-scientific. This is demonstrated by McMurtry's own example.

What, he asks (p. 172), of those societies such as the Soviet Union "where Marxist-led revolutions have apparently broken the capitalist economic form," but have not resulted in even "a proximate end to man's domination of man"? McMurtry gives several explanations designed to reconcile this with Marxian principles. First, the socialist revolution was supposed to take place in "historically advanced" societies. Since countries such as the Soviet Union and the Peoples' Republic of China are not advanced, "they simply fall outside the referential range of Marx's claim." Furthermore, "what has gone on in these societies prior to their material qualification as historically advanced societies—for example, 'forced collectivization' and 'consumer deprivation',", may "appear to involve human domination" but in fact "it is not really human domination at all, but domination by material *needs*." And finally, even if the party and state office holders do, in fact, dominate and exploit the citizenry in such societies, this is not, as it may appear on the surface, an example of "a preeminent ruling-class superstructure suspended, so to speak, in the air, with no underlying ruling-class economic infrastructure as its 'foundation'" (p. 176). Rather, it is a case of "office ownership." The profit or surplus value "belongs to an office as subject-owner; but as [the office] must be occupied by a person it is this person occupant who, *qua* occupant, receives the unearned benefits" (pp. 178–79). Thus, what appears to be a case of the superstructure dominating the base, and thus a refutation of Marx's theory, is, according to McMurtry, upon closer examination a confirmation of the theory that the base determines the superstructure.

Surely this is not only a classic case of selecting facts in light of the theory they are supposed to test but of taking imprecise concepts and stretching them so that they "fit the facts" and thus "confirm" the theory. The result is literally to render what is supposed to be an "empirical theory" immune from any empirical test. Other examples of "nonfalsifiability" are found in Marx's writings. For example, revolutions will be successful, he says, when the "objective material conditions are correct." But since the "objective material conditions," correct or otherwise, are never specified we only know whether or not they are correct by observing whether or not the revolution succeeded.

It is clear that if Marx's claim that the theory of historical materialism is an empirical theory is to be taken seriously, the concepts must be defined much more rigorously.

b. *The Meaning of "Economic"*. Sidney Hook (p. 20) observes that the term "economic" is used by Marx in at least four different senses: (1) "it is sometimes used to characterize motives, like a desire for wealth or money"; (2) it "sometimes refers to the presence or absence of land and raw materials . . . necessary for production;" (3) "more often it means the techniques, forces, and powers of production, including not only tools and instruments but skills and know-how," and (4) "what Marx calls the *mode* of economic production or the "social relations of production."

c. *The Source of Ideas*. In order to examine Marx's claim that the theory of historical materialism is empirically verifiable one must know what Marx meant by the term "economic." Since ideas are "produced" by, or "reflexes and echoes" of the base, and since human nature, itself, is, according to Marx, "conditioned" by the base, it is clear that in saying that the economic base determines the superstructure Marx cannot have in mind category (1). This is so since motives are part of the superstructure and thus derived from the base. It is clear that in saying that the base refers to the "totality" of all economic relations Marx is using the term "economic" in its broadest sense. This would include both the forces and the relations of production or categories (2), (3) *and* (4). The means of production "determine" the "relations of production." And the "totality" or "sum total of these relations of production . . . constitute the economic structure of society on which rises a legal and political superstructure" (1970, p. 21).

There is an obvious problem here. Marx says that the "totality" of "the social relations of production constitutes the economic structure of society," and that the relations of production include property relations which, he says, are a "legal" relationship. This seems to make law a part of the economic base. Yet, he also states that from the economic base "arises a legal and political superstructure," thereby making law and politics not part of the base but part of the superstructure. Similarly, Marx says that ideas and knowledge are reflexes or echoes of the base. Yet he also claims not merely that the ideological superstructure reacts upon or has an impact on the base, but that ideas are *part of* the base, that they are in fact, a "material productive force." In the *Grundrisse* (Bottomore and Rubel 1961, p. 91), for example, Marx writes that:

> Nature constructs no machines, no locomotives, railways, electric telegraphs, self-acting mules, etc. . . . They are the product of human industry, natural materials transformed into instruments of human domination of Nature, or of its activity in Nature. They are instruments of the human brain created by the human hand; they are the materialized power of

knowledge. The development of fixed capital indicates the extent to which general social *knowledge has become a direct force of production*, and thus the extent to which the conditions of the social life process have been brought under control of the general intellect and reconstructed in accordance with it. [emphasis supplied]

I simply don't know any other way to read this statement than that ideas and knowledge are a material productive force and thus part of the economic base. For Marx, legal and political relations are seen as part of the base; at other times they are viewed as part of the superstructure. At times ideas are referred to as reflexes and echoes the "material productive forces"; at other times they are viewed as an essential part of the "material productive forces." In short, the Marxian categories of base and superstructure simply do not meet the basic scientific criteria of being exhaustive and mutually exclusive. If there is virtually nothing that is not, or cannot at times be, a material productive force, if the "economic base" is so broad and fluid as to include practically anything, then the claim that the base determines the superstructure becomes an empty tautology: whatever influences the "superstructure" is, *ipso facto* part of the "economic base." Once again, a theory that claims to be empirical is constructed in such a way as to render it immune from the results of any empirical test.

Finally, it should be noted in passing that if ideas are the product of the material base and as the base changes ideas must likewise change, this means that any theory can "occupy only a transitory place in the eternal flux of facts and ideas." But this would mean that Marx's ideas, too, are no more than a product of the material base at a given point in time and are therefore destined to be replaced by other theories as the material base changes. Thus, "Marx's theory of relativity devours his own theories, the theory of relativity included" (Bober 1948, p. 381).

d. *The Forces and Relations of Production*. A second aspect of the theory of historical materialism is that the relations of production, category (4) in Hook, are "determined" by the forces of production, categories (2) and (3) in Hook. These terms, though not rigorously defined, are far more clear than the general term "economic." Since the forces of production are essentially the tools man uses, McMurtry is correct in referring to Marx as a "technological determinist" (pp. 188–239). It is clear that Marx regards the forces of production as the linchpin of his entire system. Changes in the forces of production produce "corresponding" changes in "the whole immense superstructure," although there may well be a lag time between the change in the former and the change in the latter. Changes in the forces of production, Marx says, "can be determined with the precision of natural science" (1970, p. 21). This and other similar statements, clearly imply that changes in the forces of production can be measured. Thus, one should be able to say that a 10% change in the forces of production will, at least "ultimately," result in a "corresponding" change in means of production. McMurtry (pp. 191–92) takes precisely this position. "The relations of production/economic structure correspond to a definite stage of development of the forces of production," he writes, "insofar as the *units of effective ownership* involved in the former *correspond in scale to the units of technological integration* involved in the latter" [emphasis in original].

The obvious question is how do we determine what, say, a "unit of effective ownership" is? Do we ascertain the number of factory owners in the society and divide that by, say, the square root of the number of arrests made for violation of laws protecting private property? And how do we determine what a "unit of technological integration" is? Do we calculate the average number of proletarians employed per factory and subtract from that number the average cubic feet of factory space? And would a single "unit of the forces of production" "correspond" to a single "unit of the relations of production"? Or would it be two units or even ten units? And how could we ever know? And what does it mean to say that the relations of production will "ultimately" "correspond" to the forces of production? Does "ultimately" mean two weeks, six months, or several decades? This is nothing more than meaningless, "scientistic" jargon.

e. *The Mode of Production.* Marx believed that there were several distinct modes of production or socio-economic systems and that each of these had specific "laws of motion" by which their "movements" were governed. Marx derided the "vulgar bourgeois economists" for believing that the laws of the capitalist system were "eternal" and writes (1970, pp. 188–90) that economists such as Smith and Ricardo made the mistake of dealing with "man as posited by nature," i.e., a constant, when in fact they were dealing with "the individual . . . as an historical result," as he has evolved. Thus, he says, "When we speak of production we always have in mind production at a definite stage of development." And Leontyev writes (p. 233) that "with the transition from capitalism to socialism the economic laws of socialism replace the economic laws of capitalism." But Marx does not deny that there are regularities that transcend particular systems (1970, p. 190):

> It might be thought therefore that, in order to speak of production at all we must . . . declare from the very beginning that we are examining *one* particular historical period, as for instance modern bourgeois production. . . . All periods of production, however, have certain features in common: they have certain common categories. Some elements are found in all epochs, others are common to a few epochs. The most modern period and the most ancient period will have certain categories in common. Production without them is inconceivable. But . . . it is necessary to distinguish those definitions which apply to production in general, in order not to overlook the essential differences existing despite the unity that follows from the very fact that the subject, mankind, and the object, nature, are the same. For instance, on the failure to perceive this fact depends the entire wisdom of modern economists who prove the eternity and harmony of existing social relations.

Now it is obvious that due to the variability of social conditions, of customs, cultures, etc., results we might expect, which were formed on the basis of experience in our own culture or historical period, would not coincide with the results we would get in another culture or historical period. But this does not mean that the "laws" have changed. It merely means either that the conditions under which the law applies are not present or that the scope of the law is not as broad as was originally thought and that one must therefore revise the law by narrowing the conditions under which it applies. Thus, the law would still be universal, i.e., valid whenever the conditions to which it applies are present. For example, although those laws regarding such things as the division of labor, rent and market exchange might be universally valid, they would be irrelevant to Robinson Crusoe since the conditions under which they hold simply do not exist in such a situation.

Marx does not deny this. However, since he is primarily interested in the laws peculiar to the various modes of production and since he regularly derides the bourgeois economists for believing that the "laws of the capitalist system" are universal, we are entitled to know which "laws" have universal status and which are confined to the particular mode of production. This cannot be done *a priori*. It would entail taking each "law" and examining whether the specific conditions under which a law holds are present in each mode of production. One could conclude that the "laws" of one mode of production are not relevant for another mode only if the specific conditions under which the law would apply are completely absent in the latter. Marx never attempted such a feat. He simply concluded that the laws of the capitalist system, i.e., the laws of the market, were specific to that mode of production.

The basis for this conclusion seems to come from Marx's view of human nature. Marx maintains that (1) man does have a nature but that (2) it is modified by the particular mode of production (McMurtry 1978, p. 20). According to Marx, man is, by his nature, industrious and creative. When the bourgeois form of production is "peeled away," says Marx (1964, pp. 84–45; also see Marx, 1973a, p.112–14) one sees that it is in the nature of man to produce, and to produce creatively. As McMurtry puts it (p. 26), "For Marx, then, Man the Producer is, in the end, Man the Artist." But man's nature is modified by history. All modes of production will stimulate the development of some aspects of man's nature while blocking the development of others. But capitalism seriously distorts human nature. "Political economy starts with the fact of private property," Marx says (1973a, p. 107), and thereby "sets in motion" "greed and the war *amongst the greedy—competition*" [emphasis in original]. Thus, greed and competition are not natural to man; they are, rather, a product of modes of production based on private property, in particular, capitalism.

The interesting thing about this analysis is how does Marx know what human nature really is? He derides bourgeois economists for postulating the existence of "the individual," a Robinson Crusoe. "Production by a solitary individual outside society . . . is preposterous." Man, "in the most literal sense," he says, is a "social animal." But if human nature is modified by the society in which he lives, and if the notion of a pristine man living "outside society" is "preposterous," how can Marx ever know what "human nature in general," i.e., human nature unmodified by society, really is? Since Marx provides no answer to this question, his belief that man is, by nature, productive and creative is no more than an assertion.

But it is certainly a convenient one. For the assertion that human nature changes as the means of production change, allows him to conclude, *a priori*, that "the laws of the capitalist mode of production" are not relevant to other modes of production since the conditions under which they would apply, i.e, a human nature in which greed and competition dominate, are not present. But this should be easy to test. One of the laws of the capitalist system is that a shortage of a good will, other things being equal, cause its price to rise. A corollary of this is that if the price of a good is held below the market price, a shortage will result. The historical evidence clearly shows that this is exactly what happened in ancient China and Rome, in feudal France and even in socialist Russia after the 1917 revolution. Similarly, "bourgeois economics" maintains that debasing the currency or increasing the supply of money will cause prices to rise. Again, the empirical evidence shows that this is precisely what happened in ancient Rome, in feudal France, in capitalistic United States, and, again, in socialist Russia.[2] Finally, it might be noted that, contrary to Marx's assertion, recent studies of non-capitalist village life strongly suggest that human nature, for all practical purposes, is constant (see, e.g., Popkin 1979; Mosher 1983).

f. *Conclusion*. Joseph Schumpeter (p. 10) called Marx's theory of history "one of the greatest individual achievements of sociology to this day." If this is an exaggeration, it is not much of one. The theory is breathtakingly bold in its attempt to integrate economics, sociology, politics, the natural sciences and even the arts into a single over-arching conceptual framework. It is not, however, a "scientific" theory, much less a "law of historical development." It is fertile ground for empirical research. But much depends on the ability to recast Marx's concepts into empirically falsifiable terms without doing injustice to the richness of his ideas. It is worthy of note in this context that the massive quantities of technology imported into many Third World countries since World War II did little or nothing to stimulate economic development. Since this suggests that economic development is more a product of culture, of the way people think, than vice versa, it is in direct contradiction to what at least *appears* to be the Marxian position (Sowell 1885, p. 208).

Moreover, Marx's dissatisfaction with Hegel's Idealism and the notion of the "spontaneous generation" of ideas is, I believe, well founded. The notion that anything can occur without a cause is, after all, inconceivable to the human mind (Mises 1969c, pp. 76–78). But Marx's attempt to trace back all ideas to the "material productive forces" must be pronounced a failure. It is clear that man is influenced by his material environment, but there is no reason why the material environment must be the sole, or even the "ultimate," source of all ideas.

Axiomatic Theory

Marx's theory of historical progressivity was classified as an axiomatic or "pure" theory. Beginning from certain assumptions

[2]On China see Lacy 1922; on Rome see Mises 1966, pp. 767–69; on France see White 1969; on Russia see Farbman 1937 and Dobb 1948.

Marx tried to deduce logically the "natural" course of history using the *ceteris paribus*, or other things remaining equal, qualifier. The independent variable is the state of technology which, Marx assumes, would constantly improve. From this it follows logically, he believes, that technological advancement would continually revolutionize the relations of production thereby moving society "inexorably" along the path of history from the ancient to the feudal to the capitalist and finally into the socialist/communist modes of production.

a. *The "Ceteribus Paribus" Device.* Marx's use of the *ceteribus paribus* device has a long tradition in the social sciences in general and economics in particular. It is, of course, the principle means for approximating the methods of the natural sciences. In the natural sciences extraneous data can be artificially excluded, thereby isolating the factors to be examined. This is usually not possible in the social sciences. The *ceteribus paribus* device is a method of mentally isolating the relevant factors, thereby allowing the social scientist to use the "laboratory of the mind" to conduct mental experiments by envisioning how a change in one factor would affect a second factor. Thus, the *ceteribus paribus* device allows the social scientist to approximate the laboratory experiments in the natural sciences by the use of the laboratory of the mind.

The procedure is that one stipulates certain assumptions from which certain theorems are then deduced. If the assumptions are correct and the deductions are properly drawn, then the theory *must* be correct. The theory allows one to simplify reality, thereby separating "appearances" from "essences." As the theory is further refined, more and more of the restrictive assumptions are lifted, moving the model closer to "reality." It is important to note that an axiomatic theory cannot be falsified by empirical data. If the assumptions are correct, the only question is whether or not the historical conditions correspond to the conditions for which the theory would apply (see, e.g., Marx 1970, pp. 205–14; Mises 1962, pp. 1–9, 44).

This is the procedure used, *at times*, by Marx and it is remarkably similar, in intent at least, to the "pure theory" of

Carl Menger (see, Hutchison, pp. 15–37) and especially the praxeological method of Ludwig von Mises (see, e.g., Mises 1966, pp. 1–142. Also see Rothbard 1970a, pp. 1–66; 1973, pp. 311–42; and Lachman 1951, pp. 412-27). The principle difference is that while Mises's assumptions, such as the action axiom, are *a priori*, Marx's are not. An *a priori* assumption is a "self-evident proposition" (Mises 1962, p. 4; Rothbard 1957, p. 315) and thus "not empirically falsifiable." *A priori* assumptions are not categories that are tested by recourse to human action. On the contrary, such categories are logically prior to, and therefore enable us to understand and explain, human action.

Marx, however, believed that his assumptions were in fact, *a priori*, or at least very close to it. "The premises from which we begin," write Marx and Engels, "are not arbitrary ones . . . but real premises from which abstraction can only be made in the imagination . . . The first premise of all human history is, of course, the existence of living human conditions." From this it follows that "men can be distinguished from animals . . . as soon as they begin to *produce* their means of subsistence." "The way in which men produce their means of subsistence depends first of all on the nature of the actual means they find in existence and have to reproduce." They conclude that "the nature of individuals thus depends on the material conditions determining their production" (1946, p. 6). As Engels put it (Selsam 1970, p. 35), "men must first of all eat, drink, have clothing and shelter, therefore must *work*, before they can fight for domination, pursue politics, religion, philosophy, etc." Thus, the content of the latter is a product of the process of the former.

It is indisputable that there could be no human history in the absence of human beings. That proposition would therefore have the character of an *a priori* assumption. But it is difficult to see what conclusions must *necessarily* flow from it. For example, it in no way seems to be a *logically necessary deduction* from this that man's nature "depends on the material conditions determining their production." This may be the case but it is not an *a priori* but an empirical assumption. It is *not* an assumption whose truth is self-evident but, on the contrary, one that must be established, empirically or logically. To treat it as axiomatic and thus to assume its validity, as does Marx, is simply to assume the very thing most in need of demonstration.

Marx's second major assumption is that of the inevitability of technological progress. Now Marx does not argue that technological progress *is* inevitable. Rather it is that, *for purposes of analysis*, such complicating factors as war and natural disasters, which can disrupt this process, are *temporarily* excluded. But the question is: does the exclusion of these factors render technological advance inevitable? I think the answer has to be no. First, Marx does not adequately explain the process by which technological inventions are made. His argument is that when historical conditions call for a new tool or machine, that need will prompt individuals to devote their energies to this task. That the inventions will be made is, for Marx, inevitable. As he puts it in the "Preface" (1970, p. 21), "Mankind thus inevitably sets for itself only such tasks as it is able to solve, since closer examination will always show that the problem itself arises only when the material conditions for its solution are already present." But even if one grants that this is the case (which I, by no means, do), the real question is: how are the efforts of the relevant individuals, for example, the scientists and inventors, directed into the areas where the new machines or tools are needed? "Bourgeois economists" deal with this problem by recourse to the entrepreneur. But, as Schumpeter points out (p. 32), Marx, has no place for the entrepreneur in his mechanistic view of the capitalist mode of production, where the same things are simply produced in ever expanding quantities. Thus, Marx has no way to link scientific and technological advances to economic needs. Scientific and technological advances may occur but, under Marx's view of capitalism, it is purely a fortuitive coincidence if they coincide with economic needs. The only thing Marx can say is that mankind needs them and therefore mankind invents them.

Second, and related to the first, is the question of resource depletion. Resources are depleted in the course of economic development. Instead of inevitable economic progress wouldn't it be more plausible to assume that economic progress would continue up to the point that resources became depleted, after which would follow a period of economic deterioration? Interestingly, this is the position taken by Ricardo, from whom Marx acquired much if not most of his economics (Schumpeter 1975, pp. 35-37). Ricardo believed that growing resource scarcity would cause prices to continually rise. But for Marx the essential problem for capitalism is that precisely because it is so productive the quantity of goods produced exceed the quantity demanded. Thus, the capitalists must continually lower their prices, thereby driving each other out of business. The possibility of resource depletion never seems to occur to Marx. Technological, and correspondingly economic, advances are assumed to go on indefinitely. This is not to say that resource depletion *is* inevitable, only that it is an inevitable consequence of the Marxian position. For example, if a resource is defined as something that is found in nature that we know how to use, it follows that knowledge is at least as important as the substance itself. And if one's view of the economic process leaves room for the entrepreneur to channel the energies of scientists and technicians into the areas where resources are becoming scarce, then man has the ability not merely to find additional resources but actually to *create* resources as we need them, i.e., to find uses for previously useless substances. Thus, there is then no inherent reason to believe that resources will become scarce over time (Simon 1981; Simon and Kahn 1984; and Osterfeld 1985). But by excluding the entrepreneur Marx is unable to offer any reason why resource depletion will not occur.

Finally, Marx does not deal with the affect of political policies and social attitudes. Scientific advance, and the development of knowledge in general, is a social enterprise. As Popper says (1957, pp. 154-64), "Science, and more especially scientific progress, are the results not of isolated efforts but of the *free competition of thought*. For science needs ever more competition between hypotheses and ever more rigorous tests. . . .

Ultimately, progress depends very largely on political factors: on political institutions that safeguard freedom of thought." Interestingly, the ruling class in any particular period is tenaciously trying to hold on to its position. The principle means by which it does so is to use the state to crush resistance and to prevent the emergence of dangerous ideas. Yet, Marx does not take into consideration that an environment so hostile to free thought would impede the development of science and retard, or even reverse, technological advances. For Marx, the march of science takes on the character of inevitability.

In brief, while Marx believes that his assumptions are *a priori* they are in fact empirical, and empirical assumptions of very questionable validity.

The next question is: even granting his assumptions, is the theory of historical progressivity logically deduced from those premises? Again, the answer is clearly no. Marx argues that, other things remaining equal, technological advance will produce a succession of modes of production and that each successive mode will be more productive than its predecessor. Thus, the ancient period logically flows from the Asiatic, the feudal from the ancient, etc. But neither Marx nor Engels deduce the transition from primitive communism to the ancient period from any changes in the material productive forces in that period. In *The Origin of the Family, Private Property and the State*, Engels explains the demise of primitive communism by such factors as the emergence of private property and the decline of the importance of the family. Although he does refer to the discovery of iron during this period and the significant number of industrial achievements, he does not link this change in the technological base directly to changes in the relations of production. He merely says (1942, p. 146) that as "herds began to pass into private property, exchange between individuals became more common." As to the question how and why individual ownership of herds emerged, Engels simply says "we know nothing" (p. 167). The problem here is that one appears to have a change in the relations of production that is independent of any change in the forces of production. And while he refers to the emergence of slavery during this period it is not at all clear why this necessarily or logically flows from primitive communism. He simply says that as the work to be done increased, "new labor forces were needed." Therefore, "prisoners of war were turned into slaves" (p. 147). Why they weren't enserfed or even paid wages is not explained.

Nor does there seem to be any logically necessary reason why ancient slavery should give way to medieval feudalism. Feudalism, by nearly all accounts, was not the consequence of class antagonisms between the owners and the slaves, but a product of a historically unique set of events. In particular, it was a result of the barbarian invasions which scattered the population of Europe across the continent. And the related insecurity caused by the wars forced the independent farmers, and the artisan refugees of the cities under attack, to seek protection in exchange for work. The outcome was the emergence of largely self-sufficient manors and the distinction between lords and serfs. This type of socio-economic system, as Marx himself noted, did not occur anywhere else in the world. There is, Bober observes (p. 54), no reason for a "slave mode of production [to] inevitably produce circumstances which must result in feudalism."

The transition from feudalism to capitalism is equally troublesome for Marx. For one thing the collapse of feudalism was essentially completed during the fifteenth century which means that it occurred at least a "century before the beginnings of capitalism" (Rosenberg and Birdzell 1986, p. 103). One cannot use historical data to refute an axiomatic theory. But it does raise a significant analytical problem. Marx was aware of "the 100 years hiatus" between the fall of feudalism and the rise of capitalism. He attempted to account for this hiatus by the tactical maneuver of what he called "simple commodity production," a system in which products are produced for exchange but it is exchange for subsistence and not for profit, and there is little capital accumulation. The problem with this explanation is that Marx makes it quite clear that the means of production have not yet changed (Bober 1948, p. 60). The technological revolution lay a century or more in the future. But this means that, as in the transition from primitive communism, the change in the relations of production is autonomous. It is not caused by a previous change in the means of production. In fact, it is reasonable to believe that, if anything, the change in the means of production is, itself, a result of the earlier change in the relations of production. Thus, in his attempt to extricate himself from the problem of the "100 year hiatus" Marx reverses the causal relationship stipulated by his own theory.

Marx's attempt to derive logically the emergence of socialism from the fall of capitalism is no more successful. First, there is no reason why the proletariat should be the only class contending with the bourgeoisie for power. What, for example, of the so-called "managerial class" which, to use Marxist terminology, has "grown in the womb" of the capitalist system? There may well be other possibilities.[3] The point is that even on strictly Marxian grounds there is no reason why there can be only two classes, the bourgeoisie and the proletariat. And if that is the case there is no reason why the proletariat must accede to power with the collapse of the bourgeoisie.

But there is a much more serious problem with Marx's analysis. Even if one grants Marx's economic argument that capitalism must collapse, and even if one also grants his argument, derived from the labor theory of value, that the proletariat would fare much better under socialism than under capitalism, it is simply a *non sequitur* to conclude that the proletariat would therefore fight for socialism. Capitalism, according to Marx, causes the greedy, competitive and self-interested aspects of man's nature to dominate. The question is: even if proletarians would benefit from a socialist system, why would they fight for it? Assuming there are thousands or

---

[3]Karl Popper argues that, on strictly Marxian assumptions, there could be not just two but as many as seven distinct classes in existence during the capitalist period. See Popper (1966, p. 148).

even millions of proletarians it would be reasonable for the individual proletarian to reason that his individual contribution would not affect the outcome of the revolution. He would therefore maximize his own utility by not participating in the revolution since he would then avoid any possibility of injury or even death yet, since he was a proletarian, he would still receive all the benefits of a successful proletarian revolution. But if all proletarians thought in this way, and there is no reason why they would not, the proletarian revolution would never occur (Olson 1977, pp. 98–110). The problem of establishing a socialist system is identical. Why would the victors in the revolution want to establish a classless society based on cooperation rather than competition and exploitation? They were, after all, born and bred in a society that molded their nature to be greedy, competitive and self-interested. Marx's only route out of this dilemma is to assume that the individual proletarians will place the interest of their class as a whole above their own self-interests, i.e., become a "class for itself," which means that he must assume a change in human nature *prior* to the revolution and the establishment of the socialist mode of production. But the change in human nature, according to his own theory, is supposed to be a result of, and therefore *follow*, the change in the mode of production, not precede it. In brief, Marx's attempt to show, on strictly logical grounds, that socialism must follow capitalism simply does not succeed.

On a more general level it is interesting to note that as Marx lifts the *ceteris paribus* assumptions, thereby moving it closer to "reality" his theory becomes less and less deterministic. And in the end he refers to societies that have attained an equilibrium within a particular mode of production, i.e., they have ceased to progress, and to other societies that, for one reason or another, have actually regressed to a more primitive mode.

Marx's theory of historical progressivity makes extensive use of the *ceteris paribus* device to mentally isolate the factors being examined. It purports to be based on certain self-evident premises and proceed by strictly logical deductions to the conclusion that each successive mode of production must be more productive than its predecessor. But it was shown that its premises were neither *a priori* or self-evident, nor were they empirically verified. It was also shown that the steps in the theory were not logically necessary deductions from the premises and, in some cases, they were actually inconsistent with those premises. Marx may therefore be considered a quasi-praxeologist or, perhaps more accurately, an unsuccessful practitioner of the praxeological method.

Inevitability

The last of Marx's historical theories is his theory of historical inevitability, which claims that the triumph of socialism is inevitable. The strictly logical flaws in Marx's argument that socialism must succeed capitalism were dealt with above. But there are additional reasons why Marx cannot claim that socialism is inevitable. First is the question of knowledge. Marx believes that technological advancement is inevitable. But since technological advancement assumes a prior advancement of scientific knowledge Marx must also assume that the advancement of knowledge is inevitable. But, as Popper notes (1957, pp. ix–xi), it is logically impossible to predict what inventions or discoveries will be made in the future since to do so would require that one already possesses that knowledge. As Popper puts it, "if there is such a thing as growing human knowledge, then we cannot anticipate today what we shall know only tomorrow." This means that Marx cannot scientifically predict that socialism must come or that capitalism must fall since to do so rules out the possibility of some discovery or invention that would, for example, avert the alleged Law of the Tendency for the Rate of Profit to Fall. Capitalism, according to Marx, has solved the problem of production but not the problem of distribution. But why isn't it possible, even on Marxian grounds, for someone to discover a solution to the problem of distribution while keeping the capitalistic relations of production essentially intact? Certainly this is not a logical impossibility. "Profit-sharing" is just one possibility that comes to mind. No doubt there are others. The point is not that "profit-sharing" is the solution or that a solution will necessarily be found. It is simply that Marx has not been able to show that a solution is logically inconceivable and thus cannot eliminate the possibility that a solution will be found.

The second problem is that Marx cannot claim that social-ism is inevitable because he specifically acknowledges that accidents such as wars and natural disasters can do, and in fact have actually done, so much damage to the means of production as to prevent advancement to a higher mode of production or even to cause regression to a more primitive mode. Isn't it possible on strictly Marxian grounds, therefore, for the prole-tarian revolution to cause so much damage to the means of production that it not only makes the transition to socialism impossible but actually causes society to revert to a more primi-tive mode of production. But if one cannot rule out this possibil-ity then one cannot maintain that the triumph of socialism is "inexorable."

Finally, it should be pointed out that Marx's non-teleologi-cal view of the historical process is incompatible with his tele-ological belief in history's final destination.

Part III
Marx's Taxonomy

Capitalism

Turning to Marx's taxonomy it will be recalled that his objective was to present "all possible" modes of production, although his continual revisions suggest that he was not fully satisfied that he had achieved that goal. But what is rather curious is that while he makes numerous hair-splitting distinc-tions between the various non-commodity modes of production, there is, for Marx, only a single commodity mode: capitalism. Commodity production was defined by Marx as production separated from consumption by an intervening exchange.

And capitalism was a system, in fact the only system, in which commodity production was the dominant mode. Since exchange presupposed private property and the goal of exchange was profit, capitalism was viewed by Marx as a socio-economic system based on private property and the free or unrestricted exchange of goods and services, including labor, with the goal of making a profit. Marx says, for example (1969, p. 84), that by capitalism, or "the bourgeois conditions of production" is meant "free trade, free selling and buying."

Mercantilism

This definition of capitalism in terms of the free or unhampered market is unobjectionable. But surely it is not the sole form of commodity production. It is certainly possible to conceive of a society in which relations are organized around the market, in which buying and selling permeate the society, but in which that buying and selling is restricted, or hampered, by government rules and regulations. This is not merely a logical possibility. It is a historical reality. In the seventeenth and eighteenth century England, and especially France, were notorious for the extent of their regulations. The government of England, as a matter of course, established numerous legal monopolies such as the East India Company. Competition with such companies was strictly forbidden. The American colonists, for example, were forbidden to enter numerous occupations which were reserved for inhabitants of the Mother country. Trade with "outside" countries such as France was likewise prohibited. In France, a government decree in 1666 mandated that

> Henceforth the fabrics of Dijon and Selangey are to contain 1,408 threads . . ., neither more nor less. At Auxerre, Avallon, and two other manufacturing towns, the threads are to number 1,376; at Chatillon, 1,216. Any cloth found to be objectionable is to be pilloried. If it is found three times objectionable, the merchant is to be pilloried. (Heilbroner 1972, p. 21)

Even in the supposedly *laissez faire* United States of the early-nineteenth-century government regulations, including the grant of monopolies, was far more extensive than is commonly thought. "We cannot pass the bounds of the city," complained New York locofoco leader William Leggett,

> without paying tribute to monopoly; our bread, our meat, our vegetables, our fuel, all pay tribute to monopolists. Not a road can be opened, not a bridge can be built, not a canal can be dug, but a charter of exclusive privileges must be granted to the purpose. . . . The bargaining and trucking away chartered privileges is the whole business of lawmakers.

The type of economic system characterized by such extensive government interventionism is generally referred to as mercantilism. Jacob Viner (p. 439), for example, defines mercantilism as "a doctrine of extensive state regulation of economic activity in the interest of the national economy." It was, he continues, "in sharp contrast with the later *laissez faire* doctrine." Heilbroner (p. 37) says that mercantilism is the doctrine that, by linking national power with national wealth, concluded that the focus of government policy was "how to create ever more and more wealth by assisting the rising merchant class in the furtherance of its tasks." And since it "was generally admitted that unless the poor were poor they could not be counted upon to do an honest day's toil without asking for exorbitant wages," the related problem of government policy, says Heilbroner, became "how to keep the poor poor." And Rothbard (1964, p. 146) defines mercantilism as "the use of economic regulation and intervention by the state to create special privileges for the favored groups of merchants and businessmen."

In brief, capitalism is generally defined in terms of free trade and the absence of government intervention. Mercantilism is defined in terms of highly restricted trade and extensive government regulation of economic activity. The question is: is this difference enough to justify viewing mercantilism as a distinct mode of production. Marx was certainly aware of mercantilism and it is clear that he did not think so. He describes mercantilism (1964, p. 130) as a strictly transitional phase on the road to capitalism. Perhaps it is not surprising, therefore, that mercantilism is never even mentioned in either the massive *Dictionary of Marxist Thought* (Bottomore 1983) or the almost equally massive *An Encyclopedic Dictionary of Marxism, Socialism and Communism* (Wilczynski 1981). What needs to be done is to contrast the operations of capitalism with those of mercantilism to see if there are any significant differences.

Capitalism and Mercantilism Compared

a. *Exchange: Free Versus Restricted*. Since values are subjective, any voluntary, or free, exchange will take place only when each participant expects to benefit, "The very fact that an exchange takes place," writes Professor Rothbard, "demonstrates that both parties benefit (or more strictly *expect* to benefit) from the exchange." And, since the free market is nothing more than "the array of all voluntary exchange that takes place in the world," and since "every exchange demonstrates a unanimity of benefit for both parties concerned, we must conclude that," provided all major externalities have been internalized, as they would be in a world of universal private property, "the free market benefits all its participants" (1956, p. 250. Also see Mises 1966, p. 744).

It is true, of course, that businesses go bankrupt, expected profits from investments do not always materialize and proffered exchanges are sometimes rejected. But the claim is that free exchange enables individuals to maximize their utility *ex ante*. This is certainly consistent with bankruptcy, unprofitable investments, the purchase of losing lottery tickets, etc. This can be easily demonstrated. Assume that one has a .5 percent chance of having an investment yield a profit and a .5 percent chance of suffering a loss. If the individual believed that the profit would increase his *future* utility more than a loss would decrease it, the discounted *present* value of that investment would be positive. This means that, *regardless of the actual outcome*, the decision to invest would increase one's utility *ex ante* even if it proved to be a mistaken choice and reduced it *ex post*.

The situation is similar for rejected offers. If one's offer to exchange is rejected his *actual* or *real-world* utility plane remains unchanged. What has happened is that his hoped-for increase in utility did not materialize; that is, his *actual utility plane* is lower than his hoped-for or *desired utility plane*. Of course, there must always be a discrepancy between one's actual and one's desired utility. If this were not the case, if everyone's desires were completely satisfied, all action would cease, for any action, by definition, would then entail a reduction in utility (Mises 1966, pp, 13–14).

Put differently, the free market operates to increase every individual's *actual utility plane*. To complain of a discrepancy between actual and desired utility is simply to complain that one's desires have not been fully satisfied. But this complaint reduces itself to the rather mundane observation more is better than less, that abundance is better than scarcity. But scarcity, like uncertainty, is an ineradicable element of nature that is independent of any particular economic system.

But if the market maximizes individual and, by extension, social utility, if all parties to a free exchange must benefit, it follows that government restrictions on, and prohibitions of, certain types of exchange must reduce at least one and perhaps all parties' utility to below what it would have been on the unhampered market. This is not to say that no one can benefit. Obviously, the restriction will benefit some individuals, at least in the short run, while hurting others. Thus, in contrast to capitalism, in which any exchange implies a mutuality of benefit, mercantilism is a system of exchange in which one party benefits *at the expense* of the other party or parties. Put differently, since interpersonal comparisons of utility cannot be made, one can only discuss utility in a cardinal sense. This means that since exchange under capitalism is voluntary and therefore that both parties must benefit, capitalist exchange can be described as positive-sum. In contrast, since, under mercantilism, at least one party to the exchange must be coerced, mercantilist exchange can be described as zero-sum. In fact, when one also includes exchanges that *would have been made* in the absence of mercantilist restrictions it is quite possible that the result is actually negative-sum, i.e., that more individuals are harmed by the restrictions on exchange than are benefitted by it (Osterfeld 1988, pp. 79–92. Also see Rothbard, 1970b, p. 194).

In brief, exchange under mercantilism differs significantly from exchange under capitalism.

b. *Profit: Economic Versus Political.* Since profits are a subset of exchange, there is no fundamental difference between the two. The free market is *not* a profit system but a profit *and loss* system. Profits are earned by those who are able to satisfy consumers' desires better and more cheaply than others; losses are suffered by those who fail to serve the consumers. This means that far from profits being obtained *at the expense* of the consumers, the reverse is true: the more one serves the consumers the more profit he will earn.

Profits, as Mises has noted (1969b, p. 119) are never normal. They are an indication of maladjustment, of a difference between the actual allocation of resources and the allocation that would prevail if the wishes of the consumers were satisfied to the fullest extent possible. Those entrepreneurs who are the first to spot and act on the maladjustment are the ones who earn profit. And they earn profit because their actions serve to remove the maladjustment. Those who fail to spot the maladjustment suffer losses. And if they continue to suffer losses they will go bankrupt and their capital will be transferred to others who are more adept at perceiving maladjustments. This can be easily demonstrated. Assume that the market is in equilibrium. Also assume that a new technological breakthrough has enabled the production of a new commodity highly valued by consumers. The production of the commodity, however, requires the use of factor A. Those entrepreneurs who perceive this new profit opportunity will begin to bid for the factor. The increased competition for the available supply of A will cause its price to rise, forcing some of the users of A to curtail their purchases. But who will be the ones forced to curtail their purchases? Clearly, it will be those employers of A who are receiving the least remuneration for their product from the consumers, i.e., those who are employing *A* in its least productive area. In this way units of factor *A* are channeled from uses that the consumers value less highly into uses that they value more highly. But further, the rise in the price and therefore the profit margins of *A* will encourage other entrepreneurs, also anxious to make profits, to expand the supply of *A*.

In short, "the only means to acquire wealth and to preserve it, in an economy not adulterated by government-made privileges and restrictions," Mises observed (1969a, p. 535), "is to serve the consumers in the best and cheapest way." As soon as the entrepreneurs fail to do so consumers will take their business elsewhere. It is precisely the constant threat of loss that insures that entrepreneurs remain responsive to the needs of consumers.

It is much different under a mercantilist system characterized by extensive government regulations and restrictions including tariffs, subsidies, licensing restrictions and legal monopolies. By granting such privileges to those groups favored by government, others are forced to engage in activities they consider less desirable than those they would have undertaken. Moreover, freed from competition, and thus the need to serve the consumers, the politically favored groups are able to turn out shoddy merchandise at high prices. Thus, the privileged groups are able to benefit themselves *at the expense* of the rest of society. Finally, since government interference distorts the operations of the market it must necessarily misallocate resources. Since this will lower output, the long run effect is to hurt everyone, even, in many cases, the initial beneficiaries of the privileges, by reducing their standards of living to below what they would have been on the free market.

But isn't it possible for a monopoly to emerge from the free market and then to use its position to exploit consumers? It is at least conceivable for a monopoly to emerge on the unhampered market. But the only way for this to happen is for a firm to have continually served consumers far better than any of its competitors. If it would then decide to take advantage of its new-found monopolistic position by raising prices and reducing quality, it would immediately attract competitors anxious to take advantage of the new profit opportunities, thereby forcing the would-be monopoly to reduce its prices. The case of oil is just one example. Aside from Standard Oil's unsuccessful attempt to monopolize the market in the late nineteenth century, there were numerous attempts in the early twentieth century to cartelize the domestic oil market. But these *voluntary* agreements, without exception, failed. In fact, by 1933 the price of crude oil had fallen to $.25 a barrel. It was only when the national government, with the passage of the National Recovery Act in 1933 and the Transportation of Petroleum Products Act in 1935, established a national Petroleum Code whose enforcement arm was such state agencies as the Texas Railroad Commission and Oklahoma's Corporation Commission, that cartellization of the oil industry became effective. Since the effectiveness of the cartel was directly dependent on intervention by the government, the cartel was no longer voluntary but coercive (see Osterfeld 1987). What is important is that this is not unique to the oil industry. On the contrary, it has been the monotonous story of all attempts to obtain "monopolistic profits" on the unhampered market (see Armantano 1972; Kolko 1967; Osterfeld 1976).

Because it is a profit and loss system profits, under capitalism, are directly correlated with service to consumers. In contrast, because of the network of restrictions and regulations which reduces or even eliminates competition, mercantilism is essentially a profit system, *only*. The possibility of loss is substantially reduced. But the price of this reduction is that firms no longer need to concern themselves with satisfying consumers. Thus, in contrast to capitalism which correlates profits with consumers' satisfaction, profits under mercantilism are *at the expense* of the consumers. Put differently, the source of profits under capitalism is the market; the source of profits under mercantilism is the government.

c. *Wages: Free Versus Restricted.* Since wages, like profits, are a particular type of exchange, the general principles governing exchange apply here as well. Wage rates on the unhampered market do not depend on the individual worker's "productivity," but on the marginal productivity of labor. And the marginal productivity of labor is a product of savings, on the one hand, which creates additional capital and, on the other, entrepreneurial activity which directs this additional capital into the production of those goods and services most urgently desired by consumers (Mises 1969b, p. 125). Wages rise because, in order to take advantage of new profit opportunities provided by additional capital entrepreneurs must bid workers away from their current positions. As Mises has noted (1956, pp. 88–89), there are many jobs in which the "productivity" of the worker has remained unchanged for centuries. Those of the barber, the butler and certain types of agricultural work are cases in point. Yet, he observes,

> the wage rates earned by all such workers are today much higher than they were in the past. They are higher because they are determined by the marginal productivity of labor. The employer of a butler withholds this man from employment in a factory and must therefore pay the equivalent of the increase in output which the additional employment of one man in a factory would bring about. It is not any merit on the part of the butler that causes this rise in his wages, but the fact that the increase in capital invested surpasses the increase in the number of hands.

Far from the profits of the entrepreneur or the capitalist being obtained at the expense of the worker the opposite is true. Wages increase because, in order to capitalize on profit opportunities, entrepreneurs must bid against one another in order to acquire and retain the workers they need. The irony is that while profits disappear as soon as the maladjustment is corrected, the rise in wages tends to be permanent.

But in an interventionist system like mercantilism government policy, as noted, is designed to keep wages low, to keep the poor poor and the rich rich. Wage controls, licensing restrictions, legal monopolies and the like, restrict the opportunities open to workers, thereby reducing the demand for labor. The reduced demand, in turn, reduces the wages that workers can command. Moreover, the distortions induced by the intervention of the government impedes the ability of the entrepreneurs to direct capital into its most productive uses. Since this inefficiency restricts the overall productivity of the economy, it thereby harms practically all members of society, workers in particular. Thus, while wages under capitalism are closely correlated with profits, profits under mercantilism are obtained largely *at the expense* not only of consumers but workers as well.

d. *Class Relations: Harmony Versus Conflict.* A distinction must be made between class and caste. A class is characterized by movement between economic and social groups; a caste is characterized by the absence of such movement. One born into a caste is destined to remain in that caste for life.

It is clear that capitalism is a class system. Those born into a particular class do not always remain in that class. On the free market "rich men become poor men and poor men rich" (Mises 1969c, p. 114). But the only way to become and remain wealthy under capitalism is to serve others. The genius of the market is precisely that it is able to correlate service with wealth. The more valuable one's service, the wealthier one becomes. The entrepreneur must offer goods and services that consumers want to buy at prices that they are willing to pay. Failure to do this will result in the loss of customers and, ultimately, bankruptcy. But he must also offer wages that are high enough to attract and keep the workers he needs to produce those goods and services. Failure to do so will mean the eventual loss of workers to other entrepreneurs and therefore a reduction in the quantity or quality of his goods and services. Once again, the ultimate result is bankruptcy. Similarly, the market can also make poor people rich. There is nothing to prevent any individual from saving or even borrowing enough to invest in an existing business or opening a business of his own. This is not to say that success is either easy or guaranteed. Most businesses fail, at least in the long run. But so long as one is able to provide products that consumers wish to buy, the business will prosper and grow. Individuals such as Carnegie, Rockefeller and Ford, to name but a few, all came from humble beginnings. In fact, the vast majority of immigrants to the relatively capitalistic United States were penniless upon their arrival. This was a strictly temporary phase. After adjusting to American life, which usually meant adjusting to the shock of moving from a rural to an urban environment, these individuals, and even entire ethnic and racial groups such as the Jews, the Chinese, the Italians and the West Indian blacks, to name but a few, began to ascend the economic ladder, their places at the bottom being taken by succeeding generations of immigrants. Thus, while there is a permanent "bottom twenty percent" the individual occupants of that category are constantly changing (Sowell 1981).

Under capitalism entrepreneurs compete against one another to see who best can serve the consumers. The effect of this competition is to reduce the prices of the final goods and services. Likewise, they compete against one another to obtain the labor services they require. This competition forces wage rates up. Similarly, consumers compete against one another driving the prices of goods and services up, and workers compete against one another for the available jobs, thereby reducing the remuneration to labor. It is clear that while there is competition *within* economic classes there is harmony *between* them.

Finally, it should be noted that while there is movement between classes, the efficient allocation of resources insures economic improvement which benefits all economic classes.

In short, far from a socially stratified society, capitalism is characterized by constant movement between classes, the general rise in the absolute position of all classes and class harmony.

In contrast since, under mercantilism, the class favored by government is freed from competition and the threat of economic loss, not only is it able to secure government privileges which render its socio-economic position virtually unassailable but, in the process, to benefit itself *at the expense* of the rest of society. It is able to maintain its position at the top of the economic ladder by obtaining political or government privileges which have the effect of insuring that those at the bottom of the ladder remain there. Conflict between economic groups is the inevitable result. As Mises has put it (1978, pp. 3–4),

> Under the free market the manufacturers of shoes are simply competitors. They can be welded together into a group with solidarity of interests only when privilege supervenes, e.g., a tariff on shoes or a law discriminating against them for the benefit of some other people. . . . Our age is full of serious conflicts of economic interests. But these conflicts are not inherent in the operation of the unhampered capitalist economy. They are the necessary outcome of government policies interfering with the operation of the market. . . . They are brought about by the fact that mankind has gone back to group privileges and thereby to a new caste system.

While the free market is characterized by the long run harmony of interests of all citizens, mercantilism is a system characterized by caste conflict and group antagonisms. As Mises has tersely put it (1979, p. 7), "The belief that there prevails an irreconcilable conflict of group interests is age-old. It was the essential proposition, of mercantilist doctrine. . . . mercantilism was the philosophy of war."

d. *Conclusion.* Marx did not distinguish between mercantilism and capitalism. But if the foregoing is at all correct, then the differences between capitalism and mercantilism are far greater than those between many of Marx's own non-commodity modes of production. It is fair to say, therefore, that Marx's taxonomy should have included mercantilism as a distinct mode of production. And this inclusion, as will be seen, has serious ramifications for Marx's entire socio-political analysis.

Capitalism, Mercantilism and Marxism

a. *The Economic and the Sociological Definitions.* Marx's definition of capitalism in terms of "commodity production," or the production of goods and services, including labor, for sale on the market may be termed his explicit or formal definition. But Marx also had an implicit definition of capitalism. According to

this definition capitalism is a socio-economic system characterized by conflict between the bourgeoisie, the owners of the
means of production, and the proletariat, the non-owners, and
in which the bourgeoisie constitutes the dominant, or ruling
class. The formal, explicit definition may be termed the *economic* definition while the latter, implicit definition may be
called his *sociological* definition.

That Marx subscribed to the sociological definition is beyond doubt. For example, Marx and Engels write (1969, pp.
57–59) that

> the history of all hitherto existing society is the history of class
> struggles. Freeman and slave, patrician and plebeian, lord
> and serf, guildmaster and journeyman, in a word, oppressor
> and oppressed, all stood in constant opposition to one another.
> . . . Our epoch, the epoch of the bourgeoisie has simplified the
> class antagonisms. Society as a whole is more and more split-
> ting up into two great classes directly facing each other:
> *bourgeoisie and proletariat.*

The bourgeoisie is invariably referred to as "the ruling class"
(e.g., p. 74) and as having "got the upper hand" (p. 61).

While it is not clear whether Marx realized that he had two
distinct definitions of capitalism, what is clear is that, if he did,
he did not see any incompatibility between them, for he slips
back and forth between the two without warning. References to
"free trade," and the freedom to buy and sell, are interspersed
among references to tariffs, price and wage controls and other
forms of government interventions. Marx even refers at one
point (1906, p. 809) to government policies which "compelled"
reluctant workers to "sell" their "labor-power" "voluntarily." He
saw no incompatibility between slavery and capitalism (1972b),
and this in spite of the fact that he clearly recognizes that for
the market process to work labor must be mobile or "free," as he
frequently but sarcastically refers to it. Marx also recognized
that capitalism is not possible in the absence of private property (see, e.g., Marx 1969, pp. 81–82). Yet, he did not see any
incompatibility between private ownership on the one hand
and government censorship on the other (Marx 1974b).

But the two definitions are not at all compatible. By the logic of the economic definition the more things are handled on the market, the less exchange is subject to restrictions, the more capitalistic the society. The economic definition, therefore, not only proscribes government interference for the benefit of the proletariat but government interference for the benefit of the bourgeoisie as well. Thus, Marx's economic definition makes capitalism incompatible with the interventionist state. On the other hand, Marx's sociological definition, the maintenance of the bourgeoisie in power, is not only compatible with the interventionist state, it requires it. For Marx argued that the market process, free competition among the capitalists, would reduce and ultimately eliminate the "rate of profit." [4] And this, in turn, means that the capitalist "ruling class" could maintain its position in the socio-economic hierarchy only by acquiring control of the state, for it would have to use the state to control the market in order to preserve, as much and for as long as possible, the "rate of profit." In short, Marx had two definitions of capitalism: an economic definition which is *incompatible* with the interventionist state and a *sociological* definition which requires such a state. The key question is: from which of the two definitions are Marx's key conclusions, such as the inevitability of a ruling class, class

[4] Marx denied that his "law of the tendency of the rate of profit to fall" logically entailed the elimination of profit. He argued that the decline in profit per unit would be offset by economic expansion. Thus, a fall in the profit rate is not logically incompatible with an increase in the "absolute mass" of profit. (See Marx 1974a, p. 216.)

I am not particularly impressed by this line of argument. Marx believed that competition would force prices to be reduced to their cost of production, thereby eliminating profit. It is clear that since (1) costs must eventually reach a point below which they cannot fall—theoretically, the ultimate end-point would be zero, and (2) Marx can give no reason why prices will not fall to this level, there is no reason, on Marxian grounds, to believe that "absolute profit" will increase even as the "rate of profit" declines.

It is true that one can construct a mathematical schedule in which falling prices approach the cost of production only asymptomatically, and in such a way that the decline in the rate of profit is more than offset by increases in the volume sold, so that absolute profit increases simultaneously with the decline in the rate of profit. This is what Marx had in mind as can be seen by citing his own example in volume III of *Capital* (1974, p. 217):

conflict, the source of profits and the impossibility of wages rising above the subsistence level, derived?

b. *Marx's View of the Capitalist Process.* Marx's account of the origin and early development of capitalism sheds a great deal of light on this question.

For Marx a landmark event was the enclosure movement of the fifteenth and sixteenth centuries. The rise in the price of wool provided the impetus for the "transformation of arable land into sheep-walks" (1906, pp. 789–90). The profit-hungry capitalistic landowners wanted to expand their landholding for pasturage. The government, now in the hands of the bourgeoisie, passed legislation enabling the favored members of the new ruling class to force off their land without compensation the "free peasant proprietors," i.e., those owning small plots. In this way the countryside was depopulated for the sake of the wool industry. Those who refused to leave

Period	Capital Investment	Profit	Rate of Profit
t-1	6	2	33.3%
t-2	18	3	16.7%

These figures give Marx's argument a seeming plausibility, but only because he terminates his illustration at this point. Its absurdity becomes immediately apparent as soon as one projects this process further into the future:

t-3	50	4	8.0%
t-4	125	5	4.0%
t-5	300	6	2.3%
t-6	700	7	1.0%
t-7	1,600	8	.5%
.			
.			
t-n	1,777,000	17	1/1000%

Clearly, any attempt to salvage Marx's attempt to reconcile the falling rate of profit with increasing absolute profit breaks down for not only does it require a rate of economic growth that is out of touch with reality, but a degree of economic irrationality on the part of the capitalists that borders on the absurd. For example, to increase their profits by a mere 15 units they must increase their investment by about 1,777,000 units.

their land "were systematically hunted and rooted out. Their villages," says Marx, "were destroyed and burnt, and all their fields turned to pasturage. British soldiers enforced this eviction" (p. 802). Further, in order to keep wage rates low, the dispossessed "were forbidden to emigrate from the country." They were driven "by force to Glasgow and other manufacturing cities" (p. 801).

In the cities laws were passed stipulating that "if anyone refuses to work he shall be condemned as a slave to the person who has denounced him as an idler. The master shall feed his slave on bread and water, weak broth and such refuse meat as he thinks fit. He has the right to force him to do any work, no matter how disgusting, with whip and chains" (p. 806). But since "the demand for wage-labor grew rapidly," says Marx, wages began to rise. To prevent this labor-statutes were passed which mandated "the compulsory extension of the working-day." Other legislation established maximum wages. "A maximum of wages is dictated by the State," says Marx, "but on no account a minimum." Employers paying in excess of the maximum received 10 days imprisonment, while those accepting them were sentenced to 21 days (pp. 810–11). Laws against "coalitions of workers" were imposed as were laws permitting "ear-clipping and branding of 'those no one was willing to take into service.'" Thus, Marx summarizes, "were the agricultural people first forcibly expropriated from the soil, driven from their homes, turned into vagabonds, and then whipped, branded, tortured by laws grotesquely terrible, into the discipline necessary for the wage system" (p. 809). It was, he concludes (p. 814) "the disgraceful action of the state which employed the police to accelerate the accumulation of capital for increasing the degree of exploitation of labor."

"The state," Marx writes in *A Contribution to a Critique of Political Economy* (1970 p. 214), "is the epitome of bourgeois society." In *The Communist Manifesto* Marx and Engels refer (1969, p. 61) to the state as nothing more than "a committee for handling the affairs of the whole bourgeoisie." The state, according to *Capital* (1906, pp. 838–48) is used by the capitalist as a battering-ram to knock down obstacles to foreign markets as well as an iron gate to keep foreign capitalists from entering the domestic markets. In brief, the state, according to Marx, is used by the bourgeoisie for "regulating wages, imposing protective duties, forcing sale of labor power, funding capitalist ventures, waging imperialist wars, and prosecuting dissidents." Simply put, it "adjusts whatever requires adjusting to perpetuate the ruling class's monopoly of ownership and extraction of surplus value" (McMurtry 1978, p. 105).

I am not concerned with whether Marx's account is historically accurate, but with the nature of the process as he describes it. It is abundantly clear that this account has precious little to do with "free trade, free buying and selling." It has little to do with the market. It is an account of how the bourgeoisie, by its use of the state, was able to entrench itself in power and institutionalize its economic and political position by recourse to naked force. It is an account of how the bourgeoisie relied not on the market but on the state to keep itself wealthy by keeping the poor poor. What Marx is using here is not his formal economic definition but his implicit sociological definition.

c. *Wages, Profits and Class Conflict.* Marx, as Schumpeter points out (p. 18), looks on classes as separated by an unbridgeable gulf. He assumes a "water-tight division between people who (together with their descendants) are supposed to be capitalists once and for all and others who (together with their descendants) are supposed to be proletarians once and for all." This is, as Schumpeter observes, "utterly unrealistic" in historical fact because the "salient point about social classes is the incessant rise and fall of individual families into and out of the upper strata." But it is also not derivable from Marx's own formal, economic definition of capitalism.

Marx acknowledged that "if capital is growing rapidly, wages may rise" (Arnhart 1987, p. 320). He also recognized (1972b, p. 23) that wages were high in the capitalistic United States, even despite "the wave of immigration from Europe [which] throws men on the labor market there more rapidly than the wave of immigration to the west can wash them away." And, according to Marx's own account of the origin of capitalism, wages were beginning to rise in Europe because of competition among the capitalists for available labor. This process was reversed by the intervention of the state. But what is important is that Marx can give no convincing reason why, *on the free market*, wages cannot rise above the subsistence level. And if this is the case he cannot provide any reason why there cannot be movement not only down but also up the economic ladder. If the market is free and wages begin to rise above the subsistence level why isn't it possible for some workers to save some of their income and either individually or in combination with others, invest their savings or use them to open a small business? And if that is the case, why isn't it possible for that small business to grow into a large business? Marx never considers this a possibility. But it can be regarded as impossible only if it is assumed that, to prevent the increased competition which would force prices down, thereby jeopardizing both the economic and the political positions of the ruling class, the bourgeoisie would turn to their "executive committee," the state, to impose whatever measures were necessary to quash the challenge to their position. According to Marx's account of the early days of capitalism, this is precisely what the bourgeoisie did. Thus, Marx is forced to abandon his explicit, economic, definition and rely on his implicit, sociological definition in order to obtain the conclusion he wants.

What is significant about this is that it means that, *even on Marxian assumptions*, the source of class conflict is not the market but the state. On occasion Marx refers, as already noted, to the shortage of laborers and the consequent rise in wages. This is a market relationship. Employers would only pay higher wages because they, like the workers accepting the higher pay, gain from the exchange. It is a voluntary exchange for the mutual benefit of both parties. But the rise, says Marx, is prevented and wages are forced back down not by the process of the market but by the intervention of the state. In *The Communist Manifesto* Marx and Engels note (1969, p. 73) that the "organization of the proletarians into a class . . . is continually being upset by the competition among workers themselves." And in *Capital* Marx says that the competition between capitalists forces them to lower prices, thereby driving each other out of business. "One capitalist always kills many" (1906, p. 836). Thus, even according to Marx it is competition between workers on the market that reduces wages, thereby benefitting the capitalists. But it is competition between capitalists on the market that not only reduces prices for the benefit of the consumers but raises wages for the benefit of the workers. Clearly, if there is conflict it is not conflict *between* classes but rather *within* classes. There is cooperation, or harmony, *between* classes. And, even on Marxian grounds, this intra-class competition is transformed into conflict *between* classes only through the intervention of the state. Once again, Marx can arrive at his desired conclusion that class conflict is endemic in capitalism only by resorting to his implicit definition.

Finally, it should be noted that Marx maintains that a class is only "really" a class when it is conscious of its existence, i.e., "when it carries on a common battle against another class" (Ossowski 1973b, p. 84 n). Perhaps the supreme irony is that since, according to Marx's own analysis, there is no means on the free market to prevent movement between classes, and since, again using the logic of Marx's own analysis, the free market is characterized by harmony *between* classes, this means that, according to Marx's own comments about the nature of classes, free market capitalism would have to be classified as a "classless society."

In brief, not only is Marx unable to derive any of his key conclusions—subsistence wages, permanent classes, (or, more accurately, castes), class conflict, or even, given his belief that free competition forces the rate of profit to fall, profits—from his formal economic definition, his economic definition leads to the opposite conclusions: rising wages, movement between classes, class harmony and mutually beneficial exchange. Thus, although Marx formally defines capitalism in terms of the free market, which proscribes government intervention, he in fact relies for his analysis almost entirely on his implicit, sociological definition which requires massive state intervention. It is precisely this intervention which is the source, even on Marxian grounds, for his key conclusions regarding the nature of the capitalist system.

Conclusion

Science, according to Marx, is the tool which enables one to distinguish appearance from reality, the superficial from the essence. Marx prided himself on his ability to distinguish surface appearances from their underlying essences. Yet nowhere more than in his analysis of capitalism is Marx's failure to live up to his own view of science more conspicuous. For Marx, mercantilism, like capitalism, was based on exchange relationships, on buying and selling. Because of his inability to penetrate beneath these surface appearances he was unable to perceive that there was a fundamental difference between free and restricted exchange; he was unable to distinguish between the effects of the market process, itself, and the effects of government imposed restrictions on that process. The result of this failure is nothing short of astounding. His fabled "contradictions of capitalism" are not contradictions but, for the most part, confusions stemming from his own incompatible definitions of capitalism. But, more importantly, Marx's sociological definition is identical to what is normally meant by mercantilism. This means that Marx's critique of capitalism is not a critique of capitalism at all. It is a critique of mercantilism. In fact, Marx devoted his entire life to critiquing under the name of capitalism precisely what Adam Smith and other early English and French classical liberals criticized under the name of mercantilism almost a century before.

David Osterfeld

References

Armantano, D. T. *The Myths of Antitrust*. New Rochelle, New York: Arlington House, 1972.

Arnhart, Larry. *Political Questions: Political Philosophy from Plato to Rawls*. New York: Macmillan, 1987.

Bober, M. M. *Karl Marx's Interpretation of History*. New York: Norton, 1948.

Bottomore, Tom. "Introduction," 1973a. In *Karl Marx*. Tom Bottomore, ed. New York: Spectrum, 1973, pp. 1–42.

——. Ed. *Karl Marx*. New York: Spectrum, 1973b.

——. Ed. *A Dictionary of Marxist Thought*. Cambridge: Harvard University Press, 1983.

Bottomore, Tom and Maximillien Rubel, eds. *Karl Marx, Selected Writings in Sociology and Social Philosophy*. London: Watts, 1961.

Dobb, Maurice. *Soviet Economic Development Since 1917*. New York: International Publishers, 1948.

Dunn, Stephen. *The Fall and Rise of the Asiatic Mode of Production*. London: Routledge and Kegan Paul, 1982.

Engels, Frederick. *The Origin of the Family, Private Property and the State*. New York: International Publishers, 1942.

——. *Anti-Dühring*. New York: International Publishers, 1972a.

——. *Socialism: Utopian and Scientific*. New York: International Publishers, 1972b.

Farbman, Michael. *Bolshevism in Retreat*. London: Collin's, 1937.

Hayek, F. A. *Studies in Philosophy, Politics and Economics*. New York: Simon and Schuster, 1969.

Heilbroner, Robert. *The Worldly Philosophers*. New York: Simon and Schuster, 1972.

Himmelwait, Susan. "Mode of Production." In *A Dictionary of Marxist Thought*. Tom Bottomore, ed. Cambridge: Harvard University Press, 1983 pp. 335–37.

Hobsbawm, E. J. "Introduction." In *Pre-Capitalist Economic Foundations*. Karl Marx. New York: Publishers, 1964, pp. 9–65.

Hofstadter, Richard. *The American Political Tradition*. New York: Vintage, 1948.

Hook, Sidney. *Marx and the Marxists*. New York: Van Nostrand, 1955.

Hutchison, T. W. "Some Themes from Investigations into Method." In *Carl Menger and the Austrian School of Economics*. J. R. Hicks and W. Weber, eds. London: Oxford University Press, 1973, pp. 15–37.

Kiernan, V. G. "Stages of Development." In *A Dictionary of Marxist Thought*. Tom Bottomore, ed. Cambridge: Harvard University Press, 1983, pp. 458–60.

Kolko, Gabriel. *The Triumph of Conservatism*. Chicago: Quadrangle, 1967.

Lachmann, Ludwig. "The Science of Human Action." *Economica*. (November, 1951): 412–27.

Lacy, Mary. "Food Control During Forty-Six Centuries." Address Before the Agricultural History Society. Washington, D. C., March 16, 1922.

Lenin, V. I. *Selected Works*, 3 vol. New York: International Publishers, 1967.

Leontyev, L. *A Short Course of Political Economy*. Moscow: Progress Publishers, 1968.

Lichtheim, George. "Marx and the Asiatic Mode of Production," In *Karl Marx*. Tom Bottomore, ed. Cambridge: Harvard University Press, 1973, pp. 151–71.

Lowenthal, Richard. "Karl Marx: Scholar, Prophet, Politician." *Encounter* (1984): 31–38.

Mandel, Ernest. *The Foundation of the Economic Thought of Karl Marx*. New York: Monthly Review Press, 1971.

Marx, Karl. *Capital*, Vol. 1. New York: Modern Library, 1906.

——. *Pre-Capitalist Economic Formations*. New York: International Publishers, 1964.

——. *A Contribution to the Critique of Political Economy*. Moscow: Progress Publishers, 1970.

——. *The Grundrisse*. New York: Harper and Row, 1971.

——. *Critique of the Gotha Programme*. Peking: Foreign Language Press, 1972a.

——. *On America and the Civil War*. New York: McGraw-Hill, 1972b.

——. *The Economic and Philosophic Manuscripts*. New York: International Publishers, 1973a.

——. *Wages, Price and Profit*. Peking: Foreign Language Press, 1973b.

——. *Capital*, Vol. III. New York: International Publishers, 1974a.

——. *On Freedom of the Press and Censorship*. New York: McGraw-Hill, 1974b.

Marx, Karl and Frederick Engels. *The German Ideology*. New York: International Publishers, 1947.

———. *The Communist Manifesto*. New York: Washington Square Press, 1969.

Marx, Engels and Lenin on Scientific Communism. Moscow: Progress Publishers, 1967.

McMurtry, John. *The Structure of Marx's World-View*. Princeton: Princeton University Press, 1978.

Mises, Ludwig von. *The Anti-Capitalistic Mentality*. New York: Van Nostrand, 1956.

———. *The Ultimate Foundation of Economic Science*. New York: Van Nostrand, 1962.

———. *Human Action*. Chicago: Henry Regnery, 1966.

———. *Socialism: An Economic and Sociological Analysis*. London: Jonathan Cape, 1969a.

———. *Planning For Freedom*. South Holland, Ill.: Libertarian Press, 1969b.

———. *Theory and History*. New Rochelle: Arlington House, 1969c.

———. *The Clash of Group Interests and Other Essays*. New York: Center for Libertarian Studies, 1978.

Mosher, Stephen. *Broken Earth*. New York: Free Press, 1983.

Olson, Mancur. *The Logic of Collective Action*. Cambridge: Harvard University Press, 1977.

Ossowski, Stanislaw. "The Marxian Synthesis." In *Karl Marx*. Tom Bottomore, ed. New York: Spectrum, 1973, pp. 79–92.

Osterfeld, David. "The Free Market and the 'Tyranny of Wealth'." *The Freeman*. December 1976, pp. 749–56.

———. "Resources, People and the NeoMalthusian Fallacy." *Cato Journal*. (Spring/Summer 1985): 967–102.

———. "Voluntary and Coercive Cartels: The Case of Oil." *The Freeman*. November 1987, pp. 415–25.

———. "'Social Utility' and Government Transfers of Wealth: An Austrian Perspective." *Review of Austrian Economics*. Vol. 2 (1988): 78–96.

Popkin, Samuel. *The Rational Peasant*. Berkeley: University of California Press, 1979.

Popper, Karl. *The Poverty of Historicism*. London: Routledge and Kegan Paul, 1957.

———. *The Open Society and Its Enemies*, Vol. 2. *Hegel and Marx*. Princeton University Press, 1966.

Rosenberg, Nathan and Birdzell, L. E. *How the West Grew Rich*. New York: Basic Books, 1986.

Roberts, Paul and Stephenson, Matthew. *Marx's Theory of Exchange Alienation and Crisis*. Stanford, Calif.: Hoover Institution Press, 1973.

Rothbard, Murray N. "Toward a Reconstruction of Utility and Welfare Economics." In *On Freedom and Free Enterprise*. Mary Sennholz, ed. Princeton: Van Nostrand, 1956, pp. 224–49.

——. "In Defense of 'Extreme Apriorism'." *Southern Economic Review* (January 1957): 314–20.

——. "Money, the State, and Modern Mercantilism. In *Central Planning and Neomercantilism*. Helmut Schoeck and James Wiggins, eds. New York: Van Nostrand, 1964, pp. 138–54.

——. *Man, Economy, and State*. Los Angeles: Nash, 1970a.

——. *Power and Market*. Menlo Park, Calif.: Institute for Humane Studies, 1970b.

——. "Praxeology and the Method of Economics." In *Phenomenology and the Social Sciences*. Maurice Natanson, ed. Evanston, Ill.: Northwestern University Press, 1973, Vol. II, pp. 311–42.

Selsam, Howard, Goldway, David, and Maltel, Harry, eds. *Dynamics of Social Change, A Reader in Marxist Social Science*. New York: International Publishers, 1970.

Shaw, William. "Mode of Production," In *A Dictionary of Marxist Thought*. Tom Bottomore, ed. Cambridge: Harvard University Press, 1983, pp. 335–37.

Schumpeter, Joseph. *Capitalism Socialism and Democracy*. New York: Harper and Row, 1975.

Simon, Julian. *The Ultimate Resource*. Princeton: University of Princeton Press, 1981.

Simon, Julian and Kahn, Herman, eds. *The Resourceful Earth*. New York: Basil Blackwell, 1984.

Sowell, Thomas. *Ethnic America*. New York: Basic, 1981.

——. *Marxism: Philosophy and Economics*. New York: William Morrow, 1985.

Turner, Ryan. "Asiatic Society." In *A Dictionary of Marxist Thought*. Tom Bottomore, ed. Cambridge: Harvard University Press, 1983, pp. 32–36

Viner, Jacob. "Mercantilist Thought." *International Encyclopedia of the Social Sciences*. New York: Macmillan, 1968, Vol. 4, pp. 435–43.

White, A. D. *Fiat Money Inflation in France*. Caldwell, Idaho: Caxton, 1969.

Wilczynski, Joseph. *An Encyclopedic Dictionary of Marxism, Socialism and Communism*. London: Macmillan, 1981.

Wittfogel, Karl. "The Marxist View of Russian Society and Revolution." *World Politics* (July 1960): 487–508.

~ 5 ~

Classical Liberal Roots of the Marxist Doctrine of Classes

Ralph Raico

F ew ideas are as closely associated with Marxism as the concepts of class and class conflict. It is, for instance, impossible to imagine what a Marxist philosophy of history or a Marxist revolutionary theory would be in their absence. Yet, as with much else in Marxism, these concepts remain ambiguous and contradictory.[1] For instance, while Marxist doctrine supposedly grounds classes in the process of production, *The Communist Manifesto* asserts in its famous opening lines:

> The history of all hitherto existing society is the history of class struggles. Freeman and slave, patrician and plebeian, lord and serf, guild-master and journeyman, in a word, oppressor and oppressed, stood in constant opposition to one another . . .[2]

---

[1]"The concept of class has a central importance in Marxist theory, though neither Marx nor Engels ever expounded it in a systematic form." Tom Bottomore, "Class," in idem, ed., *A Dictionary of Marxist Thought* (Cambridge, Mass.: Harvard University Press, 1983), p. 74; cf. another contemporary Marxist theoretician, Charles Bettelheim, "Reflections on Concepts of Class and Class Struggle in Marx's Work," trans. Carole Biewener, in Stephen Resnick and Richard Wolff, eds., *Rethinking Marxism: Struggles in Marxist Theory. Essays for Harry Magdoff and Paul Sweezy* (Brooklyn, N.Y.: Autonomedia, 1985), p. 22: Marx "did not arrive at a unique and coherent conception of classes and of class struggles."

[2]Karl Marx and Friedrich Engels, *Selected Works in Three Volumes* (Moscow: Progress Publishers, 1983), I, pp. 108–9.

On examination these opposed pairs turn out to be, either wholly or in part, not economic, but legal, categories.[3]

Neither Marx nor Engels ever resolved the contradictions and ambiguities in their theory in this area. The last chapter of the third and final volume of *Capital*, published posthumously in 1894, is titled, "Classes."[4] Here Marx states: "The first question to be answered is this: What constitutes a class?" "At first glance" it would seem to be "the identity of revenue and sources of revenue." That, however, Marx finds inadequate, since "from this standpoint, physicians and officials, e.g., would also constitute two classes . . ." Distinct classes would also be yielded by

> the infinite fragmentation of interest [sic] and rank into which the division of social labor splits laborers as well as capitalists and landlords—the latter, e.g., into owners of vineyards, farm owners, owners of forests, mine owners and owners of fisheries.

At this point, there is a note by Engels: "Here the manuscript breaks off." This was not on account of Marx's sudden demise, however. The chapter dates from a first draft composed by Marx between 1863 and 1867, that is, sixteen to twenty years before his death.[5] Engels's explanation is that "Marx used to leave such concluding summaries until the final editing, just before going to press, when the latest historical developments furnished him with unfailing regularity with proofs of the most laudable timeliness for his theoretical propositions."[6] This explanation would be more convincing if in the intervening years before his death Marx had elsewhere provided a clear definition of classes consistent with the other parts of his theory.

---

[3]Cf. Ludwig von Mises, *Theory and History: An Interpretation of Social and Economic Evolution* (New Haven: Yale University Press, 1957), p. 113: "Marx obfuscated the problem by confusing the notions of caste and class."

[4]Karl Marx, *Capital: A Critique of Political Economy*, III, *The Process of Capitalist Production as a Whole*, Friedrich Engels, ed. (New York: International Publishers, 1967), pp. 885–86.

[5]Ibid., Friedrich Engels, "Preface," p. 3.

[6]Ibid., p. 7.

But whatever the defects of the Marxist concept of classes and of conflicts among them, it remains the case that Marxism is so closely identified with these ideas that an important fact is often lost sight of: not only was the notion of class conflict a commonplace for decades before Marx began to write, but a quite different theory of class conflict had been worked out which itself played a role in the genealogy of Marx's ideas.

Marxism and the Classical Liberal Doctrine

Adolphe Blanqui was the protégé of Jean-Baptiste Say and succeeded him in the chair of political economy at the Conservatoire des Arts et Métiers. In what is probably the first history of economic thought, published in 1837, Blanqui wrote:

> In all the revolutions, there have always been but two parties opposing each other; that of the people who wish to live by their own labor, and that of those who would live by the labor of others. . . . *Patricians and plebeians, slaves and freemen, guelphs and ghibellines, red roses and white roses, cavaliers and roundheads, liberals and serviles, are only varieties of the same species.*[7]

Blanqui quickly makes clear what he understands to have been at issue in these social struggles:

> So, in one country, it is through taxes that the fruit of the laborer's toil is wrested from him, under pretense of the good of the state; in another, it is by privileges, declaring labor a royal concession, and making one pay dearly for the right to devote himself to it. The same abuse is reproduced under more indirect, but no less oppressive, forms, when, by means of

---

[7]Jérôme-Adolphe Blanqui, *Histoire de l'Économie Politique en Europe depuis les anciens jusqu'à nos jours* (Paris: Guillaumin, 1837), p. x. (Italics in original.) Ernst Nolte, *Marxismus und Industrielle Revolution* (Stuttgart: Klett-Cotta, 1983), p. 599, 79n, notes that Engels attacked Blanqui's "miserable history of economics" in a newspaper article shortly before he composed the *Principles of Communism*, which Marx drew upon in composing the *Manifesto*. The *Principles*, however, contains nothing similar to the opening lines of the first section of the *Manifesto*; cf. *The Communist Manifesto of Karl Marx and Friedrich Engels*, D. Ryazanoff, ed. (1930; repr., New York: Russell and Russell, 1963), pp. 319–40.

custom-duties, the state shares with the privileged industries the benefits of the taxes imposed on all those who are not privileged.[8]

Blanqui was by no means the originator of this liberal analysis of the conflict of classes; rather, he drew on a perspective that was widespread in liberal circles in the first decades of the nineteenth century. Marx and Engels were aware of the existence of at least some forms of this earlier notion. In a letter written in 1852 to his follower, Joseph Weydemeyer, the first exponent of Marxism in the United States,[9] Marx asserts:

> no credit is due to me for discovering the existence of classes in modern society or the struggle between them. Long before me bourgeois historians had described the historical development of this class struggle and bourgeois economists the economic anatomy of the classes.[10]

The two most prominent "bourgeois historians" whom he names are the Frenchmen, François Guizot and Augustin Thierry[11]; two years later, Marx referred to Thierry as "the father of the 'class struggle' in French historiography."[12]

This "bourgeois" lineage of the Marxist theory was freely

[8]Blanqui, *Histoire*, pp. x–xi.

[9]Marx to J. Weydemeyer, March 5, 1852, Karl Marx and Friedrich Engels, *Selected Correspondence* (Moscow: Progress Publishers, 1965), pp. 67–70.

[10]Ibid., p. 69. Marx here states that his own contributions are limited to having shown that classes are not a permanent feature of human society, and that the class struggle will lead to the dictatorship of the proletariat and thence to a classless society. Charles Bettelheim, "Reflections on Concepts of Class," p. 16, agrees with Marx on this point: "Lacking these elements ["polarization, historical tendency, final result"] we are faced with a conception already long defended by numerous historians who recognize the existence of class struggles and their action upon the course of history."

[11]The third is the much less significant English writer, John Wade. Later in the letter, Marx refers to the economists, Richardo, Malthus, Mill, Say, et al., who have revealed how the "economic bases of the different classes are bound to give rise to a necessary and ever-growing antagonism among them." Marx and Engels, *Selected Correspondence*, p. 69. It is worth noting that in the same letter, Marx ridicules the view of "the fatuous [Karl] Heinzen," that "the existence of classes [is connected with] the existence of political *privileges* and *monopolies* . . ." Ibid., emphasis in original.

[12]Marx to Engels, July 27, 1854, *Selected Correspondence*, p. 87.

conceded by Marx's immediate followers. Towards the end of his life, Engels suggested that so little did individuals count in history, as compared to the great underlying social forces, that even in the absence of Marx himself, "the materialist conception of history" would have been discovered by others; his evidence is that "Thierry, Mignet, Guizot, and all the English historians up to 1850" were striving towards it.[13] Franz Mehring, Plekhanov, and and other scholars of Marxism in the period of the Second International emphasized the roots of the Marxist class conflict doctrine in the liberal historiography of the French Restoration.[14] Lenin, too, credited "the bourgeoisie," not Marx, with having originated the theory of the class struggle.[15]

Sources of *Industrialisme*

Of the French historians mentioned, only Augustin Thierry had delved deeply into the subject and had, in fact, participated in shaping a coherent, radical-liberal analysis of classes and class

---

[13]Engels to H. Starkenburg, January 25, 1894, *Selected Correspondence*, p. 468.

[14]In his classic biography of Marx, Franz Mehring traces this conception to Marx's period in Paris in 1843–44: "The study of the French Revolution led him on to the historical literature of the 'Third Estate,' a literature which originated under the Bourbon restoration and was developed by men of great historical talent who followed the historical existence of their class back into the eleventh century and presented French history as an uninterrupted series of class struggles. Marx owed his knowledge of the historical nature of classes and their struggles to these historians . . . Marx always denied having originated the theory of the class struggle." Franz Mehring, *Karl Marx: The Story of His Life*, (1918) Edward Fitzgerald, trans. (Ann Arbor: University of Michigan Press, 1962), p. 75. David McLellan telescopes the process described by Mehring when he states, in *Karl Marx: His Life and Thought* (New York: Harper and Row, 1973), p. 95: "It was his [Marx's] reading of the history of the French Revolution in the summer of 1843 that showed him the role of class struggle in social development." Neither Guizot nor Thierry concentrated on the Revolution in their works; in any case, it is their emphasis on class struggle as a constant spanning centuries of medieval and modern history that is reflected in the Marxian account.

[15]V. I. Lenin, *State and Revolution* (1917) (New York: International Publishers, 1943), p. 30: "The theory of the class struggle was *not* created by Marx, but by the bourgeoisie *before* Marx and is, generally speaking, *acceptable* to the bourgeoisie." (Italics in original.) The last part of Lenin's statement, however, is problematical.

conflict. The purpose of this paper is to sketch the background and content of this original analysis and to discuss various points that arise in connection with it. The possibility that it might prove superior to Marxism as an instrument for interpreting social and political history will also be canvassed.

Liberal class conflict theory emerged in a polished form in France, in the period of the Bourbon Restoration, following the final defeat and exile of Napoleon. From 1817 to 1819, two young liberal intellectuals, Charles Comte and Charles Dunoyer, edited the journal, *Le Censeur Européen*; beginning with the second volume (issue), Augustin Thierry collaborated closely with them. The *Censeur Européen* developed and disseminated a radical version of liberalism, one that continued to influence liberal thought up to the time of Herbert Spencer and beyond. It can be viewed as a core-constituent—and thus one of the historically defining elements—of authentic liberalism.[16] In this sense, a consideration of the world-view of the *Censeur Européen* is of great importance in helping to give shape and content to the protean concept, "liberalism." Moreover, through Henri de Saint-Simon and his followers and through other channels, it had an impact on socialist thought as well. Comte and Dunoyer called their doctrine *Industrialisme*, Industrialism.[17]

---

[16]See Ralph Raico, "Review Essay: *The Rise and Decline of Western Liberalism*," *Reason Papers* 14 (Spring 1989): 163–64.

[17]Leonard P. Liggio has had the merit of recognizing the significance of the Industrialist writers and pioneering the study of their thought in recent years; see his highly important article, "Charles Dunoyer and French Classical Liberalism," *Journal of Libertarian Studies* 1, no. 3 (1977): 153–78 (the scope of which is considerably wider than is suggested by the title) and the relevant works cited in the endnotes, as well as, idem, "The Concept of Liberty in 18th and 19th Century France," *Journal des Économistes et des Études Humaines* 1, no. 1 (Spring, 1990), and idem, *Charles Dunoyer and the Censeur: A Study in French Liberalism* (forthcoming); also, Charles Dunoyer, "Notice Historique sur l'Industrialisme," *Oeuvres de Charles Dunoyer* 3, *Notices de l'Économie Sociale* (Paris: Guillaumin, 1880), pp. 173–199; Ephraïm Harpaz, "'Le Censeur Européen': Histoire d'un Journal Industrialiste," *Revue d'Histoire Économique et Sociale* 37, no. 2 (1959): 185-218, and 37, no. 3 (1959): 328-357; Élie Halévy, "The Economic Doctrine of Saint-Simon," (1907), in *The Era of Tyrannies: Essays on Socialism and War*, R. K. Webb, trans. (Garden City, N.Y.: Anchor/Doubleday, 1965), pp. 21–60; Edgard Allix, "J.-B. Say et les origines d'industrialisme," *Revue d'Économie Politique* 24 (1910): 304–13, 341–62.

There were several major sources of Industrialism. One was Antoine Destutt de Tracy, the last and most famous of the Idéologue school of French liberals, whose friend, Thomas Jefferson, arranged for the translation and publication of his *Treatise on Political Economy* in the United States before it appeared in France.[18] Tracy's definition of society was crucial:

> Society is purely and solely a continual series of exchanges. It is never anything else, in any epoch of its duration, from its commencement the most unformed, to its greatest perfection. And this is the greatest eulogy we can give to it, for exchange is an admirable transaction, in which the two contracting parties always both gain; consequently, society is an uninterrupted succession of advantages, unceasingly renewed for all its members.[19]

Tracy's position was that "commerce is society itself. . . . It is an attribute of man. . . . It is the source of all human good . . ."[20] For Tracy, in the words of a student of his thought, commerce was a "panacea," "the world's civilizing, rationalizing, and pacifying force."[21]

Comte, Dunoyer, and Augustin Thierry and his brother Amédée were frequent guests at Tracy's salon in the rue d'Anjou, a center of liberal social life in Paris. Here the young liberal intellectuals mingled with Stendhal, Benjamin Constant, Lafayette, and others.[22]

---

[18]What appealed to Jefferson was Tracy's condemnation of government squandering of social wealth through public debt, taxation, banking monopolies, and spending, which paralleled his own anti-Hamiltonian views. Emmet Kennedy, *A Philosophe in the Age of Revolution: Destutt de Tracy and the Origins of "Ideology,"* (Philadelphia: American Philosophical Society, 1978), p. 228.

[19]Antoine Destutt de Tracy, *A Treatise on Political Economy*, Thomas Jefferson, ed. (1817; New York: Augustus M. Kelley, 1970), p. 6.

[20]Emmet Kennedy, *A Philosophe in the Age of Revolution*, p. 180. This leads Kennedy to refer mistakenly to Tracy's position as a form of "economic determinism."

[21]Ibid., p. 183.

[22]Ibid., pp. 270–72. At a later point, Kennedy refers to Augustin Thierry and Dunoyer as among Destutt de Tracy's "old friends"; ibid., p. 290. See also Cheryl B. Welch, *Liberty and Utility: The French Idéologues and the Transformation of Liberalism* (New York: Columbia University Press, 1984), pp. 157–158. Augustin Thierry, in his review of Tracy's *Commentaire sur L'Esprit des Lois de Montesquieu*, states: "the principles of the Commentaire are also ours." *Censeur Européen* 7 (1818): 220.

Constant's work, *De l'esprit de conquête et de l'usurpa-tion*, which appeared in 1813, is another major source of Industrialist thought. Dunoyer credits Constant with being the first to distinguish sharply between modern and ancient civilization, thus opening up the question of the distinctive aim of modern civilization and the form of organization appropriate to that aim.[23] From the reactionary author Montlosier was derived the view of the importance of conquest in the social predominance of the nobility over the commoners. The liberal reaction against the militarism and despotism of the Napoleonic period also played a part.[24]

The Role of Jean-Baptiste Say

There is little doubt, however, that the chief influence on Industrialism was Jean-Baptiste Say's *Traité de l'économie politique*, the second edition of which appeared in 1814 and the third in 1817.[25] Comte and Dunoyer probably became personally acquainted with Say during the Hundred Days, in the spring of 1815. Together with Thierry, they were participants at Say's salon.[26] (Comte later became Say's son-in-law.) The third edition of Say's *Traité* was accorded a two-part review of over 120 pages in the *Censeur Européen*.[27]

Say held that wealth is comprised of what has value, and value is based on utility.

> [The different ways of producing] all consist in taking a product in one state and putting it into another in which it has more utility and value . . . in one way or another, from

[23]Charles Dunoyer, "Notice Historique," pp. 175–76; Ephraïm Harpaz, "'Le Censeur Européen'": 197.

[24]Allix, "J-B. Say et les origines de l'industrialisme": 305.

[25]Ibid. Michael James, "Pierre-Louis Roederer, Jean-Baptiste Say, and the Concept of Industry," *History of Political Economy* 9, no. 4 (Winter 1977): 455–75, argues for Say's indebtedness to the Idéologue Roederer for some important concepts, but grants that it was Say who directly and powerfully influenced the *Censeur Européen* group.

[26]Harpaz, "'Le Censeur Europen'": 204–05.

[27]*Censeur Européen* 1 (1817): 159–227; 2 (1817): 169–221.

the moment that one creates or augments the utility of things, one augments their value, one is exercising an industry, one is producing wealth.[28]

All those members of society who contribute to the creation of values are deemed productive, but Say awards pride of place to the entrepreneur. Say was one of the first to realize the boundless possibilities of a free economy, led by creative entrepreneurs. As one commentator summarizes his message:

> The productive power of industry is limited only by ignorance and by the bad administration of states. Spread enlightenment and improve governments, or, rather, prevent them from doing harm; there will be no limit that can be assigned to the multiplication of wealth.[29]

There exist, however, categories of persons who merely consume wealth rather than produce it. These unproductive classes include the army, the government, and the state-supported clergy[30]—what could be called the "reactionary" classes, associated by and large with the Old Regime.

However, Say was quite aware that anti-productive and anti-social activity was also possible, indeed, altogether common, when otherwise productive elements employed state power to capture privileges:

> But personal interest is no longer a safe criterion, if individual interests are not left to counteract and control each other. If one individual, or one class, can call in the aid of authority to ward off the effects of competition, it acquires a privilege and at the cost of the whole community; it can then make sure of profits not altogether due to the productive services rendered, but composed in part of an actual tax upon consumers for its private

[28]Jean-Baptiste Say, *Cathéchisme d'Économie Politique, ou Instruction Familière* (Paris: Crapelet, 1815), p. 14.

[29]Allix, "J.-B. Say et les origines de l'industrialisme,": 309. Cf. Harpaz, "'Le Censeur Européen'": 356: "The immense progress of modern material civilization is sketched, or at the very least suggested, in the twelve volumes of the *Censeur Européen.*"

[30]Allix, "J.-B. Say et les origines de l'industrialisme": 341–44.

profit;whichtaxit commonly shares with the authority that thus unjustly lends its support. The legislative body has great difficulty in resisting the importunate demands for this kind of privileges; *the applicants are the producers that are to benefit thereby, who can represent, with much plausibility, that their own gains are a gain to the industrious classes, and to the nation at large, their workmen and themselves being members of the industrious classes, and of the nation.*[31]

Thus, while there was a harmony of interest among producers (between employers and workers, for instance), a natural conflict of interests obtained between producers and non-producers, as well as between those members of the producing classes when they choose to exploit others through government-granted privilege. As one scholar has put it, the cry of Say—and of his disciples—could be, "Producers of the world, unite!"[32]

Social Philosophy of the *Censeur Européen*

The essential achievement of Comte, Dunoyer, and Thierry in the *Censeur Européen* was to have taken the ideas of Say and other earlier liberals and forged them into a fighting creed.[33]

---

[31]Jean-Baptiste Say, *A Treatise on Political Economy, or the Production, Distribution, and Consumption of Wealth*, C. R. Prinsep, trans. from 4th ed. (1880; New York: Augustus M. Kelley, 1964), pp. 146–47 (emphasis supplied). It has been persuasively argued that Say was an important source for the modern theory of "rent-seeking"; Patricia J. Euzent and Thomas L. Martin, "Classical Roots of the Emerging Theory of Rent Seeking: the Contribution of Jean-Baptiste Say," *History of Political Economy* 16, no. 2 (Summer 1984): 255–62. As Euzent and Martin point out, Say was familiar with why "those engaged in any particular branch of trade are so anxious to have themselves made the subject of regulation . . ." *Treatise*, pp. 176–77.

[32]Allix, "J.-B. Say et les origines de l'industrialisme": 312.

[33]As Dunoyer, "Notice historique," p. 179, put it: "If it is doubtful that these writers had perceived the political consequences of their observations relative to industry, these observations cast a new light upon politics that was singularly favorable to its progress. Their writings fell into the hands of several men who were making this science their special study, and effected a revolution in their ideas. Such was notably the effect that these writings produced in the authors of the *Censeur*."

Industrialism purports to be a general theory of society. Taking as its starting point man, who acts in order to satisfy his needs and desires, it posits that the purpose of society is the creation of "utility" in the widest sense: the goods and services useful to man in the satisfaction of his needs and desires. In striving to meet his needs, man has three alternative means available: he may take advantage of what nature offers spontaneously (this is pertinent only in rather primitive circumstances); he may plunder the wealth that others have produced; or he may labor to produce wealth himself.[34]

In any given society, a sharp distinction may be drawn between those who live by plunder and those who live by production. The first are characterized in several ways by Comte and Dunoyer; they are "the idle," "the devouring," and "the hornets." The second, are termed, among other things, "the industrious" and "the bees."[35] To attempt to live without producing is to live "as savages." The producers are "the civilized men."[36]

Cultural evolution has been such that whole societies may be designated as primarily plundering and idle, or as productive and industrious. Industrialism is thus not only an analysis of social dynamics, but also a theory of historical development. Indeed, much of Industrialist theory is embedded in its account of historical evolution.

The "Industrialist Manifesto"

The history of all hitherto existing society is the history of struggles between the plundering and the producing classes. Following Constant, plunder through warfare is said to have been the method favored by the ancient Greeks and Romans. With the decline of the Roman Empire in the West, Germanic

[34]Charles Comte, "Considérations sur l'état moral de la nation française, et sur les causes de l'instabilité de ses institutions," *Censeur Européen* 1: 1–2, 9. The similarity to Franz Oppenheimer's analysis is obvious. See his *The State*, John Gitterman, trans., and C. Hamilton, intro. (New York: Free Life, 1975).

[35]Charles Comte, "Considérations sur l'état moral," *Censeur Européen 1: 11.*

[36]Ibid.: 19.

barbarians established themselves, through conquest, as the lords of the land: feudalism developed—especially in France, after the Frankish invasion and in England after the Norman conquest. It was essentially a system for the spoliation of domestic peasants by the warrior elite of "noblemen."[37] Under feudalism, there was

> a kind of subordination that subjected the laboring men to the idle and devouring men, and which gave to the latter the means of existing without producing anything, or of living nobly.[38]

Throughout the Middle Ages, the nobility exploited not only its own peasants, but especially the merchants who passed through their territories. The nobles' castles were nothing but thieves' dens.[39] With the rise of the towns in the eleventh century, one may even speak of "two nations" sharing the soil of France: the plundering feudal elite and the productive commoners of the towns.

To the rapacious nobility there eventually succeeded the equally rapacious kings, whose "thefts with violence, alterations of the coinage, bankruptcies, confiscations, hindrances to industry," are the common stuff of the history of France.[40] "When the lords were the stronger, they viewed as belonging to them everything they could lay hold of. As soon as the kings were on top, they thought and acted in the same way."[41] With the growth of the wealth produced by the commoners, or Third Estate, additional riches became available for expropriation by the parasitic classes. Comte is particularly severe on royal manipulation of money and legal tender laws, and quotes a seventeenth century writer on how "discountings [*les*

---

[37]Ibid., p. 9.

[38]Charles Comte, "De l'organisation sociale considérée dans ses rapports avec les moyens de subsistance des peuples," *Censeur Européen* 2 (1817): 22.

[39]Charles Comte, "Considérations sur l'état moral," *Censeur Européen* 1: 14. Thierry's work on the Norman conquest is already foreshadowed in this early essay of Comte's, in his attack on William the Conqueror. Ibid.: 19–20.

[40]Ibid., pp. 20–21.

[41]Ibid., p. 21.

escomptes] enriched the men of money and finance at the expense of the public."[42]

In modern times, the main types of the idle classes have been the professional soldiers, monks, the nobles, bourgeois who were ennobled, and governments.[43]

"Peace and Freedom"

A pro-peace position was central to the Industrialist point of view—indeed, the motto on the title page of each issue of the *Censeur Européen* was: *paix et liberté*—"peace and freedom."

The Industrialist attack on militarism and standing armies was savage and relentless. In a typical passage, for instance, Dunoyer states that the "production" of the standing armies of Europe has consisted in

> massacres, rapes, pillagings, conflagrations, vices and crimes, the depravation, ruin, and enslavement of the peoples; they have been the shame and scourge of civilization.[44]

Particularly anathematized were wars engendered by mercantilism, or "the spirit of monopoly . . . the pretension of each to be industrious to the exclusion of all others, exclusively to provision the others with the products of its industry."[45] In the course of a jeremiad against the imperialist foreign policy of the English, Dunoyer states, significantly:

> The result of this pretension was that the spirit of industry became a principle more hostile, more of an enemy to civilization, than the spirit of rapine itself.[46]

Monasticism, in the Industrialist view, encouraged idleness and apathy.[47] In the modern period, the nobles, no longer able

---

[42]Ibid.

[43]Charles Dunoyer, "Du systéme de l'équilibre des puissances européenes," *Censeur Européen* 1 (1817): 119–26.

[44]Ibid., p. 120.

[45]Ibid., p. 131.

[46]Ibid., p. 132.

[47]Ibid., p. 120.

to live by directly robbing the industrious, began to fill government positions, and lived by a new form of tribute, "under the name of taxes."[48] Members of the bourgeoisie who achieved noble status no longer tended to their own businesses and, in the end, had no means of subsistence but the public treasury. Finally, governments, while burdening the producers with taxes, "have very rarely furnished society with the equivalent of the values they received from it for governing."[49]

The Industrialist writers anticipated that with the greater perfectioning of society would come the ultimate triumph of their cause. Comte looked forward to "the extinction of the idle and devouring class" and to the emergence of a social order in which "the fortune of each would be nearly in direct ratio to his merit, that is, to his utility, and almost without exception, none would be destitute except the vicious and useless."[50]

State Functionaries as Exploiters

The class of contemporary exploiters that the Industrialist writers investigated more than any other was the government bureaucrats. As Comte put it:

> What must never be lost sight of is that a public functionary, in his capacity as functionary, produces absolutely nothing; that, on the contrary, he exists only on the products of the industrious class; and that he can consume nothing that has not been taken from the producers.[51]

[48]Charles Comte, "De l'organisation sociale," *Censeur Européen* 2: 33.

[49]Charles Dunoyer, "Du système de l'équilibre," *Censeur Européen* 1: 124. Dunoyer goes on to state (124): "If, in precisely rendering this service [protection of liberty and property] to them [the members of society], it makes them pay more than it is worth, more than the price at which they could obtain it for themselves, then everything it takes in addition is something truly subtracted from them, and, in this respect, it acts according to the spirit of rapine." It will be noted that Dunoyer is faced with a problem here, in so far as he assents to monopoly government with taxing powers. The same is true regarding his assertion (125) that the government, in providing security, "should not have obliged them [the citizens] to pay more than it should naturally cost [ce qu'il devrait naturellement coûter]."

[50]"Considérations sur l'état moral," *Censeur Européen*, vol. 1: 88–89.

[51]"De l'organisation sociale," *Censeur Européen*, vol. 2: 29–30.

The contribution of Industrialism to the prehistory of the theory of Public Choice has received little attention.[52] True to the Industrialist concentration on the "economic factor," Dunoyer surveyed "the influence exercised on the government by the salaries attached to the the exercise of public functions."[53] In the United States—always the model Industrialist country—official salaries, even for the president, are low. Typically, American officials receive an "indemnity" for their work, but nothing that could be called a "salary."[54] In France, on the other hand, public opinion is shocked not by the exercise of power being made into "a lucrative profession," but by its being monopolized by a single social class.[55]

Public expenditures, however, bear almost an inverse relationship to the proper functioning of government: in the United States, for instance, where government costs some 40 million francs a year, property is more secure than in England, where it costs more than 3 billion.[56] The characteristics of public employment are the reverse of those in private business. For example:

> ambition, so fertile in happy results in ordinary labor, is here a principle of ruin; and the more a public functionary wishes to progress in the profession he has taken up, the more he tends, as is natural, to raise and increase his profits, the more he becomes a burden to the society that pays him.[57]

As increasing numbers of individuals aspire to government jobs, two tendencies emerge: government power expands, and the burden of government expenditures and taxation grows. In order to satisfy the new hordes of office-seekers, the government extends its scope in all directions; it begins to concern

[52]See, however, the article by Patricia J. Euzent and Thomas L. Martin, in note 31 above.

[53]"De l'influence qu'exercent sur le gouvernement les salaires attachés à l'exercice des fonctions publiques," *Censeur Européen*, vol. 11 (1819): 75–118.

[54]Ibid., p. 77.

[55]Ibid., p. 78.

[56]Ibid., p. 80.

[57]Ibid., pp. 81–82.

itself with the people's education, health, intellectual life, and morals, sees to the adequacy of the food supply, and regulates industry, until "soon there will be no means of escape from its action for any activity, any thought, any portion" of the people's existence.[58] Functionaries have become "a class that is the enemy of the well-being of all the others."[59]

Since the enjoyment of government jobs has ceased to be the private preserve of the aristocracy, it has become the object of everyone in society.[60] In France there are perhaps "ten times as many aspirants to power than the most gigantic administration could possible accommodate. . . . Here one would easily find the personnel to govern twenty kingdoms."[61]

Similarities with Marxism

The emphasis by the *Censeur Européen* liberals on the ravenous exploitation of the productive classes by the growing class of state functionaries opens another point of contact with Marxism. As has been sometimes noted,[62] Marxism contains two rather different views of the state: most conspicuously, it views the state as the instrument of domination by exploiting classes that are defined by their position within the process of social production, e.g., the capitalists. Sometimes, however, Marx characterized the state itself as the independently exploiting agent. Thus, Marx, in *The Eighteenth Brumaire of Louis Bonaparte*, writes, quite in the Industrialist spirit:

[58]Ibid., p. 86.

[59]Ibid., p. 88.

[60]Ibid., p. 89.

[61]Ibid., p. 103.

[62]Richard N. Hunt, *The Political Ideas of Marx and Engels: I Marxism and Totalitarian Democracy, 1818–1850* (Pittsburgh: University of Pittsburgh Press, 1974), pp. 124–31; David Conway, *A Farewell to Marx: An Outline and Appraisal of his Theories* (Harmondsworth: Penguin, 1987), pp. 162–64; Ralph Raico, "Classical Liberal Exploitation Theory: A Comment on Professor Liggio's Paper," *Journal of Libertarian Studies* 1, no. 3 (1977): 179–83.

This executive power, with its enormous bureaucratic and military organization, with its ingenious state machinery, embracing wide strata, with a host of officials numbering half a million, besides an army of another half million, with appalling parasitic body, which enmeshes the body of French society like a net and chokes all its pores, sprang up in the days of the absolute monarchy . . .[63]

All regimes assisted in the growth of this parasite, according to Marx. He adds:

> Every common interest was straightway severed from society, counterposed to it as a higher, *general*, interest, snatched from the activity of society's members themselves and made an object of government activity, from a bridge, a schoolhouse, and the communal property of a village community, to the railways, the national wealth, and the national university of France. . . . All revolutions perfected this machine instead of smashing it. The parties that contended in turn for domination regarded the possession of this huge state edifice as the principal spoils of the victor.[64]

In a later work, *The Civil War in France*, Marx writes of "the State parasite feeding upon, and clogging, the free movement of society." [65]

Thus, the conception of the "parasite-state" is clearly enunciated by Marx. By now it should be clear, however, how incorrect it is to assert, as does Richard N. Hunt, that Marx originated this conception.[66] Several decades before Marx wrote, the *Censeur Européen* group had already singled out the parasitic state as the major example in modern society of the plundering and "devouring" spirit.

Interestingly, another similarity between Industrialism and Marxism is in the notion of ideology.[67] According to the

[63]In Marx and Engels, *Selected Works*, vol. 1, p. 477.

[64]Ibid. See also p. 432.

[65]Ibid., vol. 2, p. 222.

[66]Hunt, *The Political Ideas of Marx and Engels*, p. 124.

[67]I am using the term here in the Marxist, not the Idéologue, sense.

Industrialist view, there are ideas and values that serve the interests of the productive and of the exploiting classes, respectively. Comte mentions, for instance, the typically feudal judgment, that those who sweat for their wealth are ignoble while those who "gain it by shedding the blood of their fellows" are glorious; such an essentially barbaric idea, he asserts, had to be hidden and veiled by placing it in the context of classical antiquity.[68]

Comte even indicates the existence of what could be called "false consciousness," that is, the harboring by members of one class of ideas contrary to their own interests and useful to the interests of an opposing class. He states:

> The war waged by the slaves against their masters has something base to our eyes. These are men who fight so that the product of their industry should not be the spoils of those who enslaved them; it is an ignoble war. The war waged by Pompey against Caesar charms us; its object is to discover who will be the party who will tyrannize the world; it takes place between men equally incapable of subsisting by their own efforts; it is a noble war. If we trace our opinions to their source, we will find that the majority have been produced by our enemies.[69]

The Early Thierry and Industrialism[70]

In the period of his association with the *Censeur Européen*, Augustin Thierry shared the Industrialist philosophy of Comte and Dunoyer, with perhaps even more radical emphases. His review-essay on Tracy's *Commentaire sur l'Esprit des Lois de*

[68]"Considérations sur l'état moral," *Censeur Européen*, 1: 29–30.

[69]Ibid., pp. 36–37n.

[70]On Thierry, see A. Augustin-Thierry, *Augustin Thierry (1795-1856), d'après sa correspondance et ses papiers de famille* (Paris: Plon-Nourrit, 1922); Kieran Joseph Carroll, *Some Aspects of the Historical Thought of Augustin Thierry (1795–1856)* (Washington, D. C.: Catholic University of America Press, 1951); Rulon Nephi Smithson, *Augustin Thierry. Social and Political Consciousness in the Evolution of Historical Method* (Geneva: Droz, 1973); and Lionel Grossman, *Augustin Thierry and Liberal Historiography, Theory and History*, Beiheft 15 (Wesleyan University Press, 1976).

Montesquieu is particularly important in this connection.[71] Thierry seconds Tracy's firm adherence to laissez-faire.

> Government should be good for the liberty of the governed, and that is when it governs to the least possible degree. It should be good for the wealth of the nation, and that is when it acts as little as possible upon the labor that produces it and when it consumes as little as possible. It should be good for the public security, and that is when it protects as much as possible, provided that the protection does not cost more than it brings in. . . . It is in losing their powers of action that governments improve. Each time that the governed gain space, there is progress.[72]

As against Montesquieu, Thierry sides with Tracy: "commerce consists in exchange; it is society itself"; and "Taxation is always an evil."[73]

The functions of government are to ensure security, "whether there is a danger from outside or whether the mad and the idle threaten to disturb the order and peace necessary for labor." In a simile freighted with meaning in the rhetoric of Industrialism, Thierry asserts that any government that exceeds these limits ceases to be a government properly speaking:

> its action can be classed with the action exerted upon the inhabitants of a land when it is invaded by soldiers; it degenerates into domination, and that occurs regardless of the number of men involved, of the arrangement in which they order themselves, or what titles they take . . .[74]

Sharing the horror of militarism of the other Industrialist authors, Thierry quotes Tracy with approval on "the absurd and ruinous wars which have been too often waged to maintain the empire and exclusive monopoly over some faraway

---

[71]*Censeur Européen*, 7: 191–260. An English version of this essay, somewhat rearranged, was translated by Mark Weinberg and published under the title, *Theory of Classical Liberal "Industrielisme,"* Preface by Leonard P. Liggio, by the Center for Libertarian Studies (New York, 1978).

[72]*Censeur Européen*, 7: 228 and 230.

[73]Ibid.: 206 and 205.

[74]Ibid.: 244.

colonies." This is not true commerce, he declares, but "the mania for domination."[75]

Thierry goes on to sketch a radical-liberal program of very great scope indeed. First of all, the spirit of the free communes of the Middle Ages, which battled the plundering nobility, must be revived; that spirit will inspire men "to oppose the league of civilization to the league of the dominators and the idle." The intellectual movement will be allied to a great social movement:

> An invisible and ever-active power, labor spurred on by industry, will precipitate at the same time all of the population of Europe into this general movement. The productive force of the nations will break all its fetters . . . Industry will disarm power, by causing the desertion of its satellites, who will find more profit in free and honest labor than in the profession of slaves guarding slaves. Industry will deprive power of its pretexts and excuses, by recalling those the police keep in check to the enjoyments and virtues of labor. *Industry will deprive power of its income, by offering at less cost the services which power makes people pay for* [*qu'il se fait payer*]. To the degree that power will lose its actual force and apparent utility, liberty will gain, and free men will draw closer together.[76]

Appropriately enough, in view of the remarkable sentence in the above passage for which emphasis has been supplied, Thierry unequivocally enunciates the cosmopolitanism of a liberalism tending towards sheer anarchism. States are merely "incoherent agglomerations that divide the European population . . . dominions formed and increased by conquests or by diplomatic donations." Eventually, the bonds linking men to states will be shed. Then

> the passage from one society to another will scarcely be felt. Federations will replace states; the loose but indissoluble chains of interest will replace the despotism of men and of laws; the tendency towards government, the first passion of

---

[75]Ibid.: 218.
[76]Ibid.: 256–57. Emphasis added.

the human race, will cede to the free community. The era of empire is over, the era of association begins.[77]

Thierry stresses the role of historical writing in aiding in the great struggle. "We are the sons of these serfs, of these tributaries, of these bourgeois that the conquerors devoured at will; we owe them all that we are." History, which should have transmitted memories of this tradition to us, "has been in the pay of the enemies of our fathers . . . Slaves emancipated only yesterday, our memory has for a long time recalled to us only the families and the acts of our masters." [78] As if presaging his own work on the chartered towns of the Middle Ages, he adds:

> If a skillful and liberal pen were finally to undertake our history, that is, the history of towns and associations . . . all of us would see in it the meaning of a social order, what gives it birth and what destroys it.[79]

Critique of Industrialism

As far as criticism of the Industrialist viewpoint is concerned, only three problems can be indicated here, and a more comprehensive discussion of its shortcomings must be postponed to another occasion.

First, it is likely that by sidestepping the issue of rights— property, Comte claims, is better called "a fact," or even a "thing," than a right[80]—the Industrialist writers set the stage for difficulties arising latter on in their theory.

Second, by concentrating on production rather than on exchange of rightful property, they create false targets of attack. Thus, "monks"—they really mean the religious altogether—are deemed "idlers," placed in the same category as feudal lords and brigands, and, quite deliberately, no distinction is made among paupers between those who live on voluntary charity and those

[77]Ibid.: 257–58.
[78]Ibid.: 251–52.
[79]Ibid.: 255.
[80]"Considerations sur l'état moral," *Censeur Européen*, 1: 6.

who live from state aid.[81] (It would seem that the Industrialists did not totally understand the implications of positing the existence of "immaterial" as well as "material" values.)

Finally, in regard to the State: again, by speaking blithely of production rather than voluntary exchange, the Industrialists appear to be trying to avoid the tricky issue of the "production" of a good—security—that is forced upon the "consumer."[82]

Guizot and Mignet

Although Franois Guizot has often been placed in the same category as Thierry as a historian of class conflict, especially by Marxists, his views were substantially different. Guizot had no connection with the *Censeur Européen* group, being a supporter instead of the *juste milieu* views of the Doctrinaire, Royer-Collard. As a leader of the Doctrinaires (of whom it has been said that no school of thought ever deserved the name less), Guizot lacked any guiding theory, such as Industrialism, to apply in his historical works. Always an eclectic, he wrote for a while in the 1820s in the then popular idiom of class conflict. But he never held that one of the competing classes would or should triumph. On the contrary, the struggle, according to Guizot, was already in his own day eventuating in a grand synthesis, whereby aristocracy and Third Estate would combine in the "French Nation."[83] Shirley M. Gruner aptly summarizes Guizot's standpoint:

> [He] liked to be popular and therefore liked to be considered up-to-date in his ideas. Nor does he wish to appear "unscientific." Therefore he never denies anything outright but seeks to modify a little here and there so that finally nothing is left of it. There is no head-on opposition . . . This is in fact

---

[81]Charles Comte, "De la multiplication des pauvres, des gens à places, et des gens à pensions," *Censeur Européen*, 7: 1n.

[82]See also note 49, above.

[83]Cf. Shirley M. Gruner, *Economic Materialism and Social Moralism* (The Hague/Paris: Mouton, 1973), pp. 108–10.

the whole problem of Guizot—his indecisive decisiveness so that not only in history but in politics the basically constitutional conservative appears at time [sic] to long for the trappings of a radical liberal. And it has also been in the interest of certain groups, for instance the Communists of 1848, to suggest that there was not much difference between Guizot and the other "bourgeois" liberals.[84]

As a thinker (and, of course, in his political role), Guizot was essentially oriented towards the state. A major purpose of his account of French history was to show that "the bourgeoisie and the power of the Crown were not only allies but forces pressing towards each other."[85] He thoroughly endorsed the historical collaboration of the Crown and the Third Estate, which reached a kind of apotheosis in the July Monarchy, particularly under Guizot's own ministry. Over the years, Guizot's influence on Thierry grew, and it was all in the direction of emphasizing the historical contributions of *all* "classes" to the creation of *la grande Nation*, especially the assistance accorded to the Third Estate by the Monarchy in its rise to recognition and preeminence. This tendency in Thierry's work culminates in his *Essai sur l'Histoire de la Formation et des Progrès du Tiers État*, which appeared as the introduction to a collection of documents whose publication was inspired by Guizot.[86]

François Mignet, a friend of Thierry and fellow historian, is often mentioned as another of the liberal precursors of Marxist class conflict theory. But although Mignet did, of course, write of the struggles of the aristocracy and the Third Estate during the Revolution, an immense gulf separated him from the original class conflict analysis of the Industrialists. A sort of *reductio ad absurdum* of the glorification of the bourgeoisie in and of itself, irrespective of any connection with production, was reached by Mignet when in 1836 he wrote of the French Revolutionary armies:

---

[84]Ibid., p. 110.

[85]Dietrich Gerhard, "Guizot, Augustin Thierry, und die Rolle des Tiers État in der französischen Geschichte," *Historische Zeitschrift*, 190, no. 2 (1960): 305.

[86]Ibid.: 307.

All the old aristocratic armies of Europe had succumbed to
these bourgeois, at first disdained and then feared, who, forced
to take up the sword and having made use of it as before of the
word, as previously of thought, had become heroic soldiers,
great captains, and had added to the formidable power of their
ideas *the prestige of military glory and the authority of their
conquests.*[87]

Mignet also chided Charles Comte for his deprecation of the
"Great Men" of history. Comte's views here were part of the
"transvaluation of all values" attempted by the Industrialists,
whereby, for instance, a small manufacturer or a shepherd was
to be more highly valued than destructive conquerors like Cae-
sar or Pompey. But Mignet was of a more Hegelian, not to say
pedestrian, turn of mind. According to him, Comte

forgot that the greatest advances of humanity have had as
their representatives and defenders the greatest captains . . .
that Napoleon's sword had, for fifteen years, led to the
principle of modern equality penetrating all of Europe. He
likewise disputed the difficult art of governing the peoples . . .[88]

Friend and collaborator of Adolphe Thiers (virtually the
personification of the corrupt bourgeois state in nineteenth
century France), and, like Thiers, a glorifier of Napoleon, Mignet simply inhabited a different intellectual world from Say,
Comte, Dunoyer, and the young Thierry.

Thierry's Defection

This is not the place to attempt a detailed account and explanation of how Thierry exchanged his relatively sophisticated Industrialist analysis of class conflict for a considerably coarser
one. At some point, Thierry seems to have come to believe that
a rigorous Industrialist interpretation "falsified" history by

---

[87]François Mignet, "Le comte Sieyès: Notice," *Notices et portraits historiques
et littéraires,* vol. 1 (Paris: Charpentier, 1854), p. 88 (emphasis supplied).

[88]François Miget, "Charles Comte: Notice," ibid., vol. 2, p. 102.

subjecting it to too rigid a theoretical scheme.[89] After his first essays on English history, in the *Censeur Européen*, he had begun to feel, he added, the need to leave to each epoch its originality: "I changed style and manner; my former rigidity became more supple . . ."[90]

> The type of general and purely political considerations to which I had confined myself up until then seemed to me for the first time too arid and limited. I felt a strong inclination to descend from the abstract to the concrete, to envisage the national life in all its facets and to take my point of departure in solving the problem of the antagonism of the different classes of men in the bosom of the same society the study of the primitive races in their original diversity.[91]

The "tinge of politics was effaced," Thierry explains, as he devoted himself more to "science."[92] In fact, he did not cease to write as the historian of the oppressed and downtrodden, as the chronicler, first, of the sufferings of defeated "races" like the Saxons at the time of the Norman Conquest, then of the rise to power and pride of the Third Estate in France.

But Thierry's treatment of class conflict in his more famous works is defective and, ultimately, fatally flawed: the conceptual apparatus he employs is too blunt an instrument for purposes of social dissection. When he deals with the history of France in the medieval and early modern period, for instance, the industrious, creative element of society is identified *tout court* with the "Third Estate," the exploiting idlers and parasites with the feudal nobility and its descendants alone. Thus, crucial distinctions existing *within* the

---

[89]"After much time and labor lost in thus obtaining artificial results, I perceived that I was falsifying history by imposing identical formulas on totally different periods." Augustin Thierry, *Dix Ans d'Études Historiques* (1834; Paris: Furne, 1851), p. 3. Of his earlier radical liberal political views, he says: "I aspired enthusiastically towards a future of which I had no very clear idea . . . [vers un avenir, je ne savais trop lequel]." Ibid., p. 7.

[90]Ibid., pp. 6–7.

[91]Ibid., p. 8.

[92]Ibid., p. 12.

Third Estate, or bourgeoisie, of the sort that Say had already exposed and drawn attention to, are omitted. The earlier analytical dividing line between those who act on the market, through exchange, and those who use force, above all through the State, disappears. Thierry thus sinned against his own methodological principle: "The great precept that must be given to historians is to distinguish instead of confounding."[93]

The Final Stage

In Thierry's last major work, *Essay on the History of the Formation and Progress of the Third Estate*, virtually nothing is left of the original Industrialist doctrine. Instead, we are presented with what amounts to a case-study in complacent and self-satisfied Whiggish historiography. It turns out that the events and figures of some 700 years of French history have all conspired to bring about the triumph of what is now Thierry's ideal, the modern, centralized French State, based on equality before the law, to be sure, but rich in power and historical glory, as well. Over and over again, the French kings are praised for having worked to elevate the Third Estate, largely by providing jobs for its members, and, in the traditional manner, for having "created" France. Richelieu is eulogized both for his foreign and domestic policies, equally admirable, and for "multiplying for the commons, besides offices, places of honor in the State."[94] Colbert, the architect of French mercantilism, is glorified as a commoner who planned "the industrial regeneration of France," and is applauded for his distribution of largesse to writers, scholars, and "all classes of men."[95] One could go on.

---

[93]Cited in Peter Stadler, "Politik und Geschichtsschreibung in der französischen Restauration 1814–1830," *Historische Zeitschrift* 180, no. 2 (1955): 283.

[94]Augustin Thierry, *Essai sur l'Histoire de la Formation et des Progrès du Tiers État* (1853), new rev. ed. (Paris: Calmann Lévy, 1894), pp. 172–73.

[95]Ibid., pp. 189 and 195.

Thierry had experienced the socialist agitation of 1848 and the June Days; the specter of social revolution haunted him to the end of his life. He was anxious that the socialist trouble-makers should not be able to draw sustenance from his work on the role of classes in French history. In the Preface to the *Essay*, Thierry implies that now, in 1853, there is no further need for the concept of classes: "the national mass" is "today one and homogeneous." Only "the prejudices spread by systems that tend to divide" the homogeneous nation into "mutually hostile classes" could suggest otherwise.[96] The present-day antago-nism between bourgeoisie and workers, which some wish to trace back for centuries, is "destructive of all public order."[97] Thus, ironically, one of thinkers who was a major inspiration for the socialist idea of class conflict ended by categorically denying any class conflict in the modern world, and he did so in part out of fear of the dangers the idea posed now that it had been reshaped by the socialists.[98]

Liberals and the July Monarchy

The July Monarchy of Louis Philippe, which came to power in 1830, was notorious for its corruption on behalf of the bourgeoi-sie, especially in the form of massive and blatant jobbery.[99] This was the regime of which Tocqueville wrote:

> [The middle class] entrenched itself in every vacant govern-ment job, prodigiously augmented the number of such jobs,

---

[96]Ibid., pp. 1–2.

[97]Ibid., p. 2.

[98]Marx discusses Thierry's *Essai* in the letter to Engels cited in tnote 12, above. Interestingly, he commends Thierry for describing "well, if not as a connected whole: (1) How from the first, or at least after the rise of the towns, the French bourgeoisie gains too much influence by constituting itself the Parliament, the bureaucracy, etc., and not as in England through commerce and industry. This is certainly still characteristic even of present-day France." Marx and Engels, *Selected Correspondence*, p. 88.

[99]See, for instance, the popular pamphlet by "Timon" (Louis-Marie Cormenin de la Haye), *Ordre du Jour sur la Corruption Électorale*, 7th ed. (Paris: Pagnerre, 1846).

and accustomed itself to live almost as much upon the Treasury as upon its own industry.[100]

Many of the liberals were major beneficiaries of the new regime, rewarded for the support they had given, and continued to give, to Louis Philippe. Dunoyer was made prefect in Moulins, and Stendhal consul at Trieste, while Daunou was reappointed as director of the National Archives.[101] Other historians of the liberal party under the Restoration did as well, or better. Guizot, of course, was one of the chief figures of the new order. With Mignet, Thiers, Villemain, he "divided up the premier offices of the State, the most brilliant favors of the regime."[102] Thierry himself, however, now blind, had to make do with occasional grants and was reduced to pleading for a steady job as research historian. At one point, a plan to eliminate literary pensions, which would have included his own, distressed him in the extreme.[103] Thus, any analysis of the reasons behind the conservative drift of many French liberals after 1830—and of their abandonment of the dangerous idea of the conflict of classes—would have to take account not only of the growing threat of socialism, but also of the new links to power and wealth that the "liberal" regime of Louis Philippe afforded them.

Back in 1817, in the heyday of the Industrialist movement, Dunoyer had lamented the fact that "the idle and devouring class has constantly been recruited from among the industrious men . . ." "The destiny of civilization," he declared, "seems to have been to raise up the men of the laboring classes only to see them betray her cause and pass to the ranks of her enemies."[104] There is perhaps a sense in which these words were prophetic of the fate of some of the Restoration liberals, including the Industrialist thinkers themselves.

[100]*Recollections*, trans. Alexander Teixeira de Mattos (New York: Meridian, 1959), pp. 2–3.

[101]Allix, "J.-B. Say et les origines d'industrialisme": 318–19.

[102]A. Augustin-Thierry, *Augustin Thierry*, p. 114.

[103]Ibid., p. 131.

[104]"Sur l'état présent," *Censeur Européen*, 2: 97.

Other Liberal Class-Conflict Theories

The Industrialist doctrine of class conflict was by no means the first or only treatment of this question in the history of liberal theory.[105] In the United States, some Jeffersonians and Jacksonians also grappled with the question of class, in the politically relevant sense, and came to conclusions reminiscent of the Industrialist school. John Taylor of Caroline, William Leggett, and John C. Calhoun were keen observers and critics of the social groups whom they believed were utilizing political power in order to exploit the rest of society, the producers.

John Taylor was outraged by what he saw as the betrayal of the principles of the American Revolution by a new aristocracy based on "separate legal interests," the bankers privileged to issue paper money as legal tender and the beneficiaries of "public improvements" and protective tariffs. American society has been divided into the privileged and the unprivileged by this "substantial revival of the feudal system."[106]

Two decades later, in the 1830s, the northern radical, William Leggett, denounced the same exploiting classes. A thoroughgoing Jeffersonian and disciple of Adam Smith and J.-B. Say, Leggett held that the principles of political economy are the same as those of the American Republic: Laissez-faire, Do not govern too much. This system of equal rights was being overthrown by a new aristocracy, among whom Leggett particularly singled out the state-connected bankers for attack.

> Have we not, too, our privileged orders? our scrip nobility? aristocrats, clothed with special immunities, who control, indirectly, but certainly, the power of the state, monopolize the most copious source of pecuniary profit, and wring the very crust from the hand of toil? Have we not, in short, like the wretched serfs of Europe, our lordly master . . . ? If any

---

[105]See Ralph Raico, "Classical Liberal Exploitation Theory": 179–83.

[106]Eugene Tenbroeck Mudge, *The Social Philosophy of John Taylor of Caroline: A Study in Jeffersonian Democracy* (1939; New York: AMS Press, 1968), pp. 151–204 and *passim*.

man doubts how these questions should be answered, let him walk through Wall-street.[107]

The American aristocracy naturally favored a strong government, including control of the banking system. Leggett, in contrast, demanded "the absolute separation of government from the banking and credit system."[108]

John C. Calhoun, in his *Disquisition on Government*, focused attention on the taxing powers of the state, "the necessary result" of which

> is to divide the community into two great classes: one consisting of those who, in reality, pay the taxes and, of course, bear exclusively the burthen of supporting the government; and the other, of those who are the recipients of their proceeds through disbursements, and who are, in fact, supported by the government; or, in fewer words, to divide it into tax-payers and tax-consumers. But the effect of this is to place them in antagonistic relations in reference to the fiscal action of the government and the entire course of policy therewith connected.[109]

Liberal class conflict rhetoric was often applied throughout the nineteenth century; in England, it is a recurrent theme in the agitation for repeal of the corn laws, used by Cobden, Bright, and others. It underlies the attack by William Graham Sumner on the "plutocrats," capitalists who use the state rather than the market to enrich themselves.[110]

Bringing the State Back In

Today a revival appears to be under way of the concept of the state as creator of classes and class conflict. For instance, a

[107]William Leggett, *Democratick Editorials: Essays in Jacksonian Political Economy*, Lawrence H. White, ed. (Indianapolis: Liberty Press, 1984), pp. 250–51. See also Lawrence H. White, "William Leggett: Jacksonian Editorialist as Classical Liberal Political Economist," *History of Political Economy* 18, no. 2 (Summer 1986): 307–24.

[108]William Leggett, *Democratick Editorials*, p. 142.

[109]John C. Calhoun, *A Disquisition on Government and Selections from the Discourse*, C. Gordon Post, ed. (Indianapolis: Bobbs-Merrill, 1953), pp. 17–18.

[110]See, e.g., Harris E. Starr, *William Graham Sumner*, (New York: Henry Holt, 1925), pp. 241 and 458.

group of scholars including Theda Skocpol, has produced an anthology with the significant title, *Bringing the State Back In.*[111] In an introductory chapter,[112] Skocpol speaks of "an intellectual sea change" taking place, by which the "society-centered ways of explaining politics and governmental activities" popular in the 1950s and 60s are being reversed, and government itself is looked upon as "an independent actor."

We must recognize, she asserts, the capacity of the state to act independently of the various groupings of "civil society" more systematically than is allowed by the Marxist notion of "relative autonomy." In particular, in regard to relations with other states, a state may often act in ways that cannot be explained by its concern for private interests, even for collective private interests. Skocpol notes that while state actions are often justified by reference to their appropriateness for the long-run interests of society or the benefits that accrue from them to various social groups (which would tend to shift the center of attention once more to society), "autonomous state actions will regularly take forms that attempt to reinforce the authority, political longevity, and social control of the state organizations whose incumbents generated the relevant policies or policy ideas." Citing Suzanne Berger, Skocpol stresses that the view that social "interests" determine politics is one-sided and shallow, if for no other reason then because

> "the timing and characteristics of state intervention" affect "not only organizational tactics and strategies," but "the content and definition of interest itself" . . . Some scholars have directly stressed that state initiatives create corporatist forms . . . the formation, let alone the political capacities, of such purely socioeconomic phenomena as interest groups and classes depends in significant measure on the structures and activities of the very states the social actors, in turn, seek to influence.[113]

---

[111]Theda Skocpol, *Bringing the State Back In: Strategies of Analysis in Current Research* (Cambridge, England: Cambridge University Press, 1985). The title derives from an earlier essay by Skocpol.

[112]Ibid., pp. 3–37.

[113]A scholar who stressed the role of the state in creating corporatist forms

Class Conflict in Marxist Regimes

From a scientific point of view, the liberal theory—which locates the source of class conflict in the exercise of state power—would seem to have at least one pronounced advantage over the conventional Marxist analysis: liberal theory is able to shed light on the structure and functioning of Marxist societies themselves. "The theory of the Communists," Marx wrote, "may be summed up in the single sentence: Abolition of private property."[114] Yet Communist societies, which have essentially abolished private property, do not appear to be on the road to the abolition of classes. This has led to some deep soul-searching and confused analysis among Marxist theoreticians and justified complaints regarding the inadequacy of a purely "economic" analysis of class conflict to account for the empirical reality of the socialist countries.[115] Yet the liberal theory of class conflict is ideally suited to deal with such problems in a context where access to wealth, prestige, and influence is determined by control of the state apparatus.

---

and hence "class interest" (although he preferred the sociologically more accurate term "caste" to "class") was Ludwig von Mises; see his *Theory and History*, pp. 113–15. Mises, who examined this topic thirty years ago, is not mentioned by Skocpol. See also Murray N. Rothbard, *Power and Market: Government and the Economy* (Menlo Park: Institute for Humane Studies, 1970): pp. 12–13, where Rothbard states: "It has become fashionable to assert that 'Conservatives' like John C. Calhoun 'anticipated' the Marxian doctrine of class exploitation. But the Marxian doctrine holds, erroneously, that there are 'classes' on the free market whose interests clash and conflict. Calhoun's insight was almost the reverse. Calhoun saw that it was the intervention of the State that in itself created the 'classes' and the conflict." Rothbard also prefers the term "caste": "castes are State-made groups, each with its own set of established privileges and tasks." Ibid., p. 198, 5n.

[114]"Manifesto of the Communist Party," in Karl Marx and Friedrich Engels, *Selected Works*, I, p. 120.

[115]George Konrad and Ivan Szelényi, *The Intellectuals on the Road to Class Power*, Andrew Arato and Richard E. Allen, trans. (New York/London: Harcourt Brace Jovanovich, 1979), pp. xiv–xvi, 39–44, and *passim*.

~ 6 ~

Karl Marx: Communist as Religious Eschatologist

Murray N. Rothbard

Marx as Millennial Communist

The key to the intricate and massive system of thought created by Karl Marx is at bottom a simple one: *Karl Marx was a communist.* A seemingly trite and banal statement set alongside Marxism's myriad of jargon-ridden concepts in philosophy, economics, and culture, yet Marx's devotion to communism was his crucial focus, far more central than the class struggle, the dialectic, the theory of surplus value, and all the rest. Communism was the great goal, the vision, the desideratum, the ultimate end that would make the sufferings of mankind throughout history worthwhile. History is the history of suffering, of class struggle, of the exploitation of man by man. In the same way as the return of the Messiah, in Christian theology, will put an end to history and establish a new heaven and a new earth, so the establishment of communism would put an end to human history. And just as for post-millennial Christians, man, led by God's prophets and saints, will establish a Kingdom of God on Earth (for *pre*-millennials, Jesus will have many human assistants in setting up such a kingdom), so, for Marx and other schools of communists, mankind, led by a vanguard of secular saints, will establish a secularized Kingdom of Heaven on earth.

In messianic religious movements, the millennium is

invariably established by a mighty, violent upheaval, an Armageddon, a great apocalyptic war between good and evil. After
this titanic conflict, a millennium, a new age, of peace and
harmony, of the reign of justice, will be installed upon the
earth.

Marx emphatically rejected those utopian socialists who
sought to arrive at communism through a gradual and evolutionary process, through a steady advancement of the good.
Instead, Marx harked back to the apocalyptics, the post-millennial coercive German and Dutch Anabaptists of the sixteenth
century, to the millennial sects during the English Civil War,
and to the various groups of pre-millennial Christians who
foresaw a bloody Armageddon at the last days, before the millennium could be established. Indeed, since the apocalyptic
post-mils refused to wait for a gradual goodness and sainthood
to permeate mankind, they joined the pre-mils in believing that
only a violent apocalyptic final struggle between good and evil,
between saints and sinners, could usher in the millennium.
Violent, worldwide revolution, in Marx's version, to be made by
the oppressed proletariat, would be the inevitable instrument
for the advent of his millennium, communism.

In fact, Marx, like the pre-mils (or "millenarians"), went
further to hold that the reign of evil on earth would reach a peak
just before the apocalypse ("the darkness before the dawn"). For
Marx as for the millenarians, writes Ernest Tuveson,

> The evil of the world must proceed to its height before, in one
> great complete root-and-branch upheaval, it would be swept
> away . . .

> Millenarian pessimism about the perfectibility of the existing
> world is crossed by a supreme optimism. History, the millenar-
> ian believes, so operates that, when evil has reached its
> height, the hopeless situation will be reversed. The original,
> the true harmonious state of society, in some kind of egalitar-
> ian order, will be re-established.[1]

---

[1]Ernest L. Tuveson, "The Millenarian Structure of "The Communist Manifesto,"

In contrast to the various groups of utopian socialists, and in common with religious messianists, Karl Marx did not sketch the features of his future communism in any detail. It was not for Marx, for example, to spell out the number of people in his utopia, the shape and location of their houses, the pattern of their cities. In the first place, there is a quintessentially crackpotty air to utopias that are mapped by their creators in precise detail. But of equal importance, spelling out the details of one's ideal society removes the crucial element of awe and mystery from the allegedly inevitable world of the future.

But certain features are broadly alike in all visions of communism. Private property is eliminated, individualism goes by the board, individuality is flattened, all property is owned and controlled communally, and the individual units of the new collective organism are in some way made "equal" to one another.

Marxists and scholars of Marxism have tended to overlook the centrality of communism to the entire Marxian system.[2] In the "official" Marxism of the 1930s and 1940s, communism was slighted in favor of an allegedly "scientific" stress on the labor theory of value, the class struggle, or the materialist interpretation of history, and the Soviet Union, even before Gorbachev, grappling with the practical problems of socialism, treated the goal of communism as more of an embarrassment than anything else.[3] Similarly, Stalinists such as Louis

---

in C. Patrides and J. Wittreich, eds., The *Apocalypse in English Renaissance Thought and Literature* (Ithaca, N.Y.: Cornell University Press, 1984), pp. 326–27. Tuveson speculates that Marx and Engels may have been influenced by the outburst of millenarianism in England during the 1840s. On this phenomenon, particularly the flareup in England and the U.S. of the Millerites, who predicted the end of the world on October 22, 1844, see the classic work on modern millenarianism, Ernest R. Sandeen, *The Roots of Fundamentalism: British and American Millenarianism, 1880–1930* (Chicago: University of Chicago Press, 1970). See Tuveson, "Millenarian Structure," p. 340 5 n.

[2] Thus, in the highly touted work of Thomas Sowell, *Marxism: The Philosophy and Economics* (London: Unwin Paperbacks, 1986), there is scarcely any consideration whatsoever paid to communism.

[3] The official Soviet textbook on Marxism treated its own proclaimed goal with brusque dismissal, insisting that all Soviets must work hard and not skip any

Althusser dismissed the pre-1848 Marx's stress on "humanism," philosophy, and "alienation," as unscientific and pre-Marxist. On the other hand, in the 1960s it became fashionable for new left Marxists such as Herbert Marcuse to dismiss the later "scientific economist" Marx as a rationalistic prelude to despotism and a betrayal of the earlier Marx's stress on humanism and human "freedom." In contrast, I hold with the growing consensus in Marxist studies[4] that, at least since 1844 and possibly earlier, there was only one Marx, that Marx the "humanist" established the goal that he would seek for the remainder of his life: the apocalyptic triumph of revolutionary communism. In this view, Marx's exploration later into the economics of capitalism was merely a quest for the mechanism, the "law of history," that allegedly makes such a triumph inevitable.

But in that case, it becomes vital to investigate the nature of this allegedly humanistic goal of communism, what the meaning of this "freedom" might be, and whether or not the grisly records of the Marxist-Leninist regime in the twentieth century was implicit in the basic Marxian conception of freedom.

Marxism is a religious creed. This statement has been common among critics of Marx, and since Marxism is an explicit enemy of religion, such a seeming paradox would offend many Marxists, since it clearly challenged the allegedly hard-headed scientific materialism on which Marxism rested. In the present day, oddly enough, an age of liberation theology and other flirtations between Marxism and the Church, Marxists themselves are often quick to make this

---

"stages" on the long road to communism. "The CPSU [the Communist Party of the Soviet Union], being a party of scientific communism, advances and solves the problem of communist construction as the material and spiritual prerequisites for them to become ready and mature, being guided by the fact that necessary stages of development must not be skipped over . . ." *Fundamentals of Marxism-Leninism*, 2nd rev. ed. (Moscow: Foreign Languages Publishing House, 1963), p. 662. Also see ibid., pp. 645–46, 666–67, and 674–75.

[4]Thus, see the illuminating work of Robert C. Tucker, *Philosophy and Myth in Karl Marx* (1970; New York: Cambridge University Press, 1961).

same proclamation. Certainly, one obvious way in which Marxism functions as a "religion" is the lengths to which Marxists will go to preserve their system against obvious errors or fallacies. Thus, when Marxian predictions fail, even though they are allegedly derived from scientific laws of history, Marxists go to great lengths to *change* the terms of the original prediction. A notorious example is Marx's law of the impoverishment of the working class under capitalism. When it became all too clear that the standard of living of the workers under industrial capitalism was rising instead of falling, Marxists fell back on the view that what Marx "really" meant by impoverishment was not immiseration but *relative* deprivation. One of the problems with this fallback defense is that impoverishment is supposed to be the motor of the proletarian revolution, and it is difficult to envision the workers resorting to bloody revolution because they only enjoy one yacht apiece while capitalists enjoy five or six. Another notorious example was the response of many Marxists to Böhm-Bawerk's conclusive demonstration that the labor theory of value could not account for the pricing of goods under capitalism. Again, the fallback response was that what Marx "*really* meant"[5] was not to explain market pricing at all, but merely to assert that labor hours embed some sort of mystically inherent "values" into goods that are, however, irrelevant to the workings of the capitalist market. If this were true, then it is difficult to see why Marx labored for a great part of his life in an unsuccessful attempt to complete *Capital* and to solve the value-price problem.

Perhaps the most appropriate commentary on the frantic defenders of Marx's value theory is that of the ever witty and delightful Alexander Gray, who also touches on another aspect of Marx as religious prophet:

> To witness Böhm-Bawerk or Mr. [H. W. B.] Joseph carving up
> Marx is but a pedestrian pleasure; for these are but pedestrian

---

[5]*What Marx Really Meant* was the title of a sympathetic work on Marxism by G. D. H. Cole (London, 1934).

writers, who are so pedestrian as to clutch at the plain meaning of words, not realising that what Marx really meant has
no necessary connection with what Marx undeniably said. To
witness Marx surrounded by his friends is, however, a joy of
an entirely different order. For it is fairly clear that none of them
really knows what Marx really meant; they are even in considerable doubt as to what he was talking about; there are hints that
Marx himself did not know what he was doing. In particular,
there is no one to tell us what Marx thought he meant by "value."
Capital is, in one sense, a three-volume treatise, expounding a
theory of value and its manifold applications. Yet Marx never
condescends to say what he means by "value," which accordingly
is what anyone cares to make it as he follows the unfolding scroll
from 1867 to 1894. . . . Are we concerned with *Wissenschaft*,
slogans, myths, or incantations? Marx, it has been said, was a
prophet . . . and perhaps this suggestion provides the best
approach. One does not apply to Jeremiah or Ezekiel the tests
to which less inspired men are subjected. Perhaps the mistake
the world and most of the critics have made is just that they
have not sufficiently regarded Marx as a prophet—a man
above logic, uttering cryptic and incomprehensible words,
which every man may interpret as he chooses.[6]

Reabsorption Theology

But the nature of Marxism-as-religion cuts deeper than the
follies and evasions of Marxists[7] or the cryptic and often unin-
telligible nature of Marxian writings. For it is the contention of
this article that the crucial goal—communism—is an atheized
version of a certain type of religious eschatology; that the alleged inevitable process of getting there—the dialectic—is an
atheistic form of the same religious laws of history; and that

[6]Alexander Gray, *The Socialist Tradition* (London: Longmans Green, 1946), pp.
321–22.

[7]Another example of what may be termed "religious" behavior by Marxists is the
insistence of thinkers who have clearly abandoned almost all the essential tenets of
Marxism on calling themselves by the magical name "Marxist." A recent case in point
is the British "analytical Marxists," such as John Roemer and Jon Elster. For a critique
of this school by an orthodox Marxist, see Michael A. Lebowitz, "Is 'Analytical
Marxism' Marxism?" *Science and Society* 52 (Summer 1988): 191–214.

the supposedly central problem of capitalism as perceived by "humanist" Marxists, the problem of "alienation," is an atheistic version of the selfsame religion's metaphysical grievance at the entire created universe.

As far as I know, there is no commonly-agreed upon name to designate this fatefully influential religion. One name is "process theology," but I shall rather call it "reabsorption theology," for the word "reabsorption" highlights the allegedly inevitable end-point of human history as well as its supposed starting point in a pre-creation union with God.

As Leszek Kolakowski points out in his monumental work on Marxism, reabsorption theology begins with the third-century Greek philosopher Plotinus, and moves from Plotinus to some of the Christian Platonists, where it takes its place as a Christian heresy. That heresy tends to bubble up repeatedly from beneath the surface in the works of such Christian mystics as the ninth-century philosopher John Scotus Erigena and the fourteenth-century Meister Johannes Eckhart.[8]

The nature and profound implications of reabsorption theology may best be grasped by contrasting this heresy to Christian orthodoxy. We begin at the beginning—with *creatology*, the science or discipline of the first days. Why did God create the universe? The orthodox Christian answer is that God created the universe out of a benevolent and overflowing love for his creatures. Creation was therefore good and wondrous; the fly in the ointment was introduced by man's disobedience to God's laws, for which sin he was cast out of Eden. Out of this Fall he can be redeemed by the Incarnation of God-in-human flesh and the sacrifice of Jesus on the Cross. Note that the Fall was a moral one, and that Creation itself remains metaphysically good. Note, too, that in orthodox Christianity, each human individual, made in the image of God, is of supreme importance, and each individual's salvation becomes of critical concern.

---

[8]Leszek Kolakowski, *Main Currents of Marxism: Its Origins, Growth and Dissolution*, vol. 1 (Oxford: Oxford University Press, 1981), pp. 9–39.

Reabsorption theology, however, originates in a very different creatology. One of its crucial tenets is that, *before* Creation, man—obviously the collective-species man and not each individual—existed in happy union, in some sort of mighty cosmic blob, united with God and even with Nature. In the Christian view, God, unlike man, is perfect, and therefore does not, like man, perform actions in order to improve his lot. But for the reabsorptionists, God acts analogously with humans: God acts out of what Mises called "felt uneasiness," out of dissatisfaction with his current lot. God, in other words, creates the universe out of loneliness, dissatisfaction, or, generally, in order to develop his undeveloped faculties. God creates the universe out of felt need.

In the reabsorptionist view, Creation, instead of being wondrous and good, is essentially and metaphysically evil. For it generates diversity, individuality, and separateness, and thereby cuts off man from his beloved cosmic union with God. Man is now permanently "alienated" from God, the fundamental alienation; and also from other men, and from nature. It is this cosmic metaphysical separateness that lies at the heart of the Marxian concept of "alienation," and *not*, as we might now think, personal griping about not controlling the operation of one's factory, or about lack of access to wealth or political power. Alienation is a cosmic condition and not a psychological complaint. For the reabsorptionists, the crucial problems of the world come not from moral failure but from the essential nature of creation itself.

Buddhism and various pantheistic religions, as well as many mystics, offer one partial way out for this cosmic alienation. To such pantheists, God-Man-and-Nature are and continue to be one, and individual men can recapture that desired unity by various forms of training until Nirvana (nothingness) has been achieved and the individual ego has been—at least temporarily—obliterated.[9]

[9]The great orthodox Christian apologist G. K. Chesterton brilliantly illuminated the difference between Christian individualism and pantheistic collectivism in the following critique of the Buddhist Mrs. Annie Besant, one of the founders of the Fabian Society:

But the Way Out offered by the reabsorptionists is different. First, it is a way offered only to man-as-species and not to any particular individuals; and second, the way is a religiously determined and inevitable Law of History. For there is one good aspect of creation, for the reabsorptionists: that God and man each get to fulfill their faculties and expand their respective potentials through history. In fact, history is a process by which these potentials are fulfilled, in which God and man both perfect themselves. Then, finally, and here we come to *eschatology*, the science of the Last Days, there will eventually be a mighty reunion, a reabsorption, in which man and God are at last not only reunited, but reunited on a higher, on a perfected level. The two cosmic blobs—God and man (and presumably Nature too)—now meet and merge on a more exalted level. The painful state of creation is now over, alienation is at last ended, and man returns Home to be on a higher, post-creation level. History, and the world, have come to an end.

A crucial feature of reabsorption is that all this "perfecting" and "reuniting" obviously takes place only on a species-collectivist level. The individual man is nothing, a mere cell in the great collective organism man; only in that way can we say that "man" progresses or fulfills "himself" over the centuries, suffers alienation from "his" pre-creation state, and finally "returns" to unity with God on a higher level. The relation to the Marxian goal of communism is already becoming clear; the "alienation" eliminated by the inevitable communist end of history is that of the collective species man, each man being finally united with other men and with Nature (which, for Marx, was "created" by the

---

According to Mrs. Besant the universal Church is simply the universal Self. It is the doctrine that we are really all one person; that there are no real walls of individuality between man and man. . . . She does not tell us to love our neighbor; she tells us to be our neighbors. . . . The intellectual abyss between Buddhism and Christianity is that, for the Buddhist or the theosophist, personality is the fall of man, for the Christian it is the purpose of God, the whole point of His cosmic idea.

G. K. Chesterton, *Orthodoxy* (New York, 1927), pp. 244–45. Quoted in Thomas Molnar, *Utopia: the Perennial Heresy* (New York: Sheed and Ward, 1967), p. 123.

collective species man, who thereby replaces God as the creator).

I shall deal later with communism as the goal of history. Here we focus on the *process* by which all these events must take place, and necessarily take place. First, there is the pre-creation cosmic blob. Out of this blob there then arises a very different state of affairs: a created Universe, with God, individual men, and nature each existing. Here are the origins of the magical Hegelian-Marxian "dialectic": one state of affairs somehow *gives rise to* a contrasting state. In the German language, Hegel, the master of the concept of the dialectic, used the crucial term *aufhebung*, a "lifting up," which is ambiguous enough to encompass this sudden shift into a very different state, this lifting up which is at one and the same time a preserving, a transcending, and creating a stark contrast to, the original condition. The standard English translation for this process in Hegel and Marx is "negating," but such translation makes the theory even more absurd than it really is—probably "transcending" would be a better term.[10] Thus, as usual, the dialectic consists of three stages. Stage One is the original state of the pre-creation cosmic blob, with man and God in happy and harmonious unity, but each rather undeveloped. Then, the magic dialectic does its work, Stage Two occurs, and God creates man and the universe. But then, finally, when the development of man and God is completed, Stage Two creates its own *aufhebung*, its transcendence into its opposite or negation: in short, Stage

---

[10]Alexander Gray has a lot of fun with the concept of "negation" in the Hegelian and Marxian dialectic. He writes that the examples of the "negation of the negation" in Engels's *Anti-Dühring* "may be sound Hegelianism, but otherwise they appear rather silly. A seed of barley falls into the ground and germinates: negation of the seed. In the autumn it produces more grains of barley: negation of the negation. A butterfly comes from an egg: negation of the egg. After many transformations, the butterfly mates and dies: negation of the negation. . . . Hegel is surely something more than this." Gray adds a comment that Marx's admiring summary of Hegelianism in his *Poverty and Philosophy* is "not without entertainment value": "yes becomes no, no becomes yes, yes becomes at the same time yes and no, no becomes at the same time no and yes, the contraries balance, neutralize, and paralyze each other." (My own translation from Gray's original French quote, which he found "especially" entertaining.) Gray, *Socialist Tradition*, p. 300 1 n and 2 n.

Three, the reunion of God and man in an "ecstasy of union," and the end of history.

The dialectical process by which one state of affairs gives rise to a very different state, if not its opposite, is, for the reabsorptionists, a mystical though inevitable development. There was no need for them to explain the mechanism. Indeed, particularly influential for Hegel and later reabsorptionist thinkers was one of the later Christian mystics in this tradition: the early seventeenth century German cobbler Jakob Boehme. Pantheizing the dialectic, Boehme declared that it was not God's will but some primal force, that launched the cosmic dialectic of creation and history. How, Boehme asked, did the world of pre-creation transcend itself into creation? Before creation, he answered, there was a primal source, an eternal unity, an undifferentiated, indistinct, literal Nothing [*Ungrund*]. Oddly enough, this Nothing possessed within itself an inner striving, a *nisus*, a drive for self-realization. That drive, Boehme asserted, gave rise to its opposite, the Will, the interaction of which with *nisus* transformed the Nothing into the Something of the created universe.[11]

Heavily influenced by Jakob Boehme was the mystical English communist, Gerrard Winstanley, founder of the Digger sect during the English Civil War. Son of a textile merchant who had failed in the cloth business and then had sunk to the status of agricultural laborer, Winstanley, in early 1649, had a mystical vision of the ideal communist world of the future. Originally, according to this vision, a version of God had created the universe; but the spirit of "selfishness," the Devil itself, had entered into man and brought about private property and a market economy. The curse of the self, opined Winstanley, was "the beginner of particular interest," or private property, with men buying and selling and saying "This is mine." The end of original communism and its breakup into private property meant that universal liberty was gone, and creation brought

---

[11]See M. H. Abrams, *Natural Supernaturalism: Tradition and Revolution in Romantic Literature* (New York: Norton, 1971), p. 161.

"under the curse of bondage, sorrow, and tears." In England, Winstanley absurdly held, property had been communist until the Norman Conquest of 1066, which created the institution of private property.[12]

But soon, declared Winstanley, universal "love" would eliminate private property, and would thus restore the earth to "a common property as it was in the beginning . . . making the earth one storehouse, and every man and woman to live . . . as members of one household." This communism and absolute equality of possessions would thus bring to the world the millennium, "a new heaven, and a new earth."[13]

At first, Winstanley believed that little or no coercion would be necessary for establishing and maintaining his communist society. Soon, however, he realized, in the completed draft of his utopia, that all wage labor and all commerce would have to be prohibited on the penalty of death. Winstanley was quite willing to go this far with his program. Everyone was to contribute to, and take from, the common storehouse, and the death penalty was to be levied on all use of money, or on any buying or selling. The "sin" of idleness would of course be combatted by forced labor for the benefit of the communist community. This all-encompassing stress on the executioner makes particularly grisly the declaration of Winstanley that "all punishments that are to be inflicted . . . are only such as to make the offender . . . to live in the community of the righteous law of love one with another." Education in "love" was to be insured by free and

---

[12]Most of the Protestants held the very different, and far more correct, view that the Norman Conquest had imposed a state-created feudal-type landed estates on an England which had been much closer to being an idyll of genuine private property.

Engels and other historians and anthropologists saw the original Early Communism, or Golden Age, in primitive pre-market tribal societies. Modern anthropological research, however, has demonstrated that most primitive and tribal societies were based on private property, money, and market economies. Thus, see Bruce Benson, "Enforcement of Private Property Rights in Primitive Societies: Law Without Government," *Journal of Libertarian Studies* 9 (Winter 1989): 1–26.

[13]In M. H. Abrams, *Natural Supernaturalism*, p. 517n.

compulsory schooling conducted by the state, mainly in useful crafts rather than in liberal arts, as well as by "ministers" elected by the public to preach secular sermons upholding the new system.[14]

Hegel as Pantheist Reabsorptionist

Everyone knows that Marx was essentially a Hegelian in philosophy, but the precise scope of Hegel's influence on Marx is less well-understood. Hegel's dubious accomplishment was to completely pantheize reabsorption theology. It is little realized that Hegel was only one, although the most elaborate and hypertrophic, of a host of writers who constituted the highly influential Romantic movement in Germany and England at the end of the eighteenth, and during the first half of the nineteenth, centuries.[15] Hegel was a theology student at the University of Tübingen, and many of his fellow Romantics, friends and colleagues, such as Schelling, Schiller, Holderlin, and Fichte, began as theology students, many of them at Tübingen.[16]

The Romantic twist to the reabsorption story was to proclaim that God is in reality Man. Man, or rather the Man-God, created the universe. But Man's imperfection, his flaw, lay in his failure to realize that he *is* God. The Man-God begins his life in history unconscious of the vital fact that he is God. He is alienated, cut off, from the crucial knowledge that he and God are one, that he created, and continues to empower, the universe. History, then, is the inevitable process by which the Man-God develops his faculties, fulfills his potential, and ad-

[14]Christopher Hill, *The World Turned Upside Down: Radical Ideas During the English Revolution* (London: Penguin Books, 1975), p. 136. Also see F. D. Dow, *Radicalism in the English Revolution, 1640-1660* (Oxford: Basil Blackwell, 1985), pp. 74–80.

[15]See the superb work by the leading literary critic of Romanticism, Abrams, *Natural Supernaturalism*.

[16]Hegel was nominally a Lutheran, but Lutheranism in Germany at that time was evidently latitudinarian enough to encompass pantheism.

vances his knowledge, *until* that blissful day when Man acquires Absolute Knowledge, that is, the full knowledge and
realization that he is God. At that point, the Man-God finally
reaches his potential, becomes an infinite being without
bounds, and thereby puts an end to history. The dialectic of
history occurs, again, in three fundamental stages: the Pre-
Creation stage; the post-Creation stage of development with
alienation; and the final reabsorption into the state of infinity
and absolute self-knowledge, which culminates, and puts an
end to, the historical process.

Why, then, did Hegel's Man-God (also termed by Hegel the
"world-self" or "world-spirit" [*Weltgeist*]) create the universe?
Not out of benevolence, but out of a felt need to become conscious of itself as a world-self. This process of growing consciousness is achieved through the creative activity by which
the world-self externalizes itself. First, this externalization
occurs by the Man-God creating nature, and next, by a continuing self-externalization through human history. By building
civilization, Man increases the knowledge of his own divinity;
in that way, through history Man gradually puts an end to his
own "self-alienation," which for Hegel was *ipso facto* the alienation of Man from God. Crucial to Hegelian doctrine is that Man
is alienated, and he perceives the world as hostile, *because* it is
not himself. All these conflicts are finally resolved when Man
realizes at long last that the world really *is* himself.

But why is Hegel's Man so odd and neurotic that he regards
everything that is not himself as alien and hostile? The answer
is central to the Hegelian mystique. It is because Hegel, or
Hegel's Man, cannot stand the idea of himself not being God,
and therefore not being of infinite space and without boundary
or limit. Seeing any other being or any other object exist, would
imply that he himself is not infinite or divine. In short, Hegel's
philosophy constitutes solipsistic megalomania on a grand and
cosmic scale. Professor Robert C. Tucker describes the situation
with characteristic acuity:

> For Hegel alienation is finitude, and finitude in turn is bond-
> age. The experience of self estrangement in the presence of an

apparent objective world is an experience of enslavement, . . .
Spirit, when confronted with an object or "other," is *ipso facto*
aware of itself as merely finite being . . . as extending only so
far and no farther. The object is, therefore, a "limit" (*Grenze*).
And a limit, since it contradicts spirit's notion of itself as
absolute being, i.e. being-without-limit, is necessarily appre-
hended as a "barrier" or "fetter" (*Schranke*). . . . In its confron-
tation with an apparent object, spirit feels imprisoned in
limitation. It experiences what Hegel calls the "sorrow of
finitude."

. . . In Hegel's quite unique conception of it, freedom means
the consciousness of self as unbounded; it is the absence of a
limiting object or non-self . . .

Accordingly, the growth of spirit's self-knowledge in history is
alternatively describable as a progress of the consciousness of
freedom.[17]

Hegel's dialectic of history did not simply have three stages;
history moved forward in a series of stages, each one of which
was moved forward dramatically by a process of *aufhebung*. It
is evident that the Man who creates the world, advances his
"self"-knowledge, and who finally "returns" "Home" in an ecstasy of self-knowledge is not puny individual Man, but Man as
collective-species. But, for Hegel, each stage of advance is pro-
pelled by great individuals, "world-historical" men, who embody
the attributes of the Absolute more than others, and act as significant agents of the next *aufhebung*, the lifting up of the Man-God's
or "world-soul's" next great advance into "self-knowledge."

Thus, at a time when most patriotic Prussians were reacting
violently against Napoleon's imperial conquests, and mobilizing
their forces against him, Hegel wrote to a friend in ecstasy about
having seen Napoleon, "the Emperor—this world-soul" riding
down the street; for Napoleon, even if unconsciously, was pursuing the world-historical mission of bringing a strong Prussian
State into being.[18] It is interesting that Hegel got his idea of the

---

[17]Robert C. Tucker, *Philosophy and Myth*, pp. 53–54.

[18]See Raymond Plant, *Hegel* (Bloomington: Indiana University Press, 1973),
p. 120.

"cunning of Reason," of great individuals acting as unconscious agents of the world-soul through history by perusing the works of the Rev. Adam Ferguson, whose phrase about events being "the product of human action but not of human design," has been so influential in the thought of F. A. Hayek and his disciples.[19] In the economic realm, as well, Hegel learned of the alleged misery of alienation in separation—that is specialization and the division-of-labor, from Ferguson himself through Friedrich Schiller and from Ferguson's good friend, Adam Smith, in his *Wealth of Nations*.[20]

It is easy to see how the reabsorptionist-Hegelian doctrine of unity-good, separation-bad, helped form the Marxian goal of communism, the end-state of history in which the individual is totally absorbed into the collective, thus attaining the state of true collective-man "freedom." But there are also more particular influences. Thus, the Marxian idea of early or primitive communism, happy and integrated though undeveloped, and then burst apart by rapacious, alienating if developing capitalism, was prefigured by Hegel's historical outlook. Following his friend and mentor the Romantic writer Friedrich Schiller, Hegel, in an article written in 1795, lauded the alleged homogeneity, harmony, and unity of ancient Greece, supposedly free of

---

[19]Ferguson, furthermore, used his phrase in a fashion very similar to that of Hegel, and was originally far from the Hayekian analysis of the free market. Ferguson, as a young Calvinist minister, enlisted in the suppression of the Jacobite rebellion of 1745 in Scotland. After the rebellion was at last put down, Ferguson preached a sermon in which he tried to solve the great puzzle: why did God permit the Catholics to pursue their evil goals and almost triumph? His answer: that the Catholics, even though consciously pursuing evil ends, served as the unconscious agents of God's good purpose: i.e., rousing the Presbyterian Church of Scotland out of its alleged apathy. Hence, a prototype of the "cunning of Reason" in history, except for theist rather than pantheist goals. See Richard B. Sher, *Church and University in the Scottish Enlightenment* (Princeton: Princeton University Press, 1985), pp. 40–44.

[20]As Paul Craig Roberts has rightly emphasized, "alienation" in Marx is not simply the capitalist wage-relation, but, more deeply, specialization, the division of labor, and the money economy itself. But as we see, alienation is even more rootedly the cosmic condition of man's state until the reabsorption of collective man-and-nature under communism. See Paul Craig Roberts, *Alienation and the Soviet Economy* (Albuquerque: University of New Mexico, 1971); and Roberts and Matthew A. Stephenson, *Marx's Theory of Exchange, Alienation and Crisis*, 2nd ed. (New York: Praeger, 1983).

the alienating division of labor. The consequent *aufhebung*, though leading to the growth of commerce, living standards, and individualism, also destroyed the wonderful unity of Greece and radically fragmented man. To Hegel, the next inevitable stage of history would reintegrate man and the State.

The State was critical for Hegel. Again foreshadowing Marx, it is now particularly important for man—the collective organism—to surmount unconscious blind fate, and "consciously" to take control of his "fate" by means of the State.

Hegel was quite insistent that, in order for the State to fulfill its vital function, it must be guided by a comprehensive philosophy, and indeed by a Great Philosopher, to give its mighty rule the necessary coherence. Otherwise, as Professor Plant explains, "such a state, devoid of philosophical comprehension, would appear as a merely arbitrary and oppressive imposition of the freedom of individuals." But, on the contrary, if armed with Hegelian philosophy and with Hegel himself as its great leader, "this alien aspect of the progressive modern state would disappear and would be seen not as an imposition but a development of self-consciousness."[21]

Armed, then, with such a philosophy and such a philosopher, the modern, especially the modern Prussian, State could take its divinely-appointed stand at the apex of human history and civilization, as God on earth. Thus: "The modern State, . . . when comprehended philosophically, could therefore be seen as the highest articulation of Spirit, or God in the contemporary world." The State, then, is "a supreme manifestation of the activity of God in the world"; "The State is the Divine Idea as it exists on earth"; "The State is the march of God through the world"; "The State is the actually existing, realized moral life"; the "State is the reality of the kingdom of heaven." And finally: "The State is God's Will."[22]

For Hegel, of all the various forms of State, monarchy—as

---

[21]Plant, *Hegel*, p. 96.

[22]See Plant, *Hegel*, pp. 122, 123, and 181. Also see Karl R. Popper, *The Open Society and its Enemies*, vol. 2 (New York: Harper Torchbooks, 1963), p. 31.

in contemporary Prussia—is best, since it permits all its subjects to be "free" (in the Hegelian sense) by submerging their
being into the divine substance, which is the authoritarian,
monarchial State. The people are only "free" as insignificant
particles of this divine substance. As Tucker writes:

> Hegel's conception of freedom is totalitarian in a literal sense
> of the word. The world-self must experience itself as the
> totality of being, or in Hegel's own words must elevate itself
> to a "self-comprehending totality," in order to achieve the
> consciousness of freedom.[23]

Every determinist creed thoughtfully provides an escape
hatch for the determinist himself, so that he can rise above the
determining factors, expound his philosophy and convince his
fellowmen. Hegel was no exception, but his was unquestionably
the most grandiose of all escape-hatches. For of all the world-historical figures, those embodiments of the Man-God, who are called
on to bring on the next stage of the dialectic, who can be greater,
more in tune with the divinity, than the Great Philosopher himself
who has brought us the knowledge of this entire process, and
thereby was able to himself complete man's final comprehension
of the Absolute and of man's all-encompassing divinity? And isn't
the great creator of the crucial philosophy about man and the
universe in a deep sense greater than the philosophy itself? And
therefore, if the species man is God, isn't he, the great Hegel, in a
profound sense God of Gods?[24] Finally, as luck and the dialectic

---

[23]Tucker, *Philosophy and Myth*, pp. 54–55. E. F. Carritt points out that, for
Hegel, "freedom" is "desiring above all things to serve the success and glory of their
State. In desiring this they are desiring that the will of God should be done." If an
individual thinks he should do something which is *not* for the success and glory of
the State, then, for Hegel, "he should be 'forced to be free.'" How does a person *know*
what action will redound to the glory of the State? To Hegel, the answer was easy.
Whatever the State rulers demand, since "the very fact of their being rulers is the surest
sign of God's will that they should be." Impeccable logic indeed! See E. F. Carritt, "Reply"
(1940), reprinted in W. Kauffmann, ed., *Hegel's Political Philosophy* (New York: Atherton
Press, 1970), pp. 38–39.

[24]Tucker offers an amusing comment on the reaction of the eminent Hegelian
W. T. Stace, who had written that "we must not jump to the preposterous conclusion
that, according to Hegel's philosophy, I, this particular human spirit, am the
Absolute, nor that the Absolute is any particular spirit, nor that it is humanity in
general. Such conclusions would be little short of shocking." Tucker adds that this

would have it, Hegel was just in time to take his place as the Great Philosopher, in the greatest, the noblest, and most developed authoritarian State in the history of the world: the existing Prussian monarchy of King Friedrich Wilhelm III. If the King would only accept his world-historical mission, Hegel, arm-in-arm with the King, would then usher in the final culminating self-knowledge of the Absolute Man-God. Together, Hegel, aided by the King, would bring an end to human history.

For his part, King Friedrich Wilhelm III was all too ready to play his divinely appointed role. When the reactionary powers took over Prussia in 1815, they needed an official philosopher to call on Prussian subjects to worship the State, and thereby to combat the French Revolutionary ideals of individualism, liberty, reason, and natural rights. Hegel was brought to the great new University of Berlin in 1818, to become the official philosopher of that academic monument to the authoritarian Prussian State.

While highly influential in Prussia and the Protestant sectors of Germany, Hegelianism was also akin to, and influential upon, the Romantic writers in England. Virtually all of Wordsworth's poetic output was designed to set forth what he called a "high Romantic argument" designed to transcend and counteract Milton's "heroic" or "great" argument expounding the orthodox Christian eschatology, that man, as individual men, will either return to Paradise or be consigned to Hell upon the Second Advent of Jesus Christ. To this "argument," Wordsworth counterposed his own pantheist vision of the upward spiral of history in which Man, as species, inevitably returns home from his cosmic alienation. Also dedicated to the Wordsworthian vision were Coleridge, Shelley and Keats. It is instructive that all of these men were Christian heretics, converts from explicitly Christian theology: Wordsworth had been trained to be an Anglican priest; Coleridge had been a lay preacher, and was steeped in neo-Platonism and the mystical works of Jakob Boehme; and

---

"argument from propriety" does not answer the question "why we must assume that Hegel could not be 'shocking.'" Or, we might add, preposterous, or megalomaniacal. Tucker, *Philosophy*, pp. 46 n. and 47 n.

Shelley had been absorbed in the study of the Bible.

Finally, the tempestuous conservative statist British writer, Thomas Carlyle, paid tribute to Hegel's mentor Friedrich Schiller by writing a biography of Schiller in 1825. From then on, Carlyle's influential writings were to be steeped in the Hegelian vision. Unity is good, diversity and separateness is evil and diseased; science as well as individualism constitutes division and dismemberment. Selfhood, Carlyle ranted, is alienation from nature, from others, and from oneself. But one day, Carlyle prophesied, the breakthrough, the world's spiritual rebirth, will arrive, led by world-historical figures ("great men"), through which man will return home to a friendly world by means of the utter "annihilation of self" (*Selbst-todtung*).[25] Finally, in *Past and Present* (1843), Carlyle applied his profoundly anti-individualist vision to economic affairs. He denounced egoism, material greed, and laissez-faire, which, by fostering man's severance from others, had led to a world "which has become a lifeless other, and in severance also from other human beings within a social order in which 'cash payment is . . . the sole nexus of man with man.'" In opposition to this evil "cash nexus" lay the familial relation with nature and fellow-men, the relation of "love." The stage was set for Karl Marx.[26]

Communism as the Kingdom of God on Earth: From Joachim to Müntzer

So far we have dealt with reabsorption theology as a crucial forerunner of Marx's religious eschatological communism. But there is another important strand sometimes woven in with the first, fused into his eschatological vision: messianic millennial-

---

[25]On the influence of Schiller's views on organicism and alienation upon Hegel, Marx and later sociology, see Leon Bramson, *The Political Context of Sociology* (Princeton: Princeton University Press, 1961), p. 30 n.

[26]See Abrams, *Natural Supernaturalism*, p. 311.

ism, or chiliasm, the establishing of a communist Kingdom of God on Earth.

Throughout its history, Christianity has had to confront the question of the millennium: the thousand-year reign of God on earth. Particularly in such murky parts of the Bible as the book of *Daniel* and the book of *Revelation*, there are suggestions of such a millennial Kingdom of God on Earth before the final Day of Judgment and the end of human history. The orthodox Christian line was set by the great Saint Augustine in the early fifth century, and has been accepted ever since by the mainstream Christian churches: Roman Catholic, Lutheran, and arguably by Calvin and at least by the Dutch wing of the Calvinist church. That orthodox line holds that the millennial Kingdom of God on Earth [KGE] is strictly a metaphor for the Christian Church, which reigns on earth only in the spiritual sense. The material realization of the Kingdom of God will only arrive upon the Day of Judgment, and is therefore to be confined to heaven alone. Orthodox Christians have always warned that taking the KGE literally, what the late orthodox Christian theorist Erich Voegelin called "immanentizing the eschaton"—bringing the eschaton down to earth—is bound to create grave social problems. For one thing, most versions of how the KGE will come into being are apocalyptic. The KGE is to be preceded by a mighty Armageddon, a titanic war of good against evil, in which the good will finally, though inevitably, triumph. One reason for the apocalypse is a fundamental problem faced by all KGE theorists. The KGE, by definition, will consist of a society of saints, of perfect people. But if this is true, what has become of the host of human sinners, of whom alas there are legion? In order to establish the KGE there must first be some sort of mighty apocalyptic purge of the sinners to clear the ground for the society of saints. "Pre-millennial" and "post-millennial" variants of apocalyptics accomplish this task in different ways. The pre-mils, who believe that Jesus's Second Advent will precede the KGE, and that Jesus will run the Kingdom with the cadre of saints at his right hand, achieve the purge by a divinely determined Armageddon between God's forces and the forces of the Beast and the Anti-Christ. The post-mils, who believe that man must establish the

KGE as a precondition of Jesus's Second Coming, have to take matters more directly in their own hands and accomplish the great purge on their own.

Thus, one disturbing aspect of the KGE is the preparatory purgation of the host of human sinners. A second problem is what the KGE is going to look like. As we might imagine, KGE theorists have been extremely cloudy about the nature of their perfect society, but one troublesome feature is that, to the extent that we know its operations at all, the KGE is almost always depicted as a communist society, lacking work, private property, or the division of labor. In short, something like the Marxian communist utopia, except run by a cadre, not of the vanguard of the proletariat, but of theocratic saints.

Any communist system faces the problem of production: who would have the incentive to produce for the communal store-house, and how would this work and its products be allocated? The first, and most highly influential, communist Christian heretic was the late twelfth-century Calabrian abbot and her-mit, Joachim of Fiore. Joachim, who almost managed to convert three popes to his heresy, adopted the thesis that there are destined to be in history, not just two Ages (pre and post-Christian) as orthodox Christians believe, but a Third Age a-borning, of which he was the prophet. The pre-Christian ara was the age of the Father, of the Old Testament; the Christian era the age of the Son, the New Testament. And now arrives the third apocalyptic age of the Holy Spirit, to be ushered in during the next half-century, an age of pure love and freedom, in which history was to come to an end. The Church, the Bible, and the State would be swept away, and man would live in a free communist community without work or property.

Joachim dispensed with the problem of production and allo-cation under communism very neatly and effectively, more so than any communist successor. In the Third Age, he declared, man's material bodies will disappear, and man will be pure spirit, free to spend all of his days in mystical ecstasy chanting praises to God for a thousand years until the Day of Judgment. Without physical bodies, there is of course precious little need for production.[27] For Joachim, the path to this kingdom of pure spirit would be blazed by a new order of highly spiritual monks, from whom would come 12 patriarchs headed by a supreme teacher, who would convert the Jews to Christianity as foretold in the book of *Revelation*. For a blazing three and a half years a secular king, the Antichrist, would crush and destroy the corrupt Christian Church, after which the Antichrist would be overthrown by the new monastic order, who would promptly establish the millennial age of the Spirit. It is no wonder that a rigorist wing of the Franciscan order, which was to emerge during the first half of the thirteenth century, and be dedicated to material poverty, should see themselves as the coming Joachimite cadre.

At the same period, the Amaurians, led by a group of theology students of Amalric at the University of Paris, carried on the Joachimite doctrine of the three Ages, and added an interesting twist: each age, they declared, has enjoyed its own Incarnation. In the age of the Old Testament, the divine Incarnation settled in Abraham and perhaps some other patriarchs; for the New Testament age, the Incarnation was of course Jesus; and now, for the dawning Age of the Holy Spirit, the Incarnation would emerge among the various human beings themselves. As might be expected, the Amaurian cadre proclaimed themselves to be living gods, the Incarnation of the Holy Spirit. Not that they would always remain a divine elite, among men; on the contrary, they were destined to be the vanguard, leading mankind to its universal Incarnation.

During the following century, a congeries of groups throughout northern Europe known as the Brethren of the Free Spirit added another important ingredient to this brew: the mystical dialectic of the "reabsorption into God." But the brethren added their own elitist twist: while the reabsorption of all men

---

[27]As the historian Norman Cohn put it, the Joachimite new "world would be one vast monastery, in which all men would be contemplative monks rapt in mystical ecstasy and united in singing the praises of God." Norman Cohn, *The Pursuit of the Millennium*, rev. ed. (New York: Oxford University Press, 1970), pp. 108–09.

must await the end of history, and the mass of the "crude in spirit" must meanwhile meet their individual deaths, there was a glorious minority, the "subtle in spirit," who could and did become reabsorbed and therefore living gods during their lifetime. This minority, of course, was the cadre of the Brethren themselves, who, by virtue of years of training, self-torture, and visions had become perfect gods, more perfect and more godlike than even Christ himself. Furthermore, once this stage of mystical union was reached, it was to be permanent and eternal. These new gods, in fact, often proclaimed themselves greater than God himself.

Being living gods on earth brought a lot of good things in its wake. In the first place, it led directly to an extreme form of the antinomian heresy; that is, if people are gods, then it is impossible for them to sin. Whatever they did is necessarily moral and perfect. This means that any act ordinarily considered to be sin, from adultery to murder, becomes perfectly legitimate when performed by the living gods. Indeed, the Free Spirits, like other antinomians, were tempted to demonstrate and flaunt their freedom from sin by performing all manner of sins imaginable.

But there was also a catch. Among the Free Spirit cultists, only a minority of leading adepts were "living gods"; for the rank-and-file cultists, striving to become gods, there was one sin and one alone which they must not commit: disobedience to their master. Each disciple was bound by an oath of absolute obedience to a particular living god. Take, for example, Nicholas of Basle, a leading Free Spirit whose cult stretched most of the length of the Rhine. Claiming to be the new Christ, Nicholas held that everyone's sole path to salvation consisted of making an act of absolute and total submission to Nicholas himself. In return for this total fealty, Nicholas granted his followers freedom from all sin.

As for the rest of mankind outside the cults, they were simply unredeemed and unregenerate beings who existed only to be used and exploited by the Elect. This gospel of total rule went hand in hand with the social doctrine of many of the fourteenth century cults of the Free Spirit: a communistic assault on the institution of private property. In a sense, however, this philosophic communism was merely a thinly camouflaged cover for the Free Spirits' self-proclaimed right to commit theft at will. The Free Spirit adept, in short, regarded all property of the non-Elect as rightfully his own. As the Bishop of Strasbourg summed up this creed in 1317: "They believe that all things are common, whence they conclude that theft is lawful for them." Or as the Free Spirit adept from Erfurt, Johann Hartmann, put it: "The truly free man is king and lord of all creatures. All things belong to him, and he has the right to use whatever pleases him. If anyone tries to prevent him, the free man may kill him and take his goods."[28] As one of the favorite sayings of the Brethren of the Free Spirit phrased it: "Whatever the eye sees and covets, let the hand grasp it."

The following century, the fifteenth, brought the first attempt to initiate the KGE, the first brief experiment in totalitarian theocratic communism. This attempt originated in the left, or extreme, wing, of the Taborites, which in turn constituted the radical wing of the revolutionary Hussite movement in Czech Bohemia of the early fifteenth century. The Hussite movement, led by Jan Hus, was a pre-Protestant revolutionary formation that blended struggles of religion (Hussite vs. Catholic), nationality (popular Czech vs. upper-class and upper-clergy German), and class (artisans cartelized in urban guilds trying to take political power from patricians). Building on the previous communist KGE movements, and especially on the Brethren of the Free Spirit, the ultra-Taborites added, with considerable enthusiasm, one extra ingredient: the duty to exterminate. For the Last Days are coming, and the Elect must go forth and stamp out sin by exterminating all sinners, which means, at the very least, all non-ultra-Taborites. For all sinners are enemies of Christ, and "accursed be the man who withholds his sword from shedding the blood of the enemies of Christ. Every believer must wash his hands in that blood." This destruction was of course not to stop at intellectual eradication. When sacking churches and monasteries, the

---

[28]Cohn, *Pursuit of the Millennium*, p. 182.

Taborites took particular delight in destroying libraries and burning books. For "all belongings must be taken away from God's enemies and burned or otherwise destroyed." Besides, the Elect have no need of books. When the Kingdom of God on Earth arrived, there would no longer be "need for anyone to teach another. There would be no need for books or scriptures, and all worldly wisdom will perish." And all people too, one suspects.

The ultra-Taborites also wove in the reabsorption theme: a return to the alleged early condition of Czech communism: a society lacking the sin of private property. In order to return to this classless society, determined the Taborites, the cities, those notorious centers of luxury and avarice, must be exterminated. And once the communist KGE had been established in Bohemia, the Elect must forge out from that base and impose such communism on the rest of the world.

The Taborites also added another ingredient to make their communist ideal consistent. In addition to the communism of property, women would also be communized. The Taborite preachers taught that "Everything will be common, including wives; there will be free sons and daughters of God and there will be no marriage as union of two—husband and wife."

The Hussite revolution broke out in 1419, and in that same year, the Taborites gathered at the town of Usti, in northern Bohemia near the German border. They renamed Usti "Tabor," i.e., the Mount of Olives where Jesus had foretold his Second Coming, was ascended to heaven, and where he was expected to reappear. The radical Taborites engaged in a communist experiment at Tabor, owning everything in common, and dedicated to the proposition that "whoever owns private property commits a mortal sin." True to their doctrines, all women were owned in common, and if husband and wife were ever seen together, they were beaten to death or otherwise executed. Characteristically, the Taborites were so caught up in their unlimited right to consume from the common store that they felt themselves exempt from the need to work. The common store soon disappeared, and then what? Then, of course, the radical Taborites claimed that their need entitled them to claim the property of the non-elect, and they proceeded to rob others at will. As a synod of the moderate Taborites complained: "many communities never think of earning their own living by the work of their hands but are only willing to live on other people's property and to undertake unjust campaigns for the sake of robbing." Moreover, the Taborite peasantry who had rejoiced in the abolition of feudal dues paid to the Catholic patricians, found the radical regime reimposing the same feudal dues and bonds only six months later.

Discredited among their moderate allies and among their peasantry, the radical communist regime at Usti/Tabor soon collapsed. But their torch was quickly picked up by a sect known as the Bohemian Adamites. Like the Free Spirits of the previous century, the Adamites held themselves to be living gods, superior to Christ, since Christ had died while they still lived (impeccable logic, if a bit short-sighted). For the Adamites, led by a peasant leader they dubbed "Adam-Moses," all goods were owned strictly in common, and marriage was considered a heinous sin. In short, promiscuity was compulsory, since the chaste were unworthy to enter the messianic Kingdom. Any man could choose any woman at will, and that will would have to be obeyed. On the other hand, promiscuity was at one and the same time compulsory and severely restricted; since sex could only take place with the permission of the leader Adam-Moses. The Adamites added a special twist: they went around naked most of the time, imitating the original state of Adam and Eve.

Like the other radical Taborites, the Adamites regarded it as their sacred mission to exterminate all the unbelievers in the world, wielding the sword, in one of their favorite images, until blood floods the world up to the height of a horse's bridle. The Adamites were God's scythe, sent to cut down and eradicate the unrighteous.

Pursued by the Hussite military commander, Jan Zizka, the Adamites took refuge on an island in the river Nezarka, from which they went forth in commando raids to try their best, despite their relatively small number, to fulfill their twin pledge of compulsory communism and extermination of the non-elect. At night, they raided the mainland—in forays they called a "Holy War"—to rob everything they could lay their hands on and to exterminate their victims. True to their creed, they murdered every man, woman, and child they could find.

Finally, in October 1421, Zizka sent a force of 400 hundred trained soldiers to besiege the Adamite island, soon overwhelming the commune and massacring every last Adamite. One more hellish Kingdom of God on Earth had been put to the sword.

The moderate Taborite army was, in turn, crushed by the Hussites at the Battle of Lipan in 1434, and from then on, Taborism declined and went underground. But Taborite and millennialist ideas continued to pop up, not only among the Czechs, but also in Bavaria and in other German lands bordering Bohemia.

Sometimes Martin Luther must have felt that he had loosed the whirlwind, even opened the Gates of Hell. Shortly after Luther launched the Reformation, Anabaptist sects appeared and spread throughout Germany. Anabaptists believed that they were the Elect, and that the sign of that election was an emotional, mystical conversion experience, the process of being "born again," or baptized in the Holy Spirit. For groups of the Anabaptist elect finding themselves within a corrupt and sinful society, there were two routes to take. One, the voluntary Anabaptists, such as the Amish or Mennonites, became virtual anarchists, striving to separate themselves as much as possible from a sinful State and society. The other wing, the theocratic Anabaptists, sought to seize power in the State and to shape up society by extreme coercion. As Monsignor Knox has pointed out, this ultra-theocratic approach must be distinguished from the sort of theocracy (what has recently been called *theonomy*—the rule of God's Law) imposed by Calvin in Geneva or by the Calvinistic Puritans in the seventeenth century North America. Luther and Calvin, in Knox's terminology, did not pretend to be "prophets" enjoying continuing personal divine revelation; they were only "pundits," scholarly experts in interpreting the Bible, and in applying Biblical law to man.[29] But the coercive Anabaptists were led by men claiming mystical illumination and revelation and deserving therefore of absolute power.

The wave of theocratic Anabaptism that swept over Germany and Holland with hurricane force may be called the "Müntzer-Münster era," since it was launched by Thomas Müntzer in 1520, and ended in a holocaust at the city of Münster 15 years later. A learned young theologian and graduate of the Universities of Leipzig and Frankfurt, Müntzer was selected by Luther to become a Lutheran pastor in the city of Zwickau. Zwickau, however, was near the Bohemian border, and there Müntzer was converted by the weaver and adept Niklas Storch, who had lived in Bohemia, to the old Taborite creed. In particular: continuing personal divine revelation to the prophet of the cult, and the necessity for the elect to seize power and impose a society of theocratic communism by brutal force of arms. In addition, there was to be communism of women: marriage was to be prohibited, and each man was to be able to have any woman at will.

Thomas Müntzer now claimed to be the divinely chosen prophet, destined to wage a war of blood and extermination by the elect against the sinners. Müntzer claimed that the "living Christ" had permanently entered his own soul; endowed thereby with perfect insight into the divine will, he asserted himself to be uniquely qualified to fulfill the divine mission. He even spoke of himself as "becoming God." Having graduated from the world of learning, Müntzer was now ready for the world of action.

Müntzer wandered around central Germany for several years, gaining adepts and inspiring uprisings that were quickly suppressed. Gaining a ministerial post in the small Thuringian town of Allstedt, Müntzer gained a wide popular following by preaching in the vernacular, attracting a large number

[29]Ronald A. Knox, *Enthusiasm: A Chapter in the History of Religion* (1950; New York: Oxford University Press, 1961), pp. 132–34.

of uneducated miners, whom he formed into a revolutionary organization called "The League of the Elect." A turning point in Müntzer's career came in 1524, when Duke John, brother of the Elector of Saxony and a Lutheran, came to town and asked Müntzer to preach him a sermon. Seizing his opportunity, Müntzer laid it on the line: the Saxon princes must take their stand as either servants of God or of the Devil. If they would do the former, they must "lay on with the sword" to "exterminate" all the "godless" and "evil-doers," especially including priests, monks, and godless rulers. If the Saxon princes failed in this task, Müntzer warned, "the sword shall be taken from them. . . . If they [the princes] resist, let them be slaughtered without mercy. ..." Such extermination, performed by the princes and guided by Müntzer, would usher in a thousand-year-rule by the Elect.

Duke John's reaction to this fiery ultimatum was surprisingly blasé, but, warned repeatedly by Luther that Müntzer was becoming dangerous, the Duke finally ordered Müntzer to refrain from any provocative preaching until his case was decided by the Elector.

This reaction by the Saxon princes, however mild, was enough to set Thomas Müntzer onto his final revolutionary road. The princes had proved themselves untrustworthy: it was now up to the mass of the poor to make the revolution. The poor, the Elect, would establish a rule of compulsory egalitarian communism, where all things would be owned in common by all, where everyone would be equal in all things and each person would receive according to his need. But not yet. For even the poor must first be broken of worldly desires and frivolous enjoyments, and they must recognize the leadership of a new "servant of God" who "must stand forth in the spirit of Elijah . . . and set things in motion." It was not difficult to guess who that Leader was supposed to be.

Seeing Allstedt as inhospitable, Müntzer moved to the Thuringian city of Muhlhausen, where he found a friendly home in a land in political turmoil. Under Müntzer's inspiration, a revolutionary group took over Muhlhausen in February 1525, and Müntzer and his allies proceeded to impose a communist regime upon that city.

The monasteries of Muhlhausen were seized, and all property was declared to be in common; as a consequence, as a contemporary observer noted, the regime "so affected the folk that no one wanted to work." As under the Taborites, the regime of communism and love soon became, in practice, a systemic excuse for theft:

> when anyone needed food or clothing he went to a rich man and demanded it of him in Christ's name, for Christ had commanded that all should share with the needy. And what was not given freely was taken by force. Many acted thus. . . . Thomas [Müntzer] instituted this brigandage and multiplied it every day.[30]

At that point, the great Peasants' War erupted throughout Germany, a rebellion by the peasantry in favor of their local autonomy, and opposing the new centralizing, high tax rule of the German princes. In the process of crushing the feebly armed peasantry, the princes came to Muhlhausen on May 15, and offered amnesty to the peasants if they would hand over Müntzer and his immediate followers. The peasants were tempted, but Müntzer, holding aloft his naked sword, gave his last flaming speech, declaring that God had personally promised him victory; that he would catch all the enemy cannon-balls in the sleeves of his cloak; and that God would protect them all. At a climactic moment in Müntzer's speech, a rainbow appeared in the heavens. Since Müntzer had adopted the rainbow as the symbol of his movement, the credulous peasantry naturally interpreted this event as a veritable Sign from heaven. Unfortunately, the Sign failed to work, and the princes' army crushed the peasantry, killing 5,000 while losing only half a dozen men. Müntzer himself fled and hid, but was captured soon after, tortured into confession, and duly executed.

---

[30]Quoted in Igor Shafarevich, *The Socialist Phenomenon* (New York: Harper and Row, 1980), p. 57.

Communism as the Kingdom
of God on Earth:
The Takeover of Münster

Thomas Müntzer and his Sign may have gotten short shrift, and his body be a-mouldrin' in the grave, but his soul kept marching on. His cause was soon picked up by a Müntzer disciple, the bookbinder Hans Hut. Hut claimed to be a prophet sent by God to announce that Christ would return to earth at Whitsuntide, 1528, and would give the power to enforce justice to Hut and to his following of rebaptized saints. The saints would then "take up double-edged swords" and wreak God's vengeance upon priests, pastors, kings, and nobles. Hut and his men would then "establish the rule of Hans Hut on earth," with Muhlhausen, as one might expect, as the world's capital. Christ, aided by Hut and company, would then establish a millennium of communism and free love. Hut was captured in 1527 (unfortunately before Jesus had a chance to return), imprisoned at Augsburg, and killed allegedly trying to escape. For a year or two, Huttian followers popped up throughout southern Germany, threatening to set up a communist Kingdom of God by force of arms. In 1530, however, they were smashed and suppressed by the alarmed authorities. Müntzerian-type Anabaptism would now move to northwestern Germany.

Northwestern Germany was dotted by a number of small ecclesiastical states, each run by a prince-bishop, bishops who were secular aristocratic lords not ordained as priests. The ruling clergy of the state exempted themselves from taxation, while imposing heavy taxes on the rest of the populace. Generally, the capital cities of each state were run by an oligarchy of guilds who cartelized their crafts, and who battled the state clergy for a degree of autonomy.

The largest of these ecclesiastical states in northwest Germany was the bishopric of Münster; its capital city of Münster, a town of some 10,000 people, was run by the town guilds. During and after the Peasants' War, the guilds and clergy battled back and forth, until, in 1532, the guilds, supported by the people, were able to take over the town, soon forcing the Catholic bishop to recognize Münster officially as a Lutheran city.

Münster was not destined to remain Lutheran for long, however. From all over the northwest, hordes of Anabaptist crazies flooded into the city of Münster, seeking the onset of the New Jerusalem. Anabaptism escalated when the eloquent and popular young minister Bernt Rothmann, a highly educated son of a town blacksmith, converted to Anabaptism. Originally a Catholic priest, Rothmann had become a friend of Luther and a head of the Lutheran church in Münster. But now he lent his eloquent preaching to the cause of communism as it had supposedly existed in the primitive Christian Church, with everything being held in common, with no mine or thine, and each man receiving according to his "need." Rothmann's widespread reputation attracted thousands more into Münster, largely the poor, the rootless, and those hopelessly in debt.

The leader of the horde of Münster Anabaptists, however, was destined to be not Rothmann but a Dutch baker from Haarlem, Jan Matthys. In early 1534, Matthys sent out missionaries or "apostles" to rebaptize everyone they could into the Matthys movement, and his apostles were greeted in Münster with enormous enthusiasm. Even Rothmann was rebaptized once again, followed by many former nuns and a large part of the population. The leader of the Matthys movement soon arrived, a young Dutchman of 25 named Jan Bockelson (Jan of Leyden). Bockelson quickly married the daughter of the wealthy cloth merchant, Bernt Knipperdollinck, the leader of the Münster guilds, and the two men, leading the town in apocalyptic frenzy, led a successful uprising to dominate the town. The two leaders sent messengers outside the town urging all followers to come to Münster. The rest of the world, they proclaimed, would be destroyed in a month or two; only Münster would be saved, to become the New Jerusalem. Thousands poured in from as far away as Frisia in the northern Netherlands. As a result, the Anabaptists were able to impose absolute rule on the city, with the incoming Matthys, aided by Bockelson, becoming the virtual dictators of Münster. At last,

Anabaptism had seized a real-life city; the greatest communist experiment in history to that date could now begin.

The first cherished program of this new communist theocracy was, of course, to purge the New Jerusalem of the unclean and the ungodly, as a prelude to their ultimate extermination throughout the world. Matthys, therefore, called for the execution of all remaining Catholics and Lutherans, but Knipperdollinck, slightly more politically astute, warned Matthys that such immediate slaughter might bring down the wrath of the rest of the world. Matthys therefore did the next best thing, and on February 27 the Catholics and Lutherans were driven out of the city, in the midst of a horrendous snowstorm. Prefiguring the actions of communist Cambodia in the 1970s, all non-Anabaptists, including old people, invalids, babies, and pregnant women, were driven into the snowstorm, and all were forced to leave behind all their money, property, food, and clothing. The remaining Lutherans and Catholics were compulsorily rebaptized, all those refusing being put to death. The mass expulsion of non-Anabaptists was enough for the bishop, who began a long military siege of Münster the next day.

With every person in the city drafted for siege work, Jan Matthys launched his totalitarian communist social revolution. The first step was to confiscate the property of the expellees. All their worldly goods were placed in central depots, and the poor were encouraged to take "according to their needs," the "needs" to be interpreted by seven appointed "deacons" chosen by Matthys. When a blacksmith protested at these measures imposed, particularly gallingly, by a group of Dutch foreigners, Matthys arrested the courageous smithy. Summoning the entire population of the town to be witness, Matthys personally stabbed, shot, and killed the "godless" blacksmith, and then threw into prison several leading citizens who protested his treatment. The crowd was warned to profit by this public execution, and they obediently sang a hymn in honor of the killing.

A crucial part of the Anabaptist reign of terror was their decision, again prefiguring that of the Khmer Rouge regime in Cambodia, to abolish all private ownership of money. With no money to purchase any good, the population became slavishly dependent on handouts or rations from the power elite. Accordingly, Matthys, Rothmann and the rest launched a propaganda campaign that it was un-Christian to own money privately; and that all money should be held "in common," which in practice meant that all money whatsoever must be handed over to Matthys and his ruling clique. Several Anabaptists who kept or hid their money were arrested and terrorized into crawling to Matthys on their knees, begging forgiveness, which Matthys graciously granted them.

After two months of unremitting propaganda, combined with threats and terror against those who disobeyed, the private ownership of money was effectively abolished in Münster. The government seized all the money and used it to buy goods or hire workers from the outside world. Wages were doled out in kind by the only employer: the theocratic Anabaptist State.

Food was confiscated from private homes, and rationed according to the will of government deacons. Also, to accommodate the host of immigrants, all private homes were effectively communized, with everyone permitted to quarter themselves everywhere; it was now illegal to close, let alone lock, one's doors. Compulsory communal dining-halls were established, where people ate together to the readings from the Old Testament.

The compulsory communism and reign of terror was carried out in the name of community and Christian "love." This communization was considered the first giant steps toward egalitarian communism, where, as Rothmann put it, "all things were to be in common, there was to be no private property and nobody was to do any more work, but simply trust in God." Somehow, the workless part never seemed to arrive.

A pamphlet sent by the Matthys regime to other Anabaptist communities hailed their new order of Christian love through terror:

> For not only have we put all our belongings into a common pool under the care of deacons, and live from it according to our need; we praise God through Christ with one heart and

mind and are eager to help one another with every kind of
service.

And accordingly, everything which has served the purposes
of self-seeking and private property, such as buying and
selling, working for money, taking interest and practicing
usury . . . or eating and drinking the sweat of the poor . . .
and indeed everything which offends us against love—all
such things are abolished amongst us by the power of love
and community.

At the end of March 1534, however, Matthys's swollen *hu-
bris* brought him down. Convinced at Easter time that God had
ordered him and a few of the faithful to lift the Bishop's siege
and liberate the town, Matthys and a few others rushed out of
the gates at the besieging army, and were literally hacked to
pieces in response.

The death of Matthys left Münster in the hands of young
Bockelson. And if Matthys had chastised the people of Münster
with whips, Bockelson would chastise them with scorpions.
Bockelson wasted little time in mourning his mentor. He
preached to the faithful: "God will give you another Prophet
who will be more powerful." How could this young enthusiast
top his master? Early in May, Bockelson caught the attention of
the town by running naked through the streets in a frenzy,
falling then into a silent three-day ecstasy. When he rose on the
third day, he announced to the entire populace a new dispensation that God had revealed to him. With God at his elbow,
Bockelson abolished the old town offices of Council and burgor-
master, and installed a new ruling council of 12 Elders headed
by himself. The Elders were given total authority over the life
and death, the property and spirit, of every inhabitant of Münster. The old guilds were abolished, and a strict system of
forced labor was imposed. All artisans not drafted into the
military were now public employees, working for the community for no monetary reward.

Totalitarianism in Münster was now complete. Death was
now the punishment for virtually every independent act. Capital punishment was decreed for the high crimes of: murder,

theft, lying, avarice, and quarrelling. Death was also decreed for every conceivable kind of insubordination: the young against the parents, wives against their husbands, and, of course, anyone at all against the chosen representative of God on earth, the government of Münster. Bernt Knipperdollinck was appointed high executioner to enforce the decrees.

The only aspect of life previously left untouched was sex, and this deficiency was now made up. The only sexual relation now permitted by the Bockelson regime was marriage between two Anabaptists. Sex in any other form, including marriage with one of the "godless," was a capital crime. But soon Bockelson went beyond this rather old-fashioned credo, and decided to enforce compulsory polygamy in Münster. Since many of the expellees had left their wives and daughters behind, Münster now had three times as many marriageable women as men, so that polygamy had become technologically feasible. Bockelson convinced the other rather startled preachers by citing polygamy among the patriarchs of Israel, reinforcing this method of persuasion by threatening any dissenters with death.

Compulsory polygamy was a bit a much for many of the Münsterites, who launched a rebellion in protest. The rebellion, however, was quickly crushed and most of the rebels put to death. And so, by August 1554, polygamy had been coercively established in Münster. As one might expect, young Bockelson took an instant liking to the new regime, and before long he had amassed a harem of 15 wives, including Divara, the beautiful young widow of Jan Matthys. The rest of the male population also began to take enthusiastically to the new decree. Many of the women reacted differently, however, and so the Elders passed a law ordering compulsory marriage for every woman under (and presumably also over) a certain age, which usually meant becoming a compulsory third or fourth wife.

Since marriage among the godless was not only invalid but also illegal, the wives of the expellees became fair game, and they were forced to "marry" good Anabaptists. Refusal of the women to comply with the new law was punishable, of course, with death, and a number of women were actually executed as a result. Those "old" wives who resented the new competitors in their households were also cracked down on, and their quarrelling was made a capital crime; many women were thereupon executed for quarrelling.

Bockelsonian despotism could only reach so far, however, and general resistance forced the regime to relent and permit divorce. In an aboutface, not only divorce was now permitted, but all marriage was now outlawed totally, and divorce made very easy. As a result, Münster now became a regime of what amounted to compulsory free love. Thus, within the space of a few months, a rigid puritanism had been transmuted into a system of compulsory promiscuity.

Bockelson proved to be an excellent organizer of a besieged city. Compulsory labor was strictly enforced, and he was also able to induce many of the Bishop's poorly paid mercenaries to quit by offering them regular pay—with *money*, of course, that had been confiscated from the citizens of Münster. When the Bishop fired pamphlets into the town offering a general amnesty in return for surrender, Bockelson made reading such pamphlets a crime punishable by death. As a result, the Bishop's armies were in disarray by the end of August, and the siege was temporarily lifted.

Jan Bockelson took the opportunity to triumphantly carry his "egalitarian" communist revolution one crucial step further: he had himself proclaimed King and Messiah of the Last Days.

Bockelson realized that proclaiming *himself* King might have appeared tacky and unconvincing, even to the Bockelsonian faithful. And so he arranged for one Dusentschur, a goldsmith from a nearby town and self-proclaimed prophet, to do the job for him. At the beginning of September, Dusentschur announced to one and all a new revelation: that Jan Bockelson was to be the King of the whole world, the heir of King David, destined to keep that throne until God himself came to reclaim His Kingdom. Unsurprisingly, Bockelson confirmed that he himself had had the very same revelation. After a moment's coyness, Bockelson accepted the Sword of Justice and anointment as King of the World from Dusentschur, and Bockelson announced to the crowd that God had now given him "power over all the nations of the earth," and that anyone who might dare to resist God's will "shall without delay be put to death with the sword." The Anabaptist preachers of Münster dutifully explained to their bemused flock that Bockelson was indeed the Messiah as foretold in the Old Testament, and therefore the rightful ruler, both temporal and spiritual, of the entire world.

It often happens with self-proclaimed "egalitarians" that a special escape hatch from the drab uniformity of life is created—for themselves. And so it was with King Bockelson. It was important to emphasize in every way the importance of the Messiah's Advent. And so Bockelson wore the finest robes, metals and jewelry; he appointed courtiers and gentlemen-at-arms, who also appeared in splendid finery. King Bockelson's chief wife, Divara, was proclaimed Queen of the World, and she too was dressed in great finery and enjoyed a suite of courtiers and followers. The new luxurious court included two hundred people housed in fine requisitioned mansions. King Bockelson would hold court on a throne draped with a cloth of gold in the public square, wearing a crown and carrying a sceptre. Also garbed in finery were Bockelson's loyal aides, including Knipperdollinck as chief minister, and Rothmann as royal orator.

If communism is the perfect society, *somebody* must be able to enjoy its fruits; and who better than the Messiah and his courtiers? Though private property in money was abolished, the confiscated gold and silver was now minted into ornamental coins in honor of the new King. All horses were confiscated for the King's armed squadron. Names in revolutionary Münster were also transformed; all the streets were renamed; Sundays and feast days were abolished; and all new-born children were named personally by the King in accordance with a special pattern.

In order that the King and his nobles might live in high luxury, the subject population were now robbed of everything above the bare minimum; clothing and bedding were severely rationed, and all "surplus" turned over to King Bockelson on pain of death.

It is not surprising that the deluded masses of Münster began to grumble at being forced to live in abject poverty while King Bockelson and his courtiers lived in great luxury on the proceeds of their confiscated belongings. Bockelson responded by beaming propaganda to justify the new system. The justification was this: it was all right for Bockelson to live in pomp and luxury because he was already "dead" to the world and the flesh. Since he was dead to the world, in a deep sense his luxury didn't count. In the style of every guru who has ever lived in luxury among his poor credulous followers, he explained that for him material objects had no value. More importantly perhaps, Bockelson assured his subjects that he and his court were only the advance guard of the new order; soon, *they* too would be living in the same millennial luxury. Under their new order the people of Münster would soon forge outward, armed with God's will, and conquer the entire world, exterminating the unrighteous, after which Jesus would return and they will live in luxury and perfection. Equal communism with great luxury for all would then be achieved.

Greater dissent meant, of course, escalated terror, and King Bockelson's reign of "love" and death intensified its course of intimidation and slaughter. As soon as he proclaimed the monarchy, the prophet Dusentschur announced a new divine revelation: that all who persisted in disagreeing with or disobeying King Bockelson shall be put to death, and their very memory extirpated forever. Many of the victims executed were women, who were killed for denying their husbands marital rights, insulting a preacher, or daring to practice polygyny— which was considered to be a solely male privilege.

The Bishop was beginning to resume his siege, but Bockelson was able to use much of the expropriated gold and silver to send apostles and pamphlets out to surrounding areas, attempting to rouse the masses to Anabaptist revolution. The propaganda had considerable effect, leading to mass uprisings throughout Holland and northwestern Germany during January 1535. A thousand armed Anabaptists gathered under the leadership of someone who called himself Christ, Son of God;

and serious Anabaptist uprisings took place in West Frisia, in the town of Minden, and even the great city of Amsterdam, where the rebels managed to capture the town hall. All these uprisings were eventually suppressed, with the help of betrayal of the names of the rebels and the location of their munition dumps.

By this time, the princes of northwestern Europe had had enough; and all the states of the Holy Roman Empire agreed to supply troops to crush the hellish regime at Münster. By late January, Münster was totally and successfully blockaded and cut off from the outside world. Food shortages appeared immediately, and the crisis was met by the Bockelson regime with characteristic vigor: all remaining food was confiscated, and all horses killed, for the benefit of feeding the king, his royal court, and his armed guards. At all times throughout the siege the king and his court managed to eat and drink well, while famine and devastation swept through the town of Münster, and the masses ate literally anything, even inedible, they could lay their hands on.

King Bockelson maintained his rule by beaming continual propaganda and promises to the starving masses. God would definitely save them by Easter, or else Bockelson would have himself burnt in the public square. When Easter came and went, and no salvation had appeared, Bockelson craftily explained that he had meant only "spiritual" salvation, which had indeed occurred. He then promised that God would change the cobblestones to bread, and this of course did not happen either. Finally, Bockelson, long fascinated by the theater, ordered his starving subjects to engage in three days of dancing and athletics. Dramatic performances were held, as well as a Black Mass.

The poor starving people of Münster were now doomed totally. The Bishop kept firing leaflets into the town promising a general amnesty if they would only depose King Bockelson and his court and hand them over to the princely forces. To guard against this threat, Bockelson stepped up his reign of terror still further. In early May, Bockelson divided the town into 12 sections, and placed a "Duke" over each section with an armed force of 24 men. The Dukes were foreigners like himself, and as Dutch immigrants would be more likely to be loyal to King Bockelson. Each Duke was strictly forbidden to leave his own section, and they, in turn, prohibited any meetings of even a few people. No one was allowed to leave town, and anyone caught attempting or plotting to leave, helping anyone else to leave, or criticizing the King, was instantly beheaded—mainly by King Bockelson himself. By mid-June such deeds were occurring daily, with the body often quartered in sections and nailed up as a warning to the Münster masses.

Bockelson would undoubtedly have let the entire population of the city starve to death rather than surrender; but two escapees betrayed weak spots in the town's defenses and on the night of June 24, 1535, the nightmare New Jerusalem of communism and "love" at last came to a bloody end. The last several hundred Anabaptist fighters surrendered under an amnesty and were promptly massacred, and Queen Divara was beheaded. As for King Bockelson, he was led about on a chain, and, the following January, he and Knipperdollinck were publicly tortured to death, and their bodies suspended in cages from a church-tower.

The old establishment of Münster was duly restored and the city became Catholic once more. The stars were again in their courses, and the events of 1534–35 understandably led to an abiding distrust of mysticism and enthusiast movements throughout Protestant Europe.

It is instructive to understand the attitude of all Marxist historians toward Münster and the other millennialist movements of the early sixteenth century. The Marxists have always understandably lauded these movements and regimes, (a) for being communist, and (b) for being revolutionary movements from below. Marxists have invariably hailed these movements as forerunners of their own.

Ideas are notoriously difficult to kill, and Anabaptist communism was one such idea. One of Müntzer's collaborators, Henry Niclaes, who had been born in Münster, survived to found Familism, a pantheistic creed claiming that Man *is* God, and calling for the establishment of the Kingdom of God on Earth as the only place that it would ever exist. A key to that kingdom would be a system in which all property would be held in common, and all men would attain the perfection of Christ. Familist ideas were carried to England by a Dutch joiner, Christopher Vittels, a disciple of Niclaes, and familism spread in England during the late sixteenth century. A center of familism in early seventeenth century England was the Grindletonians, in Grindleton, Yorkshire, led, in the decade after 1615, by the curate, the Rev. Roger Brearly. Part of the attraction of familism was its antinomianism, the view that a truly godly person—such as themselves—could never, by definition, commit a sin, and antinomian behavior usually flaunted what most people considered sins in order to demonstrate to one and all their godly and sin-free status.

During the English Civil War, of the 1640s and 1650s, many radical religious groups bubbled to the surface, including Gerrard Winstanley and the pantheist communist Diggers noted above. Featuring extreme antinomianism combined with pantheism and communism including communism of women, were the half-crazed Ranters, who urged everyone to sin so as to demonstrate their purity.

The Reappearance of Communism in the French Revolution

In times of trouble, war, and social upheaval, millennial and messianic sects have always appeared and burgeoned. After the English Civil War subsided, millennialist and communist creeds vanished, only to appear again in force at the time of the French Revolution. The difference was that now, for the first time, secular rather than religious communist movements appeared. But the new secular communist prophets faced a grave problem: What was their agency for social change? The agency acclaimed by the religious millennialists had always been God and his Providential Messiah or vanguard prophets and destined, apocalyptic tribulations. But what could be the agency for a secular millennium and how could secular prophets drum up the necessary confidence in their foreordained triumph?

The first secularized communists appeared as two isolated individuals in mid-eighteenth century France. One was the aristocrat Gabriel Bonnot de Mably, elder brother of the laissez-faire liberal philosopher Etienne Bonnot de Condillac. Mably's major focus was to insist that all men are "perfectly" equal and uniform, one and the same everywhere. As in the case of many other communists after him, Mably found himself forced to confront one of the greatest problems of communism: if all property is owned in common and every person is equal, then there can be little or no incentive to work. For only the common store will benefit from anyone's work and not the individual himself. Mably in particular had to face this problem, since he also maintained that man's natural and original state was communism, and that private property arose to spoil everything precisely out of the indolence of some who wished to live at the expense of others. As Alexander Gray points out, "the indolence that ruined primitive communism would probably once again ruin communism, if reestablished."

Mably's two proposed solutions to this crucial problem were scarcely adequate. One, was to urge everyone to tighten their belts, to want less, to be content with Spartan austerity. The other was to come up with what Che Guevara and Mao Tsetung would later call "moral incentives": to substitute for crass monetary rewards the recognition of one's merits by one's brothers—in the form of ribbons, medals, etc. In his devastatingly witty and perceptive critique, Alexander Gray writes that:

> The idea that the world may find its driving force in a Birthday Honors List (giving to the King, if necessary, 365 birthdays a year) occurs with pathetic frequency in the more Utopian forms of socialist literature ...

> But obviously, if any were wise or depraved enough to say that they preferred indolence to a ribbon (and there would be many such) they would have to be allowed to continue to lead idle lives, sponging on their neighbors; perhaps some who had at last attained the ribbon might burst into a blaze of *faineantise* (laziness) in order that they might without distraction savor the pleasure which accompanies consideration.

Gray goes on to point out that the more "distinctions" are handed out as incentives, the less they will truly distinguish, and the less influence they will therefore exert. Furthermore, Mably "does not say how or by whom his distinctions are to be conferred." Gray goes on:

> it is assumed, and always is assumed, that there will be a universal and unquestioning belief that the fountain of honor has sprayed its refreshing waters on all the most deserving and on none but the most deserving. This naively innocent faith does not exist in the world we know, nor is it likely to exist in any earthly paradise that many may imagine.

Gray concludes that in a communist society in the real world, many people who *don't* receive honors may and probably will be disgruntled and resentful at the supposed injustice: "A general or a civil servant, kept waiting unduly in the queue for the Bath, may find his youthful ardour replaced by the sourness of hope deferred, and zeal may flag."[31]

Thus, in his two preferred solutions, Gabriel de Mably was resting his hope on a miraculous transformation of human nature, much as the Marxists would later look for the advent of the New Socialist Man, willing to bend his desires and incentives to the requirements of, and the baubles conferred by, the collective. But for all his devotion to communism, Mably was at the bottom a realist, and so he held out no hope for communist triumph. Man is too steeped in the sin of selfishness and private property for a victory to occur. Clearly, Mably had scarcely begun to solve the secularist problem of social change or to inspire the birth and flowering of a revolutionary communist movement.

If Mably's pessimism was scarcely suitable for inspiring a movement, the same was not true of the other influential secular communist of mid-eighteenth century France, the unknown writer Morelly. Though personally little known, Morelly's *La Code de la Nature*, published in 1755, was highly influential,

---

[31]Gray, *The Socialist Tradition*, pp. 90–91.

going into five more editions by 1773. Morelly had no doubts about the workability of communism; for him there was no problem of laziness or negative incentive, and therefore no need for the creation of a New Socialist Man. To Morelly, man is everywhere good, altruistic, and dedicated to work; only *institutions* are degrading and corrupt, specifically the institution of private property. Abolish that, and man's natural goodness would easily triumph. (Query: where did these corrupt human institutions come from, if not from man?)

Similarly, for Morelly, as for Marx and Lenin after him, the administration of the communist utopia would be absurdly easy as well. Assigning to every person his task in life, and deciding what material goods and services would fulfill his needs, would apparently be a trivial problem for a Ministry of Labor or of Consumption. For Morelly, all this is merely a matter of trivial enumeration, listing things and persons.

And yet, somehow things are not going to be *that* easy in the Morelly utopia. While Mably, the pessimist, was apparently willing to leave society to the voluntary actions of individuals, the optimist, Morelly, was cheerfully prepared to employ brutally coercive methods to keep all of his "naturally good" citizens in line. Morelly worked out an intricate design for his proposed ideal government and society, all allegedly based on the evident dictates of natural law, and most of which were supposed to be changeless and eternal.

In particular, there was to be no private property, except for daily needs; every person was to be maintained and employed by the collective. Every man is to be forced to work, to contribute to the communal storehouse, according to his talents, and then will be assigned goods from these stores according to his presumed needs. Marriages are to be compulsory, and children are to be brought up communally, and absolutely identically in food, clothing, and training. Philosophic and religious doctrines are to be absolutely prescribed; no differences are to be tolerated; and children are not to be corrupted by any "fable, story, or ridiculous fictions." All trade or barter is to be forbidden by "inviolable law." All buildings are to be the same, and grouped in equal blocks; all clothing is to be made out of the same fabric (a proposal prophetic of Mao's China). Occupations are to be limited and strictly assigned by the state.

Finally, the imposed laws are to be held sacred and inviolable, and anyone attempting to change them is to be isolated and incarcerated for life.

It should be clear that these utopias are debased, secularized versions of the visions of the Christian millennialists. Not only is there no ordained agency of social change to achieve this end-state, but they lack the glitter of messianic rule or glorification of God to disguise the fact that these utopias are static states, in which, as Gray puts it, "Nothing ever happens; no one ever disagrees with any one; the government, whatever its form may be, is always so wisely guided that there may be room for gratitude but never for criticism. . . . Nothing happens, nothing can happen in any of them." Gray concludes that even though, according to the utopian writers, "we are assured that never was there such a happy population," that "in fact no Utopia has ever been described in which any sane man would on any conditions consent to live, if he could possibly escape . . ."[32]

We must not think, however, that Christian communist millennialism had disappeared. On the contrary, heretical Christian messianism was also revived in the stormy times of the middle and late eighteenth century. Thus, the Swabian Pietist Johann Christoph Otinger, in the mid-eighteenth century, prophesied a coming theocratic world-kingdom of saints, living communally, without rank or property, as members of a millennial Christian commonwealth. Particularly influential among later German Pietists was the French mystic and theosophist Louis Claude de Saint-Martin, who in his influential *Des Erreurs et la Verite* (1773) portrayed an "inner church of the elect" allegedly existing since the dawn of history, which soon would take power in the coming age. This "Martinist" theme was developed by the Rosicrucian movement, concentrated in

---

[32] Gray, *Socialist Tradition*, pp. 62–63.

Bavaria. Originally alchemist mystics during the seventeenth and eighteenth centuries, the Bavarian Rosicrucians began to stress the coming to world power by the church of the elect during the dawning millennial age. The most influential Bavarian Rosicrucian author, Carl von Eckartshausen, expounded on this theme in two widely read works, *Information on Magic* (1788-92) and *On Perfectibility* (1797). In the latter work, he developed the idea that the inner church of the elect had existed backward in time to Abraham and then to go forward to a world government ruled by these keepers of the divine light. The third and final Age of History, the Age of the Holy Spirit, was now at hand. The illuminated elect destined to rule the new communal world order were, fairly obviously, the Rosicrucian Order, since major evidence for the dawn of the Third Age being imminent was the rapid spread of Martinism and Rosicrucianism itself.

And these movements were indeed spreading during the 1780s and 1790s. The Prussian King Frederick William II and a large portion of his court were converted to Rosicrucianism in the late 1780s, as was the Russian Czar Paul I a decade later, based on his reading of Saint-Martin and Eckartshausen, both of whom Paul considered to be transmitters of divine revelation. Saint-Martin was also influential through his leadership of the Scottish Rite Masonry in Lyons, and was the major figure in what might be called the apocalyptic-Christian wing of the Masonic movement.[33]

The leading communist movement during the French Revolution, however, was secularized. The ideas of Mably and Morelly could not hope to be embodied in reality in the absence of a concrete ideological *movement*, and the task of applying these ideas in movement form was seized by a young journalist and commissioner of land deeds in Picardy, Francois Noel ("Caius Gracchus") Babeuf, who came to Paris at the age of 26 in 1790, and imbibed the heady revolutionary atmosphere in

---

[33]See the revealing article by Paul Gottfried, "Utopianism of the Right: Maistre and Schlegel," *Modern Age* 24 (Spring 1980): 150–60.

that city. By 1793, Babeuf was committed to egalitarianism and communism; two years later, he founded the secret Conspiracy of the Equals, a conspiratorial revolutionary organization dedicated to the achievement of communism. The Conspiracy was organized around his new journal, *The Tribune of the People.* The *Tribune*, in a prefigurement of Lenin's *Iskra* a century later, was used to set a coherent line for his cadre as well as for his public followers. Babeuf's *Tribune* "was the first journal in history to be the legal arm of an extralegal revolutionary conspiracy."[34]

The ultimate ideal of Babeuf and his conspiracy was absolute equality. Nature, they claimed, calls for perfect equality; all inequality is injustice; therefore community of property is to be established. As the Conspiracy proclaimed emphatically in its *Manifesto of Equals*—written by one of Babeuf's top aides, Sylvain Marechal—"We demand real equality, or Death; that is what we must have." "For its sake," the *Manifesto* went on, "we are ready for anything; we are willing to sweep everything away. Let all the arts vanish, if necessary, as long as genuine equality remains for us."

In the ideal communist society sought by the Conspiracy, private property would be abolished, and all property would be communal, and stored in communal storehouses. From these storehouses, goods would be distributed "equitably" by the superiors—oddly enough, there would apparently be a cadre of "superiors" in this "equal" world! There was to be universal compulsory labor, "serving the fatherland . . . by useful labor." Teachers or scientists "must submit certifications of loyalty" to the superiors. The *Manifesto* acknowledged that there would be an enormous expansion of government officials and bureaucrats in the communist world, inevitable where "the fatherland takes control of an individual from his birth till his death." There would be severe punishments consisting of forced labor against "persons of either sex who set society a bad example by absence of civic-

[34]James H. Billington, *Fire in the Minds of Men: Origins of the Revolutionary Faith* (New York: Basic Books, 1980), p. 73.

mindedness, by idleness, a luxurious way of life, licentious-
ness." These punishments, described, as one historian notes
"lovingly and in great detail"[35] consisted of deportation to
prison islands. Freedom of speech and the press are treated as
one might expect. The press would not be allowed to "endanger
the justice of equality" or to subject the Republic "to interminable
and fatal discussions." Moreover, "No one will be allowed to utter
views that are in direct contradiction to the sacred principles of
equality and the sovereignty of the people." In point of fact, a work
would only be allowed to appear in print "if the guardians of the
will of the nation consider that its publication may benefit the
Republic."

All meals would be eaten in public in every commune, and
there would, of course, be compulsory attendance imposed on
all community members. Furthermore, everyone could only
obtain "his daily ration" in the district in which he lives; the
only exception would be "when he is traveling with the permission of the administration." All private entertainment would be
"strictly forbidden," lest "imagination, released from the super-
vision of a strict judge, should engender abominable vices contrary to the commonweal." And, as for religion, "all so-called
revelation ought to be banned by law."

Important as an influence on later Marxism-Leninism was
not only the communist goal, but also Babeuf's strategic theory
and practice in the concrete organization of revolutionary activity. The unequal, the Babouvists proclaimed, must be de-
spoiled, the poor must rise up and sack the rich. Above all, the
French Revolution must be "completed" and redone; there must
be total upheaval (*bouleversement total*), a total destruction of
existing institutions so that a new and perfect world can be
built from the rubble. As Babeuf called out, at the conclusion of
his own *Plebeian Manifesto*: "May everything return to chaos,
and out of chaos may there emerge a new and regenerated

---

[35]For this phrase and other translated quotes from the *Manifesto*, see Shafarevich, *The Socialist Phenomenon*, pp. 121–24. Also see Gray, *Socialist Tradition*,
p. 107.

world."[36] Indeed, the *Plebian Manifesto*, published slightly earlier than the *Manifesto of Equals* in November 1795, was the first in a line of revolutionary manifestos that would reach a climax in Marx's *Communist Manifesto* a half-century later.

The two Manifestos, the *Plebeian* and the *Equals*, revealed an important difference between Babeuf and Marechal which might have caused a split had not the Equals been crushed soon afterward by police repression. For in his *Plebeian Manifesto*, Babeuf had begun to move toward Christian messianism, not only paying tribute to Moses and Joshua, but also particularly to Jesus Christ as his, Babeuf's, "co-athlete." In prison, furthermore, Babeuf had written *A New History of the Life of Jesus Christ*. Most of the Equals, however, were militant atheists, spearheaded by Marechal, who liked to refer to himself with the grandiose acronym l'HSD, *l'homme sans Dieu* [the Man without God].

In addition to the idea of a conspiratorial revolution, Babeuf, fascinated by military matters, began to develop the idea of people's guerilla warfare: of the revolution being formed in separate "phalanxes" by people whose permanent occupation would be making revolution—whom Lenin would later call "professional revolutionaries." He also toyed with the idea of military phalanxes securing a geographical base, and then working outward from there.

A secret, conspiratorial inner circle, a phalanx of professional revolutionaries—inevitably this meant that Babeuf's strategic perspective for his revolution embodied some fascinating paradoxes. For in the name of a goal of harmony and perfect equality, the revolutionaries were to be led by a hierarchy commanding total obedience; the inner cadre would work its will over the mass. An absolute leader, heading an all-powerful cadre, would, at the proper moment, give the signal to

---

[36]Billington, *Fire in the Minds*, p. 75. Also see Gray, *Socialist Tradition*, p. 105n. As Gray comments, "what is desired is the annihilation of all things, trusting that out of the dust of destruction a fair city may arise. And buoyed by such a hope, how blithely would Babeuf bide the stour." Ibid., p. 105.

usher in a society of perfect equality. Revolution would be made to end all further revolutions; an all-powerful hierarchy would be necessary, allegedly to put an end to hierarchy forever.

But of course, there was no real paradox here because Babeuf and his cadre harbored no real intention to eliminate hierarchy. The paeans to "equality" were a flimsy camouflage for the real objective—a permanently entrenched and absolute dictatorship.

After suffering police repression at the end of February, 1796, the Conspiracy of the Equals went further underground, and, a month later, constituted themselves as the Secret Directory of Public Safety. The seven secret directors, meeting every evening, reached collective and anonymous decisions, and then each member of this central committee radiated activity outward to 12 "instructors," each of whom mobilized a broader insurrectionary group in one of the 12 districts of Paris. In this way, the Conspiracy managed to mobilize 17,000 Parisians, but the group was betrayed by the eagerness of the secret directorate to recruit within the army. An informer led to the arrest of Babeuf on May 10, followed by the destruction of the Conspiracy of the Equals. Babeuf was executed the following year.

Police repression, however, almost always leaves pockets of dissidents to rise again, and the new carrier of the torch of revolutionary communism became a Babouvist and was arrested with the leader but who managed to avoid execution. Filippo Guiseppe Maria Lodovico Buonarroti was the oldest son of an aristocratic but impoverished Florentine family, and a direct descendant of the great Michelangelo. Studying law at the University of Pisa in the early 1780s, Buonarroti was converted by disciples of Morelly on the Pisa faculty. As a radical journalist and editor, Buonarroti then participated in battles for the French Revolution against Italian troops. In the spring of 1794, he was put in charge of the French occupation in the Italian town of Oneglia, where he announced to the people that all men must be equal, and that any distinction whatever among men is a violation of natural law. Back in Paris, Buonarroti successfully defended himself in a trial against his use of terror in Oneglia, and finally plunged into Babeuf's Conspiracy of Equals. His friendship with Napoleon allowed him to escape execution, and eventually to be shipped from a prison camp to exile in Geneva.

For the rest of his life, Buonarroti became what his modern biographer calls "The First Professional Revolutionist," trying to set up revolutions and conspiratorial organizations throughout Europe. Before the execution of Babeuf and others, Buonarroti had pledged his comrades to write their full story, and he fulfilled that pledge when, at the age of 67, he published in Belgium *The Conspiracy for Equality of Babeuf* (1828). Babeuf and his comrades had been long forgotten, and this massive work now told the first and most thoroughgoing narrative of the Babouvist saga. The book proved to be an inspiration to revolutionary and communist groupings, and sold extremely well, the English translation of 1836 selling 50,000 copies in a short space of time. For the last decade of his life, the previously obscure Buonarroti was lionized throughout the European ultra-left.

Brooding over previous revolutionary failures, Buonarroti counselled the need for iron elite rule immediately after the coming to power of the revolutionary forces. In short, the power of the revolution must be immediately given over to a "strong, constant, enlightened immovable will," which will "direct all the force of the nation against internal and external enemies," and very gradually prepare the people for their sovereignty. The point, for Buonarroti, was that "the people are incapable either of regeneration by themselves or of designating the people who should direct the regeneration."

The Burgeoning of Communism in the 1830s and 1840s

The 1830s and 1840s saw the burgeoning of messianic and chiliastic communist and socialist groups throughout Europe: notably in France, Belgium, Germany and England. Owenites, Cabetists, Fourierites, Saint Simonians, and many others sprouted and interacted, and we need not examine them or their nuanced variations in detail. While the Welshman Robert Owen was the first to use the word "socialist" in print in 1827, and also toyed with "communionist," the word "communist" finally caught on as the most popular label for the new system. It was first used in popular printed work in Etienne Cabet's utopian novel, *Voyage in Icaria* (1839),[37] and from there the word spread like wildfire across Europe, spurred by the recent development of a regular steamboat mail service and the first telegraphy. When Marx and Engels, in the famous opening sentence of their *Communist Manifesto* of 1848, wrote that "A spectre is haunting Europe—the spectre of Communism," this was a bit of hyperbolic rhetoric, but still was not far off the mark. As Billington writes, the talismanic word "communism" "spread throughout the continent with a speed altogether unprecedented in the history of such verbal epidemics."[38]

Amid this welter of individuals and groups, some interesting ones stand out. The earliest German exile group of revolutionaries was the League of the Outlaws, founded in Paris by Theodore Schuster, under the inspiration of the writings of Buonarroti. Schuster's pamphlet, *Confession of Faith of an Outlaw* (1834) was perhaps the first projection of the coming revolution as a creation of the outlaws and marginal outcasts of society, those outside the circuit of production whom Marx would understandably dismiss brusquely as the *"lumpenproletariat."* The *lumpen* were later emphasized in the 1840s by the leading anarcho-communist, the Russian Mikhail Bakunin, foreshadowing various strains of the New Left during the late 1960s and early 1970s.

The Outlaws was the first international organization of

---

[37]Cabet had been a distinguished French lawyer and attorney-general of Corsica, but was ousted for radical attitudes toward the French government. After founding a journal, Cabet fled into exile in London during the 1830s and initially became an Owenite. Despite Cabet's nationality, the book was originally written and published in English and a French translation was published the following year. A peaceful communist rather than a revolutionary, Cabet tried to establish utopian communes in various failed projects in the United States, from 1848 until his death 8 years later.

[38]Billington, *Fire in the Minds*, p. 243.

communist revolutionaries, comprised of about 100 members in Paris and almost 80 in Frankfurt am Main. The League of Outlaws, however, disintegrated about 1838, many members, including Schuster himself, going off into nationalist agitation. But the League was succeeded quickly by a larger group of German exiles, the League of the Just, also headquartered in Paris. The German communist groups always tended to be more Christian than the other nationalities. Thus, Karl Schapper, leader of the Paris headquarters section of the League of the Just, addressed his followers as "Brothers in Christ," and hailed the coming social revolution as "the great resurrection day of the people." Intensifying the religious tone of the League of the Just was the prominent German communist, the tailor Wilhelm Weitling. In the manifesto that he wrote for the League of the Just, *Humanity as it is and as it ought to be* (1838), which though secret was widely disseminated and discussed, Weitling proclaimed himself a "social Luther," and denounced money as the source of all corruption and exploitation. All private property and all money was to be abolished and the value of all products to be calculated in "labor-hours"—the labor theory of value taken all too seriously. For work in public utilities and heavy industry, Weitling proposed to mobilize a centralized "industrial army," fueled by the conscription of every man and woman between the ages of 15 and 18.

Expelled from France after revolutionary troubles in 1839, the League of the Just moved to London, where it also established a broader front group, the Educational Society for German Workingmen in 1840. The three top leaders of the Society, Karl Schapper, Bruno Bauer, and Joseph Moll, managed to raise their total to over 1000 members by 1847, including 250 members in other countries in Europe and Latin America.

A fascinating contrast is presented by two young communists, both leaders of the movement during the 1840s, and both of whom have been almost totally forgotten by later generations—even by most historians. Each represented a different side of the communist perspective, two different strands of the movement.

One was the English Christian visionary and fantast, John

Goodwyn Barmby. At the age of 20, Barmby, then an Owenite, arrived in Paris in 1840 with a proposal to set up an International Association of Socialists throughout the world. A provisional committee was actually formed, headed by the French Owenite Jules Gay, but nothing came of the scheme. The plan did, however, prefigure the First International. More importantly, in Paris Barmby discovered the word "communist," and adopted and spread it with enormous fervor. To Barmby, "communist" and "communitarian" were interchangeable terms, and he helped organize throughout France what he reported to the English Owenites were "social banquet(s) of the Communist or Communitarian school." Back in England, Barmby's fervor was undiminished. He founded a Communist Propaganda Society, soon to be called the Universal Communitarian Society, and established a journal, *The Promethean or Communitarian Apostle*, soon renamed *The Communist Chronicle*. Communism, to Barmby, was both the "societarian science" and the final religion of humanity. His *Credo*, propounded in the first issue of *The Promethean*, avowed that "the divine is communism, that the demonic is individualism." After that flying start, Barmby wrote communist hymns and prayers, and called for the building of Communitariums, all directed by a supreme Communarchy headed by an elected Communarch and Communarchess. Barmby repeatedly proclaimed "the religion of Communism," and made sure to begin things right by naming himself "Pontifarch of the Communist Church."

The subtitle of *The Communist Chronicle* revealed its neochristian messianism: "The Apostle of the Communist Church and the Communitive Life: Communion with God, Communion of the Saints, Communion of Suffrages, Communion of Works and Communion of Goods." The struggle for communism, declared Barmby, was apocalyptic, bound to end with the mystical reunion of Satan into God: "In the holy Communist Church, the devil will be converted into God. . . . And in this conversion of Satan doth God call peoples. . . . in that communion of suffrages, of works, and of goods both spiritual and material . . .

for these latter days."[39] The arrival in London of Wilhelm Weitling in 1844 led him and Barmby to collaborate on promoting Christian communism, but by the end of 1847, they had lost out and the communist movement was shifting decisively toward atheism.

The crucial turn came in June 1847, when the two most atheistical of communist groups—the League of the Just in London, and the small, fifteen-man Communist Correspondence Committee of Brussels, headed by Karl Marx, merged to form the Communist League. At its second congress in December, ideological struggles within the League were resolved when Marx was asked to write the statement for the new party, to become the famed *Communist Manifesto*.

Cabet and Weitling, throwing in the towel, each left permanently for the United States in 1848, to try to establish communism there. Both attempts foundered ignominiously amid America's expanding and highly individualistic society. Cabet's Icarians settled in Texas and then Nauvoo, Illinois, then split and split again, until Cabet, ejected by his former followers in Nauvoo, left for St. Louis and died, spurned by nearly everyone, in 1856. As for Weitling, he gave up more rapidly. In New York, he became a follower of Josiah Warren's individualistic though left-Ricardian labor-money scheme, and in 1854 he deviated further to become a bureaucrat with the U.S. Immigration Service, spending most of his remaining 17 years trying to promote his various inventions. Apparently, Weitling, willy-nilly, had at last "voted with his feet" to join the capitalist order.

Meanwhile, Goodwyn Barmby sequestered himself in one after another of the Channel Islands to try to found a utopian community, and denounced a former follower for setting up a more practical *Communist Journal* as "an infringement of his copyright" on the word "communism." Gradually, however, Barmby abandoned his universalism and began to call himself a "National Communist." Finally, in 1848, he went to France,

[39]Billington, *Fire in the Minds*, p. 257.

became a Unitarian minister and friend of Mazzini's and abandoned communism for revolutionary nationalism.

On the other hand, a leading young French communist, Theodore Dezamy, represented a competing strain of militant atheism and a tough, cadre approach. In his early youth the personal secretary of Cabet, Dezamy led the sudden communist boom launched in 1839 and 1840. By the following year, Dezamy became perhaps the founder of the Marxist-Leninist tradition of ideologically and politically excommunicating all deviationists from the correct line. In fact, in 1842, Dezamy, a highly prolific pamphleteer, turned bitterly on his old mentor Cabet, and denounced him, in his *Slanders and Politics of Mr. Cabet*, for chronic vacillation. In *Slanders*, Dezamy, for the first time, argued that ideological as well as political discipline is requisite for the communist movement.

More importantly, Dezamy wanted to purge French communism of the influence of the quasi-religious poetic and moralistic communist code propounded by Cabet in his *Voyage in Icaria* and especially in his *Communist Credo* of 1841. Dezamy therefore countered with his *Code of the Community* the following year. Dezamy attempted to be severely "scientific" and claimed that communist revolution was both rational and inevitable. It is no wonder that Dezamy was greatly admired by Marx.

Furthermore, pacific or gradual measures were to be rejected. Dezamy insisted that a communist revolution must confiscate all private property and all money immediately. Half measures will satisfy no one, he claimed, and, furthermore, as Billington paraphrases it, "Swift and total change would be less bloody than a slow process, since communism releases the natural goodness of man."[40] It was from Dezamy, too, that Marx adopted the absurdly simplistic view that the operation of communism was merely a clerical task of bookkeeping and registration of people and resources.[41]

---

[40]Billington, *Fire in the Minds*, p. 251.

[41]See the standard biography of Marx by David McLellan, *Karl Marx: His Life and Thought* (New York: Harper and Row, 1973), p. 118.

Not only would revolutionary communism be immediate and total; it would also be global and universal. In the future communist world, there will be one global "congress of humanity," one single language, and a single labor service called "industrial athletes," who will perform work in the form of communal youth festivals. Moreover, the new "universal country" would abolish not only "narrow" nationalism, but also such divisive loyalties as the family. In stark practical contrast to his own career as ideological excommunicator, Dezamy proclaimed that under communism conflict would be logically impossible: "there can be no splits among Communists; our struggles among ourselves can only be struggles of harmony, or reasoning," since "communitarian principles" constitute "the solution to all problems."

Amidst this militant atheism there was, however, a kind of religious fervor and even faith. For Dezamy spoke of "this sublime devotion which constitutes socialism," and he urged proletarians to reenter "the egalitarian church, *outside of which there can be no salvation.*"

Dezamy's arrest and trial in 1844 inspired German communists in Paris such as Arnold Ruge, Moses Hess, and Karl Marx, and Hess began to work on a German translation of Dezamy's Code, under the encouragement of Marx, who proclaimed the Code "scientific, socialist, materialist, and real humanist."[42]

Karl Marx:
Apocalyptic Reabsorptionist Communist

Karl Marx was born in Trier, a venerable city in Rhineland Prussia, in 1818, son of a distinguished jurist, and grandson of a rabbi. Indeed, both of Marx's parents were descended from rabbis. Marx's father Heinrich was a liberal rationalist who felt no great qualms about his forced conversion to official Lutheranism in 1816. What is little known is that, in his early years,

---

[42]See J. L. Talmon, *Political Messianism: The Romantic Phase* (New York: Praeger, 1960), p. 157.

the baptized Karl was a dedicated Christian.[43] In his graduation essays from Trier *gymnasium* in 1835, the very young Marx prefigured his later development. His essay on an assigned topic, "On the Union of the Faithful with Christ" was orthodox evangelical Christian, but it also contained hints of the fundamental "alienation" theme that he would later find in Hegel. Marx's discussion of the "necessity for union" with Christ stressed that this union would put an end to the tragedy of God's alleged rejection of man. In a companion essay on "Reflections of A Young Man on the Choice of a Profession," Marx expressed a worry about his own "demon of ambition," of the great temptation he felt to "inveigh against the Deity and curse mankind."

Going first to the University of Bonn and then off to the prestigious new University of Berlin to study law, Marx soon converted to militant atheism, shifted his major to philosophy, and joined a *Doktorklub* of Young (or Left) Hegelianism, of which he soon became a leader and general secretary.

The shift to atheism quickly gave Marx's demon of ambition full rein. Particularly revelatory of Marx's adult as well as youthful character are volumes of poems, most of them lost until a few were recovered in recent years.[44] Historians, when they discuss these poems, tend to dismiss them as inchoate Romantic yearnings, but they are too congruent with the adult Marx's social and revolutionary doctrines to be casually dismissed. Surely, here seems to be a case where a unified (early plus late) Marx is vividly revealed. Thus, in his poem "Feelings," dedicated to his childhood sweetheart and later wife Jenny von Westphalen, Marx expressed both his megalomania and his enormous thirst for destruction:

[43]Friedreich Engels was the son of a leading industrialist and cotton manufacturer, who was also a staunch Pietist from the Barmen area of the Rhineland in Germany. Barmen was one of the major centers of Pietism in Germany, and Engels received a strict Pietist upbringing. An atheist and then a Hegelian by 1839, Engels wound up at the University of Berlin and the Young Hegelians by 1841, and moved in the same circles as Marx, becoming fast friends in 1844.

[44]The poems were largely written in 1836 and 1837, in Marx's first months in Berlin. Two of the poems constituted Marx's first published writings, in the *Berlin Atheneum* in 1841. The others have been mainly lost.

> *Heaven I would comprehend*
> *I would draw the world to me;*
> *Loving, hating, I intend*
> *That my star shine brilliantly ...*

and

> *... Worlds I would destroy forever,*
> *Since I can create no world;*
> *Since my call they notice never ...*

Here, of course, is a classic expression of Satan's supposed reason for hating, and rebelling against, God.

In another poem Marx writes of his triumph after he shall have destroyed God's created world:

> *Then I will be able to walk triumphantly,*
> *Like a god, through the ruins of their kingdom.*
> *Every word of mine is fire and action.*
> *My breast is equal to that of the Creator.*

And in his poem "Invocation of One in Despair," Marx writes:

> *I shall build my throne high overhead,*
> *Cold, tremendous shall its summit be.*
> *For its bulwark—superstitious dread.*
> *For its marshal—blackest agony.*[45]

The Satan theme is most explicitly set forth in Marx's "The Fiddler," dedicated to his father.

> *See this sword?*
> *The prince of darkness*
> *Sold it to me.*

and

> *With Satan I have struck my deal,*
> *He chalks the signs, beats time for me*
> *I play the death march fast and free.*

Particularly instructive is Marx's lengthy unfinished poetic drama of this youthful period, *Oulanem, A Tragedy*. In the

[45]Richard Wurmbrand, *Marx and Satan* (Westchester, Ill.: Crossway Books, 1986), pp. 12–13.

course of this drama his hero, Oulanem, delivers a remarkable soliloquy, pouring out sustained invective, a deep hatred of the world and of mankind, a hatred of creation, and a threat and a vision of total world destruction.

Thus Oulanem pours out his vials of wrath:

> *I shall howl gigantic curses on mankind.*
> *Ha! Eternity! She is an eternal grief. ...*
> *Ourselves being clockwork, blindly mechanical,*
> *Made to be foul-calendars of Time and Space,*
> *Having no purpose save to happen, to be ruined,*
> *So that there shall be something to ruin ...*
> *If there is a Something which devours,*
> *I'll leap within it, though I bring the world to ruins—*
> *The world which bulks between me and the Abyss*
> *I will smash to pieces with my enduring curses.*
> *I'll throw my arms around its harsh reality:*
> *Embracing me, the world will dumbly pass away,*
> *And then sink down to utter nothingness,*
> *Perished, with no existence—that would be really living!*

And

> *... the leaden world holds us fat,*
> *And we are chained, shattered, empty, frightened,*
> *Eternally chained to this marble block of Being, . . . and we—*
> *We are the apes of a cold God.*[46]

All this reveals a spirit that often seems to animate militant atheism. In contrast to the non-militant variety, which expresses a simple disbelief in God's existence, militant atheism seems to believe implicitly in God's existence, but to hate Him and to wage war for His destruction. Such a spirit was all too clearly revealed in the retort of militant

---

[46]For the complete translated text of *Oulanem*, see Robert Payne, *The Unknown Karl Marx* (New York: New York University Press, 1971), pp. 81–83. Also excellent on the poems and on Marx as a messianist is Bruce Mazlish, *The Meaning of Karl Marx* (New York, Oxford University Press, 1984).

Pastor Wurmbrand points out that *Oulanem* is an anagram of Emmanuel, the Biblical name for Jesus, and that such inversions of holy names are standard practice in Satanic cults. There is no real evidence, however, that Marx was a member of such a cult. Wurmbrand, *Marx and Satan*, pp. 13–14 and *passim*.

atheist and anarcho-communist Bakunin to the famous pro-theist remark of Voltaire: "If God did not exist, it would be necessary to create Him." To which the demented Bakunin retorted: "If God did exist, it would be necessary to destroy Him." It was this hatred of God as a creator greater than himself that apparently animated Karl Marx.

When Marx came to the University of Berlin, the heart of Hegelianism, he found that doctrine regnant but in a certain amount of disarray. Hegel had died in 1831; the Great Philosopher was supposed to bring about the end of History, but now Hegel was dead, and History continued to march on. So if Hegel himself was not the final culmination of history, then perhaps the Prussian State of Friedrich Wilhelm III was not the final stage of history either. But if he was not, then mightn't the dialectic of history be getting ready for yet another twist, another *aufhebung*?

So reasoned groups of radical youth, who, during the late 1830s and 1840s in Germany and elsewhere, formed the move-ment of the Young, or Left, Hegelians. Disillusioned in the Prus-sian State, the Young Hegelians proclaimed the inevitable coming apocalyptic revolution that would destroy and transcend that State, a revolution that would *really* bring about the end of History in the form of national, or world, communism. After Hegel, there was one more twist of the dialectic to go.

One of the first and most influential of the Left Hegelians was a Polish aristocrat, Count August Cieszkowski, who wrote in German and published in 1838 his *Prolegomena to a Historiosophy*. Cieszk-owski brought to Hegelianism a new dialectic of history, a new variant of the three ages of man. The first age, the age of antiquity, was, for some reason, the Age of Emotion, the epoch of pure feeling, of no reflective thought, of elemental immediacy and hence unity with nature. The "spirit" was "in itself" (*an sich*). The second age, the Christian Era, stretching from the birth of Jesus to the death of the great Hegel, was the Age of Thought, of reflection, in which the "spirit" moved "toward itself," in the direction of abstraction and universality. But Christianity, the Age of Thought, was also an era of intolerable duality, of alienation, of man separated from God, of spirit separated from matter, and thought from action. Finally, the third and culminating age, the Age a-borning, heralded (of course!) by Count Cieszkowski, was to be the Age of Action. The third post-Hegelian age would be an age of practical action, in which the thought of both Christianity and of Hegel would be transcended and embodied into an act of will, a final revolution to overthrow and transcend existing institutions. For the term "practical action," Cieszkowski borrowed the Greek word *praxis* to summarize the new age, a term that would soon acquire virtually talismanic influence in Marxism. This final age of action would bring about, at last, a blessed unity of thought and action, spirit and matter, God and earth, and total "freedom." With Hegel and the mystics, Cieszkowski stressed that *all* past events, even those seemingly evil, were necessary to the ultimate and culminating salvation.

In a work published in French in Paris in 1844, Cieszkowski also heralded the new class destined to become the leaders of the revolutionary society: the *intelligentsia*, a word that had recently been coined by a German-educated Pole, B. F. Trentowski.[47] Cieszkowski thus proclaimed and glorified a development that would at least be implicit in the Marxist movement (after all, the great Marxists, from Marx and Engels on down, were all bourgeois intellectuals rather than children of the proletariat). Generally, however, Marxists have been shamefaced about this reality that belies Marxian proletarianism and equality, and the "new class" theorists have all been critics of Marxian socialism, (e.g. Bakunin, Machajski, Michels, Djilas).

Count Cieszkowski, however, was not destined to ride the wave of the future of revolutionary socialism. For he took the Christian messianic, rather than the atheistic, path to the new society. In his massive, unfinished work of 1848, *Our Father* (*Ojcze nasz*), Cieszkowski maintained that the new age of revolutionary communism would be a Third Age, an Age of the Holy

---

[47]In B. F. Trentowski, *The Relationship of Philosophy to Cybernetics* (Poznan, 1843), in which the author also coined the word "cybernetics" for the new, emerging form of rational social technology which would transform mankind. See Billington, *Fire in the Minds*, p. 231.

Spirit (shades of Joachimism!), an era that would be the Kingdom of God on earth "as it is in heaven." This final Kingdom of God on earth would reintegrate all of "organic humanity," and would be governed by a Central Government of All Mankind, headed by a Universal Council of the People.

At that time, it was by no means clear which strand of revolutionary communism, the religious or the atheist, would ultimately win out. Thus, Alexander Ivanovich Herzen, a founder of the Russian revolutionary tradition, was entranced by Cieszkowski's brand of Left Hegelianism, writing that "the future society is to be the work not of the heart, but of the concrete. Hegel is the new Christ bringing the word of truth to men."[48] And soon, Bruno Bauer, friend and mentor of Karl Marx and leader of the *Doktorklub* of Young Hegelians at the University of Berlin, hailed Cieszkowski's new philosophy of action in late 1841 as "The Trumpet Call of the Last Judgment."

But the winning strand in the European socialist movement, as we have indicated, was eventually to be Karl Marx's atheism. If Hegel had pantheized and elaborated the dialectic of the Christian messianics, Marx now "stood Hegel on his head" by atheizing the dialectic, and resting it not on mysticism or religion or "spirit" or the Absolute Idea or the World-Mind, but on the supposedly solid and "scientific" foundation of philosophical materialism. Marx adopted his materialism from the Left Hegelian Ludwig Feuerbach, particularly from his work *The Essence of Christianity* (1843). In contrast to the Hegelian emphasis on "spirit," Marx would study the allegedly scientific laws of matter in some way operating through history. Marx, in short, took the dialectic and made it into a "materialist dialectic of history."

By recasting the dialectic onto materialist and atheist terms, however, Marx gave up the powerful motor of the dialectic as it supposedly operated through history: either Christian

[48]Billington, *Fire in the Minds*, p. 225.

messianism or Providence or the growing self-consciousness of the World-Spirit. How could Marx find a "scientific" materialist replacement, newly grounded in the ineluctable "laws of history," that would explain the historical process thus far, and also—and most importantly—explain the inevitability of the imminent apocalyptic transformation of the world into communism? It is one thing to base the prediction of a forthcoming Armageddon on the Bible; it is quite another to deduce this event from allegedly scientific law. Setting forth the specifics of this engine of history was to occupy Karl Marx for the rest of his life.

Although Marx found Feuerbach indispensable for adopting a thoroughgoing atheist and materialist position, Marx soon found that Feuerbach had not gone nearly far enough. Even though Feuerbach was a philosophical communist, he basically believed that if man foreswore religion, then man's alienation from his self would be over. To Marx, religion was only one of the problems. The entire world of man (the *Menschenwelt*) was alienating, and had to be radically overthrown, root and branch. Only apocalyptic destruction of this world of man would permit true human nature to be realized. Only then would the existing un-man (*Unmensch*) truly become man (*Mensch*). As Marx thundered in the fourth of his "theses on Feuerbach," "One must proceed to destroy the 'earthly family' as it is 'both in theory and in practice.'"[49]

In particular, declared Marx, true man, as Feuerbach had argued, is a "communal being" (*Gemeinwesen*) or "species being" (*Gattungswesen*). Although the state as it exists must be negated or transcended, man's participation in the state comes as such a communal being. The major problem comes in the private sphere, the market, or "civil society," in which un-man acts as an egoist, as a private person, treating others as means, and not collectively as masters of their fate. And in existing society, unfortunately, civil society is primary, while

[49]Tucker, *Philosophy and Myth*, p. 101.

the State, or "political community," is secondary. What must be done to realize the full nature of mankind is to transcend the State and civil society by politicizing all of life, by making all of man's actions "collective." Then real individual man will become a true and full species being.[50,51]

But only a revolution, an orgy of destruction, can accomplish such a task. And here, Marx harkened back to the call for total destruction that had animated his vision of the world in the poems of his youth. Indeed, in a speech in London in 1856, Marx gave graphic and loving expression to this goal of his "praxis." He mentioned that in Germany in the Middle Ages there existed a secret tribunal called the *Vehmgericht*. He then explained:

> If a red cross was seen marked on a house, people knew that its owner was doomed by the *Vehm*. All the houses of Europe are now marked with the mysterious red cross. History is the judge—its executioner the proletarian.[52]

Marx, in fact, was not satisfied with the philosophical communism to which he and Engels had separately been converted by the slightly older Left Hegelian Moses Hess in the early 1840s. To Hess's communism, Marx, by the end of 1843, added the crucial emphasis on the *proletariat*, not simply as an economic class, but as destined to become the "universal class" when communism was achieved. Ironically, Marx acquired his vision of the proletariat as the key to the communist revolution from an influential book published in 1842 by a youthful enemy of socialism, Lorenz von Stein. Stein interpreted the socialist and communist movements of the day as rationalizations of the class interests of the propertyless proletariat. Marx discovered in Stein's attack the "scientific" engine for the inevitable coming of the communist

---

[50]Tucker, *Philosophy and Myth*, p. 105.

[51]It is both ironic and fascinating that the dominant intellectuals in contemporary Hungary who are leading the drive away from socialism and toward freedom are honoring the Marxian concept of "civil society" as what they are moving toward while going away from the collective and the communal.

[52]Tucker, *Philosophy and Myth*, p. 15.

revolution.[53] The proletariat, the most "alienated" and allegedly "propertyless" class, would be the key.

We have been accustomed, ever since Stalin's alterations of Marx, to regard "socialism" as the "first stage" of a communist-run society, and "communism" as the ultimate stage. This is not the way Marx saw the development of his system. Marx, as well as all the other communists of his day, used "socialism" and "communism" interchangeably to describe their ideal society. Instead, Marx foresaw the dialectic operating mysteriously to bring about the first stage, of "raw" or "crude" communism, to be magically transformed by the workings of the dialectic into the "higher" stage of communism. It is remarkable that Marx, especially in his "Private Property and Communism," accepted the horrendous picture that von Stein drew of the "raw" stage of communism. Stein forecast that communism would attempt to enforce egalitarianism by wildly and ferociously expropriating and destroying property, confiscating it, and coercively communizing women as well as material wealth. Indeed, Marx's evaluation of raw communism, the stage of the dictatorship of the proletariat, was even more negative than Stein's: "In the same way as women abandon marriage for general [i.e., universal] prostitution, so the whole world of wealth, that is, the objective being of man, is to abandon the relation of exclusive marriage with the private property owner for the relation of general prostitution with the community." Not only that, but, as Professor Tucker puts it, Marx concedes that "raw communism is not the real transcendence of private property but only the universalizing of it, and not the abolition of labor but only its extension to all men. It is merely a new form in which the vileness of private property comes to the surface."

---

[53]Stein was a conservative Hegelian monarchist, who had been assigned by the Prussian government to study the unsettling new doctrines of socialism and communism becoming rampant in France. Marx displayed a "minute textual familiarity" with Stein's book, Lorenz von Stein, *Der Socialismus und Communismus des heutigen Frankreichs* (Liepzig, 1842), a book that remains untranslated. Stein spent his mature years as professor of public finance and public administration at the University of Vienna. See Tucker, *Philosophy and Myth*, pp. 114–17.

In short, in the stage of communalization of private property, what Marx himself considers the worst features of private property will be maximized. Not only that: but Marx concedes the truth of the charge of anti-communists then and now that communism and communization is but the expression, in Marx's words, of "envy and a desire to reduce all to a common level." Far from leading to a flowering of human personality, as Marx is supposed to claim, he admits that communism will negate that personality totally. Thus Marx:

> In completely negating the *personality* of man, this type of communism is really nothing but the logical expression of private property. General *envy*, constituting itself as a power, is the disguise in which *greed* reestablishes itself and satisfies itself, only in *another way*. . . . In the approach to *woman* as the spoil and handmaid of communal lust is expressed the infinite degradation in which man exists for himself.[54]

Marx clearly did not stress this dark side of communist revolution in his later writings. Professor Tucker explains that "these vivid indications from the Paris manuscripts of the way in which Marx envisaged and evaluated the immediate post-revolutionary period very probably explain the extreme reticence that he always later showed on this topic in his published writings."[55]

But if this communism is admittedly so monstrous, a regime of "infinite degradation," why should anyone favor it, much less dedicate one's life and fight a bloody revolution to establish it? Here, as so often in Marx's thought and writings, he falls back on the mystique of the "dialectic"—that wondrous magic wand by which one social system inevitably gives rise to its victorious transcendence and negation. And, in this case, by which total evil—which turns out, interestingly enough, to be the post-revolutionary dictatorship of the proletariat and *not* previous capitalism—becomes transformed into total good, a never-never land absent the division of labor and all

---

[54]Quoted in Tucker, *Philosophy and Myth*, p. 155. Italics are Marx's.
[55]Tucker, *Philosophy and Myth*, pp. 155–56.

other forms of alienation. The curious point is that while Marx attempts to explain the dialectic movement from feudalism to capitalism and from capitalism to the first stage of communism in terms of class struggle and the material productive forces, both of these drop out once raw communism is achieved. The allegedly inevitable transformation from the hell of raw communism to the alleged heaven of higher communism is left totally unexplained; to rely on *that* crucial transformation, we must fall back on pure faith in the mystique of the dialectic.

Despite Marx's claim to be a "scientific socialist," scorning all other Socialists whom he dismissed as moralistic and "utopian," it should be clear that Marx himself was even more in the messianic utopian tradition than were the competing "Utopians." For Marx not only sought a desired future society that would put an end to history, he claimed to have found the path toward that utopia inevitably determined by the "laws of history."

But a utopian, and a fierce one, Marx certainly was. A hallmark of every utopia is a militant desire to put an end to history, to freeze mankind in a static state, to put an end to diversity and man's free will, and to order everyone's life in accordance with the utopian's totalitarian plan. Many early communists and socialists set forth their fixed utopias in great and absurd detail, determining the size of everyone's living quarters, the food they would eat, etc. Marx was not silly enough to do that, but his entire system, as Professor Thomas Molnar points out, is "the search of the utopian mind for the definitive stabilization of mankind or, in gnostic terms, its reabsorption into the timeless." For Marx, his quest for utopia was, as we have seen, an explicit attack on God's creation and a ferocious desire to destroy it. The idea of crushing the many, the diverse facets of creation, and of returning to an allegedly lost Unity with God began, as we have seen, with Plotinus. As Molnar summed up:

> In this view, existence itself is wound on nonbeing. Philosophers from Plotinus to Fichte and beyond have held that the

reabsorption of the polichrome universe in the eternal One would be preferable to creation. Short of this solution, they propose to arrange a world in which change is brought under control so as to put an end to a disturbingly free will and to society's uncharted moves. They aspire to return from the linear Hebrew-Christian concept to the Greco-Hindu cycle— that is, to a changeless, timeless permanence.

The triumph of unity over diversity means that, for the utopians including Marx, "civil society, with its disturbing diversity, can be abolished."[56]

Substituting in Marx for God's will or the Hegelian dialectic of the World-Spirit or the Absolute Idea, is monist materialism, its central assumption, as Molnar puts it, being "that the universe consists of matter plus some sort of one-dimensional law immanent in matter." In that case, "man himself is reduced to a complex but manipulable material aggregate, living in the company of other aggregates, and forming increasingly complex super aggregates called societies, political bodies, churches." The alleged laws of history, then, are derived by scientific Marxists as supposedly evident and immanent within this matter itself.

The Marxian process toward utopia, then, is man acquiring insights into his own true nature, and then rearranging the world to accord with that nature. Engels, in fact, explicitly proclaimed the Hegelian concepts of the Man-God: "Hitherto the question has always stood: What is God?—and German Hegelian philosophy has revolved it as follows: God is man. . . . Man must now arrange the world in a *truly* human way, according to the demands of his *nature*."[57]

---

[56]Thomas Molnar, "Marxism and the Utopian Theme," *Marxist Perspectives* (Winter 1978): 153–54. The economist David McCord Wright, while not delving into the religious roots of the problem, stressed that one group in society, the statists, seeks "the achievement of a fixed ideal static pattern of technical and social organization. Once this ideal is reached, or closely approximated, it need only be repeated endlessly thereafter." David McCord Wright, *Democracy and Progress* (New York: Macmillan, 1948), p. 21.

[57]Molnar, "Marxism," pp.149, 150–51.

But this process is rife with self-contradictions; for example, and centrally, how can mere matter gain insights into his [its?] nature? As Molnar puts it: "for how can matter gather insights? And if it has insights, it is not entirely matter, but matter *plus*."

In this allegedly inevitable process, of arriving at the proletarian communist utopia after the proletarian class becomes conscious of its true nature, what is supposed to be Karl Marx's own role? In Hegelian theory, Hegel himself is the final and greatest world-historical figure, the Man-God of man-gods. Similarly, Marx in his own view stands at a focal point of history as the man who brought to the world the crucial knowledge of man's true nature and of the laws of history, thereby serving as the "midwife" of the process that would put an end to history. Thus Molnar:

> Like other utopian and gnostic writers, Marx is much less interested in the stages of history up to the present (the egotistic *now* of all utopian writers) than the final stages when the stuff of time becomes more concentrated, when the drama approaches its denouement. In fact, the utopian writer conceives of history as a process leading to himself since he, the ultimate *comprehensor*, stands in the center of history. It is natural that things accelerate during his own lifetime and come to a watershed: he looms large between the Before and the After.[58]

Thus, in common with other utopian socialists and communists, Marx sought in communism the apotheosis of the collective species-mankind as one new super-being, in which the only meaning possessed by the individual is as a negligible particle of that collective organism. Many of Marx's numerous epigones carried out his quest. One incisive portrayal of Marxian collective organicism—what amounts to a celebration of the New Socialist Man to be created during the communizing process—was that of a top Bolshevik theoretician of

[58]Molnar, "Marxism," pp. 151–52.

the early twentieth century, Alexander Alexandrovich Bogdanov. Bogdanov, too, spoke of "three ages" of human history.
First was a religious, authoritarian society and a self-sufficient
economy. Next came the "second age," an exchange economy,
marked by diversity and the emergence of the "autonomy" of
the "individual human personality." But this individualism, at
first progressive, later becomes an obstacle to progress as it
hampers and "contradicts the unifying tendencies of the machine age." But then there will arise the Third Age, the final
stage of history, communism. This last stage will be marked by
a collective self-sufficient economy, and by

> the fusion of personal lives into one colossal whole, har-
> monious in the relations of its parts, systematically
> grouping all elements for one common struggle—struggle
> against the endless spontaneity of nature. . . . An enor-
> mous mass of creative activity . . . is necessary in order
> to solve this task. It demands the forces not of man but
> of mankind— and only in working at this task does man-
> kind as such emerge.[59]

Finally, at the apex of Marxian messianic communism is a
man who fuses all the tendencies and strands analyzed thus
far. A blend of Christian messianist *and* devoted Marxist-Len-
inist-Stalinist, the twentieth century German Marxist Ernst
Bloch set forth his vision in his recently translated three-volume phantasmagoria *The Principle of Hope* (*Daz Prinzip
Hoffnung*). Early in his career, Bloch wrote a laudatory study of
the views and life of the coercive Anabaptist communist,
Thomas Müntzer, whom he hailed as magical, or "theurgic."
The inner "truth" of things, wrote Bloch, will only be discovered
after "a complete transformation of the universe, a grand
apocalypse, the descent of the Messiah, a new heaven and a
new earth." There is more than a hint in Bloch that disease,

---

[59]Quoted in S. V. Utechin, "Philosophy and Society: Alexander Bogdanov," in
Leopold Labedz, ed., *Revisionism: Essays on the History of Marxist Ideas* (New York:
Praeger, 1962), p. 122.

nay death itself, will be abolished upon the advent of communism.[60] God is developing; "God himself is part of the Utopia, a finality that is still unrealized." For Bloch mystical ecstasies and the worship of Lenin and Stalin went hand in hand. As J. P. Stern writes, Bloch's *Principle of Hope* contains such remarkable declarations as *"Ubi Lenin, ibi Jerusalem"* [Where Lenin is, there is Jerusalem], and that "the Bolshevist fulfillment of Communism" is part of "the age-old fight for God."

In the person of Ernst Bloch, the old grievous split within the European communist movement of the 1830s and 1840s between its Christian and atheist wings was at last reconciled. Or, to put it another way, in a final bizarre twist of the dialectic of history, the total conquest by 1848 of the Christian variants of communism at the hands of the superior revolutionary will and organizing of Karl Marx, was now transcended and negated. The messianic eschatological vision of heretical religious and Christian communism was now back in full force, within the supposed stronghold of atheistic communism, Marxism itself. From Ernst Bloch to the fanatical cults of personality of Stalin and Mao to the genocidal vision and ruthlessness of Pol Pot in Cambodia and the Shining Path guerrilla movement in Peru, it seems that, within the body and soul of Marxism, Thomas Müntzer had at last triumphed conclusively over Feuerbach.

---

[60]J. P. Stern, "Marxism on Stilts: Review of Ernst Bloch, "The Principle of Hope," *The New Republic* 196 (March 9, 1987): 40, 42. Also see Kolakowski, *Main Currents*, vol. 3, pp. 423–24.

Index

Contributors

David Gordon is senior fellow at the Ludwig von Mises Institute.

Hans-Hermann Hoppe is professor of economics at the University of Nevada, Las Vegas.

Yuri N. Maltsev, a former Soviet economist, is associate professor of economics at Carthage College, Kenosha, Wisconsin.

Gary North is president of the American Bureau of Economic Research, Fort Worth, Texas, and publishes the *Remnant Review*.

David Osterfeld is assistant professor of political science at St. Joseph's College, Renselaer, Indiana.

Ralph Raico is associate professor of history at the State University College, Buffalo, New York.

Murray N. Rothbard is S. J. Hall distinguished professor of economics at the University of Nevada, Las Vegas, and editor of the *Review of Austrian Economics*.